James Wilson Pierce

Story of Turkey and Armenia

James Wilson Pierce

Story of Turkey and Armenia

ISBN/EAN: 9783743316683

Manufactured in Europe, USA, Canada, Australia, Japa

Cover: Foto ©ninafisch / pixelio.de

Manufactured and distributed by brebook publishing software (www.brebook.com)

James Wilson Pierce

Story of Turkey and Armenia

STORY

OF

TURKEY AND ARMENIA

With a full and accurate account of the recent massacres written by eye witnesses.

EDITED BY
REV. JAMES WILSON PIERCE D. D.

A SKETCH OF CLARA BARTON AND THE RED CROSS.

ILLUSTRATED.

BALTIMORE:
R. H. WOODWARD COMPANY,
1896.

COPYRIGHT, 1896, BY
R. H. WOODWARD COMPANY.

PUBLISHERS' NOTE.

In the preparation of this book great care and pains has been taken to use only such information of the massacres and condition of the country as were known to be trustworthy. Many hundreds of letters, written by eye-witnesses, have been placed at our disposal; but nearly all of these we are unable to publish. Nearly all which are given were furnished by private parties, who had friends in Armenia, or were written by missionaries. We are compelled to withhold in nearly every instance the names of the writers of these letters on account of their personal safety. The illustrations, which greatly increase the value of this book, have been secured through the kindness of former residents in that country and also by direct importation from Constantinople, and furnish the reader a truthful knowledge of the country and its people.

The publishers desire to make a public acknowledgment of the kindness of the editors of the Review of Reviews, Independent, and Outlook, of New York. They kindly gave permission to make use of articles which had appeared in their papers.

CONTENTS.

CHAPTER I.
Introductory, ... 1

CHAPTER II.
The Evil of the Turk, ... 25

CHAPTER III.
Abdul Hamid, Sultan of Turkey, . . 37

CHAPTER IV.
The People of Turkey—Their Home-Life and Religion, . . 105

CHAPTER V.
Constantinople, . . 208

CHAPTER VI.
The Armenians—Who Are They? 220

CHAPTER VII.
The Armenian Church, ... 231

CHAPTER VIII.
A Trip Through Armenia, 253

CONTENTS.

CHAPTER IX.
Gladstone on the Armenian Question, ... 291

CHAPTER X.
The Kurds, ... 304

CHAPTER XI.
Home-Life of the Armenians, ... 318

CHAPTER XII.
Opinions of Distinguished Writers, . 332

CHAPTER XIII.
The Armenian Outrages, ... 364

CHAPTER XIV.
The Condition of Armenia, ... 379

CHAPTER XV.
Story of the Massacres—How Caused, ... 445

CHAPTER XVI.
Clara Barton and the Red Cross, ... 487

LIST OF ILLUSTRATIONS.

A Wealthy Turkish Gentleman and His Friends....	Frontispiece.
Fountain of Achmet III, Constantinople..................	5
Constantinople—Pedestal of Obelisk.....................	11
Constantinople—Sweet Waters of Asia...................	11
Palace of Beylerbey, Constantinople.....................	17
The Execution of Criminals at City Gate, Tabriz..........	23
A Turkish Cawas.......................................	29
Abdul Hamid, Sultan of Turkey.........................	35
Head Bishop of the Armenian Church....................	35
Beggars	41
Khalil Rifaat Pasha, the New Grand Vizier, on his way to take up his Post.......................................	47
Mosque of the Sultan at Sweet Waters of Europe..........	53
Entrance to a Mosque..................................	59
Imperial Kiosk of Sweet Waters of Asia—Constantinople...	65
Interior of Mosque of St. Sophia, Constantinople...........	71
Palace of Balarius, Constantinople......................	77
Seven Towers of Constantinople........................	83
Gate to a Palace.......................................	89
Interior of Mosque of St. Sophia.........................	89
Gate of Seraskierat, Constantinople.....................	95
A Scene in Turkey.....................................	101
Roberts College..	107
Imperial Palace of Dolman Baytche, Constantinople.......	113
Great Mosque, Tomb of John the Baptist, Damascus.......	119
Tomb of Sultan Mahmaud..............................	119
Massacre in the Streets of Marash.......................	125

LIST OF ILLUSTRATIONS.

	PAGE.
Mosque of the Sultan Valide	131
Bosphorus	131
An Oriental Funeral	137
Burned Column of Constantine	145
Temple of Jupiter—East End of Peristyle, Baalbak	145
Kiosk of the Reviews	153
Interior of Mosque, Soliman	153
Interior of a Mosque	161
A Turkish Cart	169
Damascus—Group of Tombs of Damasquins Emir	169
Mosque of Solimar, Constantinople	177
Dancing Dervishes	185
Turkish Ladies	185
Howling Dervish	193
A Turkish Lady of Wealth	193
Mohammedans at Prayer	201
View of Constantinople	209
A Turkish Feast	217
Armenian Women in Walking Costume	225
Obelisk, Constantinople	233
An Armenian High Priest	241
An Armenian Woman	249
Armenian School Children	257
A Street in the City of Van, Armenia	265
Armenian Princess	273
Turkish High Priest	273
An Armenian City	281
Armenian Women Making Bread	289
A Group of Kurds, Armenia	289
An Armenian Village	297
A "Mollah" Narrating the Battle of Kerbala in the Bazar at Tabriz, Persia	305
In a Kurdish Camp	313

LIST OF ILLUSTRATIONS.

	PAGE.
A Kurd Capturing an Armenian Woman	313
Mt. Ararat	321
A Newspaper Reporter Being Pursued by Turkish Soldiers	329
Armenian Peasant Women Weaving Turkish Carpets	337
Kurdish Bandits	337
A Rural Scene in Armenia	345
Vestibule of Palace of Dolma Baytche	353
Map of Turkey in Asia	361
Armenian Villagers Pursued by Kurds	369
Armenians Being Sent Away to Exile	377
A Group of Villagers, Armenia	385
A Harvest Scene	385
Armenian Refugees	393
A Scene in Armenia	401
An Armenian Family	409
Koor-se, Armenia	417
Carrying Presents to the Shah of Persia on Birthday	425
Baalbets—Sculpture of Ceiling of Temple of Jupiter	433
Tower of Galata	433
Wall and Gate of Libasgun	441
Armenians Slain in the Streets of Baiburt	449
Armenian Mother and Children	457

Story of Turkey and Armenia.

CHAPTER I.

INTRODUCTORY.

One of the three most remarkable epochs in the world's history was the Gothic age. With it we irresistibly associate the barons of Runnymede, the great names of Saint Louis and Saint Ferdinand, the greater name of Dante. We rarely remember to put with them another name, representing, it is true, no Christian advance; instead, one in Islam. The name is Othman or Osman, and from that name is derived Ottoman or Osmanli. Othman's father was the leader of a wild heathen band from Central Asia. Until recently the subjects of the Ottoman Empire have recognized only the name Ottomans or Osmanlis, not that of Turk, which applies to a wider race. The Uighurs, or Turks, were pushed forth from Central Asia by the Mongols. The Turks gradually came west, and were probably, like the Kurds of today, a wild race supplying neighboring rulers with mercenary troops. They settled in Khorasan (the northeastern province of Persia). They began their career first as slaves and then as mercenary soldiers. Being of great beauty and vigor, they were favorites with all the princes with whom they came in contact, and whom they well served. They developed before long into a military aristocracy, and ended in becoming Seljuk Sultans, governing most of the Khalifs' dominions in Asia. They even controlled the power of the Persians and Arabs. Out of the many tribes of Turks, one came into Asia Minor, and it was the good fortune of its leader to help the Seljuk Sultan in battle against the Mongols at Angora (1250). Gaining the victory through his help, the Sultan gave to his supporters a few square miles of land under Bithynian Olympus; the name of the place was Sugat, and these few square miles became the nucleus of the Ottoman Empire.

The leader of the Turks had managed affairs so well as to obtain for his son Othman the succession of the Seljuk Sultan. Othman—a prince of much physical prowess, bravery and patience, qualities which he transmitted to his descendants—continually advanced his small domain (making Brusa his capital), until it absorbed northwestern Asia Minor. One of the cleverest methods of conquest was in the formation of the Janissaries (new troops), composed of children taken when young from conquered races, generally Christians. The new soldiers were compelled to become Moslems and to undergo a life of severe discipline. Separated from family and country, given great pay, and opportunity for the gratification of ambition and of pleasure, this military organization became a redoubtable instrument. Seventy years ago the Janissaries were suppressed; they had grown too arrogant. The Ottoman civil and military government was regarded in such a friendly way that the Greek Emperor did not even object when the Turks crossed the Hellespont, and for the first time took possession of European soil. About this time a convenient earthquake happened, and the walls of Gallipoli fell down. The Turks immediately marched in, declaring that Providence had opened the city to them, and they could not think of disregarding so clear an instance of divine interposition. From Gallipoli in a few years the Turks had spread over all what is now known as Turkey in Europe, and then began to conquer the outlying provinces—Servia, Bulgaria, Rumania.

This development of Turkish aggrandizement had been a wonderful one, and it occupied only a century and one-half. We shall look far and wide to find a parallel. The reason for this growth was not in the circumstances which surrounded the Turks, but in the great abilities which each of their rulers represented. Cruel they were, and rudely ruled a rude race; yet there is no question as to their pre-eminent power in militarism and statecraft. Now, however, there came an event which not only delayed by fifty years the capture of Constantinople, but seemed to blot out the Ottoman Empire. It was the descent of Tamerlane. This great warrior was himself of Mongol-Turkish race, and had established his dominion throughout lower Russia, Central Asia, India, Persia and Syria, but he had been resisted by the Mamluk Sultans of Egypt and by the Ottoman Sultan of Turkey. The latter was crushed by Tamerlane on that same plain of Angora where the Ottoman Empire had taken its start. The Moslems, believers in fate, regarded the empire doomed where it had begun.

Yet by the energy of a great man—the Sultan Mohammed —the start was made all over again, and only half a century sufficed to rebuild the empire, to overwhelm the Christians with just retribution for their perfidy, and to capture Constantinople. How could all this be done, and so soon? First, because of the superiority in physical and moral worth of the Ottoman Turks; because they represented a better government than those about them; because the disintegrated peoples of Asia Minor in the south and the conquered Christians in the north had become so impressed with these things that they were ready to fuse with the turks, even to accepting the religion of the latter; and because the clever Ottomans made no difference between born and converted Moslems in preferment; indeed, most of the Grand Viziers have been of Christian or of Jewish birth.

After Constantinople, the Crimea, Greece, Armenia and Kurdistan were taken, while a foothold was gained on the Italian coast at Otranto. Many important conquests now followed—those of Mesopotamia, Syria, Arabia and Egypt; this was not only a vast addition, but, what was of infinitely greater moment, gave to the Ottoman Sultan the title of Khalif, for by the conquest of the Mamluks he succeeded to their supremacy over the sacred cities of Mecca and Medina, while the last of the Baghdad Khalifs made over to the Ottoman Sultan the symbols of his high office—namely, the cloak and the standard of the Prophet himself. Then came the conquest of Hungary; but when Suleiman the Magnificent would take Vienna, his siege came to naught, and the Ottoman Empire met its first rebuff. Still, its conquests increased, as a rule, in spite of a second check—this time at Lepanto; Cyprus, Tunis, and Georgia were added to the

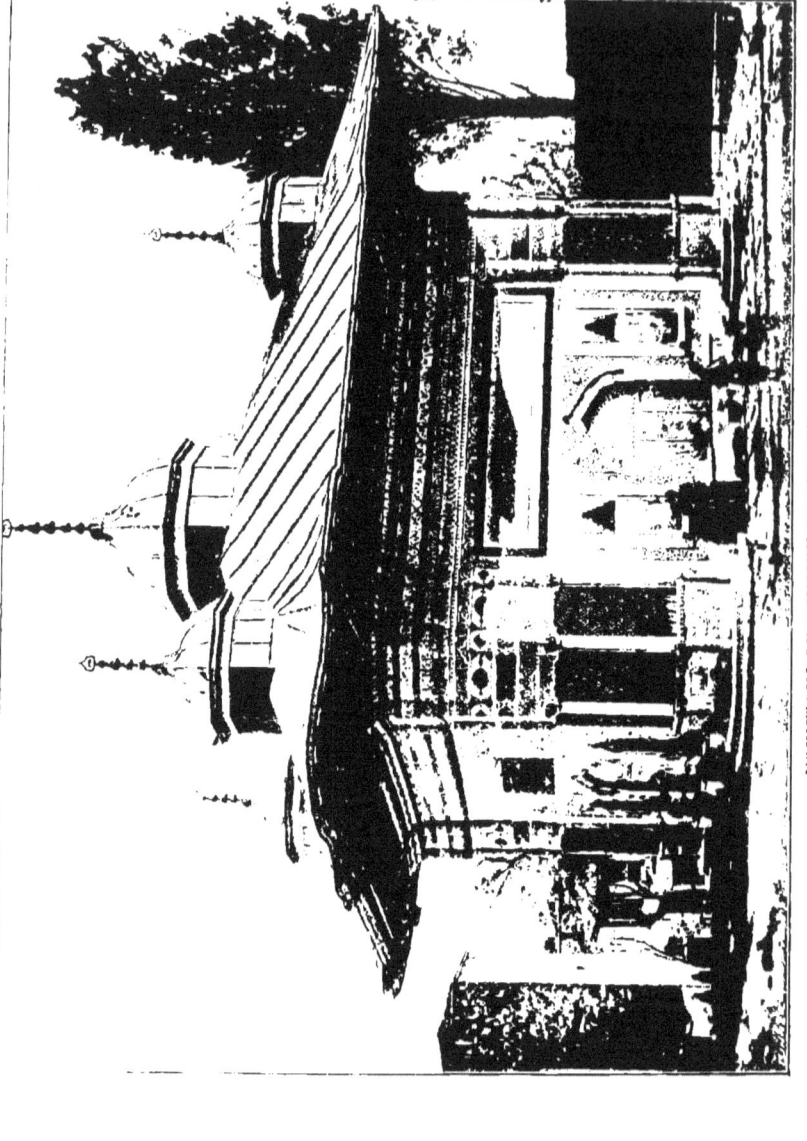

FOUNTAIN OF ACHMET III. CONSTANTINOPLE.

empire, and the first conflict experienced with Russia. The year 1600 marked the point of greatest territorial extent.

Then followed a decline; Turkey itself receded, then it was dismembered. Hungary was first lopped off, then Transylvania, then Wallachia, and so on; and the empire had to acknowledge the independence of peoples once subject to it. We have noted the causes of growth; those of decline are no less evident. In the first place, Turkey has ever been a consumer, not a producer; a military power, she has fattened on what conquered lands could give her; she gave them nothing. Often she gave them worse than nothing—cruelty, brutal lust, slavery. After Suleiman—a prince who held his own in that Renaissance age which saw a Charles V, an Elizabeth, a Francis I, a Leo X—there was, in place of barbaric but direct government, indirection and the growing seclusion of the Sultan, induced largely by the pernicious harem influence. The first ten sultans had been robust, able, cruel; the last twenty-five (save Mahmud II) have been no less cruel, but no longer robust, no longer able. There were now, however, external causes to accentuate the internal, the chief of which was Russia's rise. By 1700 the Turkish dominions in Europe had shrunk to half their former extent. The next century saw Russian aggrandizement come to such a point that not only did the Crimean Khanate become independent of Turkey, but gates at Moscow and Kherson were inscribed "The Way to Constantinople," and Constantine became henceforth an honored name in the Russian Imperial family. Later events—Navarino, the disaffection of Egypt, the treaty of Unkiar-Skelessi lately rumored to have been readopted), the

Crimean war reaction, quickly followed by the Lebanon affair, the independence of Rumania, the successive revolts of the Herzegovina, of Bulgaria, Servia and Montenegro, resulting in the Russo-Turkish war, and the further dismemberment of Turkey in both Europe and Asia—are not these summed up in Lord Beaconsfield's phrase, "Peace with honor?"—a phrase which has meant so much peace to some of the European States, little and big, so little honor to Great Britain and Turkey. The latter's hold in Europe, both in area and population, is now reduced to less than one-fourth of what it once was. It still has much of its vast area and population in Asia; but in Africa the loss of Algiers, Tunis and Egypt takes away two-thirds of its area and twelve times the present population in Tripoli.

Fifty years ago the Emperor Nicholas said to Sir Hamilton Seymour: "We have on our hands a sick man, a very sick man." The present invalid is the Sultan Abdul-Hamid II. He succeeded to the throne in 1876, on the deposition of his older brother, Murad V, who was declared to be suffering from idiocy, and has since been kept in strict seclusion. Abdul-Hamid is the thirty-fifth sovereign in uninterrupted male descent of the House of Othman, the founder of the empire. No family in European history can show such an example of continuous authority. The crown is inherited by the eldest male descendant in the imperial line, no matter whether he be the Sultan's son, uncle, cousin, or nephew.

The government of Turkey is often called the "Sublime Porte." This name is taken from the only gate in general use along the quay which runs outside the whole length of the sea-wall of Constantinople. It is called Bab-i-Humayum (the great gate of the Seraglio), or the Sublime Porte. In the old days, just without this gate pyramids of heads used to be piled up, trophies of war. The Sublime Porte really means the Sultan. He is absolute in matters both temporal and spiritual. He delegates his authority in temporal things to his Grand Vizier, and in religious affairs to the Sheik-ul-Islam. In connection with the Sultan and Grand Vizier is the Privy Council, the ministers of which, however, are little more than secretaries. Connected with the Sheik-ul-Islam is the Ulema, a body comprising priests and lawyers, and also the Mufti, the interpreters of the Koran. The government is thus before everything a theocracy, and is irreformable to any permanent degree. True, a constitution was proclaimed in 1876, but it lasted only a few months. There can be no equality of Moslem and Christian before the law. Yet the Sultan has repeatedly promised "perfect equality of civil rights" to all his subjects. What he really has had to do, however, is to exercise his Khalifate. By its votaries the Mohammedan religion is believed to be God's last expression of His will. Therefore, the Sultan, the Moslem counterpart of papal vicegerency and infallibility, is not only a sovereign, he is also an Inquisitor. He must needs compel all to embrace Islam; if the "heathen" will not, then death to them; if Christians and Jews will not, then servitude to them. The Turkish dominion in Europe is about equally divided between Mohammedans and Christians, but in Asia the former form a vast majority. The Christians number those who use the Roman Catholic liturgy, the Greeks, Armenians, Bulgarians, Syrians, Maronites, and Protestants.

The empire is partitioned into thirty-one departments called Vilayets. These are subdivided into provinces (Sanjaks), and these in turn into districts (Kazaks), and these again into subdistricts and communities. The Governor of a Vilayet is called a Vali, and is assisted by a Provincial Council. The provinces, districts, etc., are governed by authorities, and the names of the Governors of sub-districts and of communes—Mudir and Muktar—have lately become familiar. The making and carrying out of Turkish law have not yet come to such a state of perfection that foreigners feel like giving up their own consular courts, which they retain, and by means of which are under the same laws as in their respective countries. Cases between foreign and Turkish subjects, however, are tried in the Ottoman courts. Through the prevailing dishonesty, foreign governments are also compelled to maintain their own postoffices in Turkey. Yet, by England at least, Turkish government is apparently thought good enough for unarmed Christians, since, in spite of solemn obligations incurred eighteen years ago, not one thing has the British government done to succor those Christians.

The Turks today are still nomadic. Their agriculture is backward, not so much from soil-sterility in Albania or in Asia Minor as from the apathy of the inhabitants to settled vocations. In Macedonia and in Thrace the soil is fertile, but the same poverty is seen. The people have ruthlessly destroyed their forests. Their mines are unworked despite

CONSTANTINOPLE—PEDESTAL OF OBELISK.

CONSTANTINOPLE—SWEET WATERS OF ASIA.

the gold, silver, copper and salt known to exist abundantly.
With an empire possessing every kind of soil and climate,
vegetable, animal and mineral product, the Ottomans are
bankrupt; they seem as alien as when, six hundred years ago,
they emerged from obscurity.

Armenia is a country lying about Mount Ararat as a central point. The country is now partly in Russia, partly in Persia, partly in Asia Minor. Turkish Armenia is about the size of New England; it is a mountain land, some of the Taurus peaks rising over 10,000 feet. There are a few valleys in which scant rice and cotton may be grown, but the high plateau is mostly a grazing place. As in the rest of the Ottoman Empire, agriculture is in a pitifully primitive state, and, though there are abundant deposits, mining does not exist. The climate is one of extremes of cold and heat. The sources of the Euphrates and Tigris are in Armenia, and there is also Lake Van, a salt lake. The roads are nothing but bridle-paths; they are infested with brigands, and there are no inns. Geographical isolation is not the least of the hardships in the present crisis.

The Armenians represent an ancient civilization, and have kept their individuality through all ages. Their name comes from an early king, Haik, a descendant of Japhet. Armenia is mentioned several times in the Old Testament; for instance (2 Kings xix, 37), when the sons of Sennacherib are said to have escaped thither. The best known Armenian king, Tigranes I, was an ally of Cyrus the Great, and in Xenophon's

Retreat of the Ten Thousand we have a description of Armenia as it might be today. Then came Alexander's conquest, followed by those of the Parthians, Romans, Byzantines, Saracens and Turks. The latter overran the country in the eleventh century.

The Armenian language is, like the Greek, an independent branch of the Indo-Germanic. The Gothic Bishop Ulfilas was the first to give form to the early German, by his translation of the Bible, and so did the Armenian Bishop Mesrob to Armenian; he invented the Armenian alphabet, and then translated the Bible into that tongue. The language is distinguished by two characteristics: there is no gender, and all words are accented on the last syllable.

There are now about four million Armenians, of whom only 600,000 are in Armenia—a fourth of the entire number in all Turkey. There are 1,250,000 in Russian Armenia, and they are fairly prosperous there; 150,000 in Persian Armenia; 100,000 in Europe, and about 5000 in this country. The saying runs that if it takes ten Christians to cheat a Jew, it takes ten Jews to cheat an Armenian, and the cleverness of the latter in trade is well known. They go to Constantinople, and the great cities whenever possible, and often become affluent. The stay-at-homers attend to their flocks, till their soil, make their honey, and weave their carpets and rugs.

Half the population of Armenia is Moslem, and it is made up of Kurds and Turks. The former are by nature brave and hospitable, but are still unsubjugated, and have become brutal through contact with the degenerate Turk. Contrary to the customs of other Mohammedans, their women go about unveiled and enjoy much liberty. The Kurds are now organized into guerrilla regiments of the Turkish army.

According to legend, the Apostle Thaddeus founded the Armenian Church; according to history, St. Gregory the Illuminator, in 289, when the king was baptized and Christianity became the national religion. The Armenian is supposed to be the oldest of any national church. As they were at war during the Council of Chalcedon, the Armenians did not attend it and did not approve its decrees. This led to a separation, and, about 500 years ago, a division in the Armenian Church itself occurred, when a branch of it acknowledged the Pope's supremacy. The highest Armenian ecclesiastical dignitary is called Katholikos. He resides near Erivan, the capital of Russian Armenia, and at least once in their lives all Armenians must journey thither. There is a belief in the worship of saints in the Armenian Church, but none in purgatory; there are ignorance and superstition, but the work of foreign missionaries is doing much to break through the dry ecclesiastical crust. In Armenia and Asiatic Turkey there are about 250 Americans, who hold over $2,000,000 worth of property for religious, medical and educational uses. These figures do not cover our large commercial interests there.

Until the Crimean war, Russia had exercised a hundred years a kind of protectorate over the Ottoman Christians, but in 1856 she was deprived of that protectorate, and the Great Powers of Europe, in a collective protectorate, took her place. Russia had always accomplished something with the Sultan; he never forgot that, with one exception, for two centuries Russia had defeated him in every war. Therefore he was delighted at the chance of escaping from dealing with one Power to dealing with a number, for what was everybody's business was nobody's business. Furthermore, he was convinced that the integrity of his empire was essential to the balance of power in Europe. The best proof of this was the fact that Turkey had been admitted into the comity of nations. British preponderance was meanwhile growing, and in 1880 England bound herself to defend the Armenian frontier against Russia, and to see that reforms were carried out in Armenia. The curious situation is that, should Russia decide to interfere with the awful iniquities which have been going on in Armenia, the Sultan could, under this convention, call upon England to protect him. An added responsibility of England's is found in the Treaty of Berlin. The sixty-first clause of that treaty declares that the Porte shall carry out the reforms demanded by local requirements in Armenia. As a part of that agreement, the Sultan guarantees the security of Armenia against the Circassians and the Kurds, and agrees that he "will periodically make known the steps taken to this end to the Powers, who will superintend their application." Not once has Turkey announced any reforms; there have been none. In the Russo-Turkish Treaty of San Stefano the Sultan had bound himself to introduce reforms in Armenia, and the Russian troops were to remain in that province until such reforms were established. To her shame be it said, England was the only Power insisting upon the submission of the Treaty of San Stefano to the revision of the Congress at Berlin.

PALACE OF BEYLERBEY, CONSTANTINOPLE.

Thus, eighteen years ago, England and Turkey made their compact. Neither the Christian nor the Moslem Power has since done anything to relieve the situation. For England there is no excuse; for Turkey, the only apology has been that the population of Armenia, being mixed, reforms cannot be instituted applicable to Christians and Mussulsmans alike; but, as Canon MacColl points out, precisely the same objections were made to the constitution which Lord Dufferin drew up for the Lebanon after the Syrian massacres in 1860. That, however, did not prevent Great Britain insisting that the constitution should be accepted by the Porte, and events since then have abundantly justified such firmness. During these eighteen years, despite the Berlin Treaty, the Armenians have suffered as much as ever—latterly, far more. Their testimony is rarely taken in the courts; it is never acted on (while the uncorroborated evidence of a Mussulman is enough to send a Christian to jail). They may not bear arms. They are harassed by intolerable taxes. In addition to ordinary taxation (the assessing and collecting of which are outrageously performed), for all Christians who refuse to embrace Islam there is either death or the ransom from death, a capitation tax. Christians are excluded from the Ottoman army; in place of that service a tax is put on all males from three months old. There are extraordinary taxes for temporary purposes, which are never removed—we learn that the extraordinary tax levied in 1867 to pay the cost of the Sultan's visit to England is still being imposed, though the promise was that it should be levied only for that year. Taxes are often demanded a year in advance, a promise being made that the interval shall be exempted—a promise never kept. Then there is the dreaded hospitality tax. Every Christian subject of the Sultan is legally bound to provide three days' gratuitous hospitality for any Moslem traveler who may chance to demand it. These Mohammedan guests are as unwelcome as they are omnipresent. They require not only the best the house affords in food, drink and shelter, but they regard no sanctity of person as inviolable; indeed, Canon MacColl sees nothing improbable in the allegation that there is scarcely a Christian woman in Armenia who has not been outraged. While this is probably an exaggeration, we know that failure to pay a tax is regarded by Turkish law as rebellion. The penalty is forfeiture of property or of life. The Armenians have long been compelled to pay blackmail to the tax-gatherers, so that property and life, and that which is dearer than life—the dignity of their women—might be preserved. The Christians have now become so impoverished that they cannot meet all these extortions, for, after paying ordinary taxes, the peasant's share of his crop is but one-third.

This impoverishment was the cause of the Sassun massacre a year and one-half ago. The Christians had no money. The Kurds stole flocks from the villages. The Armenians tried to recover the flocks, and a fight took place, in which some Kurds were killed. Then it transpired that the latter were enrolled as soldiers. This was exactly what was wanted. The Christians had doubly forfeited their right to life, and an imperial order went forth to diminish the population. The population was diminished by just so much; it would not do to exterminate the Armenians—the milch-cow business is too good to be destroyed—but the Armenians must be cut down to a certain level. Killing goes on, say from ten to four, when the level is supposed to be reached, but woe to a Turk who kills after four; he himself is summarily shot.

The Turks allege that the Armenians were preparing for a general uprising, and that their minds had been inflamed by paid agitators. The first charge was that the Armenians wished to set up an autonomous government, eventually comprising their co-religionists in Russia and Persia. The next was that the agitators were trying to sow the seed of discontent and anarchy in order to prepare the way for a strong power (Russia) to step in and keep order. A third charge was that the agitators were Nihilists. It is true, as we are told, that the real aim of the Armenians, as a whole, is somewhat obscured by the utterances and acts of a few irresponsible Armenian hotheads.

Whatever may be said about a choice of evils as between Russia and Turkey, in the case of the Armenians there is no longer any question. In his recent book, Mr. Frederick Greene well says: "Russia is crude, stupid, and, in certain respects, brutal; but she is not decrepit, debauched and doting like official Turkey. * * * Christians and Mohammedans cannot live together on equal terms under a Mohammedan government, because the Mohammedan religion forbids that shey should; but Mohammedans and Christians may perfectly well live together under a Christian government. They do so under the governments both of England and of Russia."

While there are undoubtedly some honest Turks, no reliance may be placed on any promise of the Sultan, for no Sultan could ever carry them out. Religious principle and temporal policy alike forbid. Reform in the Ottoman dominions cannot come from within; it must come from without.

THE EXECUTION OF CRIMINALS AT CITY GATE, TAURIZ.

CHAPTER II.

THE EVIL OF THE TURK.
By an Armenian.*

The questions are often asked, "Why does Turkey wage perpetual war against her Christian subjects? What are some of the grievances to which they are subjected and of which they complain? And why are the Turkish displays of barbarism allowed to go unchecked and unpunished at the close of the enlightened nineteenth century?"

I would answer these questions from the standpoint of one reared in that country, and under those conditions of enslavement and persecution that surround all Christians there. The answer to the first question may be found in the teachings of the dominating religion of the government, Mohammedanism, whose watchword from the past to the present has been, "The sword is the key of heaven and hell"—meaning that those who accepted Mohammedanism, even from the terrors of the sword, should be saved, while those rejecting it should die by the same weapon and be damned. This is the only means used in propagating the religion of Islam. On either side of the pulpits of St. Sophia and the Mosque of Eyub are two flags hanging; one representing Judaism, and the other Christianity. When the imam goes up to the pulpit, he carries a wooden sword in one hand and the Koran in the other,

---

*The author of the article is a recent graduate of one of the leading theological seminaries.

to indicate that the conquest of the Koran over Judaism and Christianity is to be accomplished by the sword, teaching the people that their wars are holy wars, and that the Mohammedan soldier is the executor of God's will and vengeance.

No military service is required of either Jews or Christians, as they cannot be depended upon to defend Mohammedanism. Indeed, the government goes so far as to prohibit Armenians from possessing arms of any kind, even a penknife being forbidden them.

This freedom from military service, which is a mark of degradation in the eyes of a Turk, has had some compensations. It has saved the Christians from the "wasting influences and destructive diseases of the camp and the battle-field, and has accustomed them to industry and thrift." But while they are free from military service, a special tax is imposed upon them for the support of the Turkish army and State. The taxes are classified as follows: (1) One-tenth of all the crops and fruits; (2) four per cent. of the renting value of houses and lands; (3) five per cent. on every transfer; (4) an animal tax of thirty-three pence on every sheep and goat. Besides these, there are the road and labor taxes on the imaginary earnings of the Christians, and the military tax laid upon every male.

The tithes are sold to the highest bidder, and the competition is so keen that the successful bidder is forced to pay more than the entire just amount of the tax. Consequently the tithe-farmers are forced to resort to the worst form of extortion from the poor Christians, and, instead of making a careful and honest estimate of the taxable produce, assess it without examination, often to more than double its amount. If the farmer has reaped his grain, he cannot store it in his barn until the tax-gatherer has surveyed it and taken out his lion's share. If the official is busy elsewhere, or is waiting for a bribe, the grain must be left on the field for days or weeks, exposed to drenching rain and scorching sun, until the whole crop becomes spoiled or is carried away by the rapacious Kurds.

If the farmer is then unable to pay the tithe in kind, he is obliged to pay in ready cash. But as he rarely has enough to meet these exactions, his household utensils are seized and sold. The tax-gatherer, with his zabtiehs (policemen), is an ever-present scourge to the country. He is heartless and without honor. During the business transactions he must be entertained and provided for, with all his retinue and horses. If the farmer can by any means raise the money, he is only too glad to do so and free himself from this burden; but if he is unable, he is often maltreated and thrown into prison. False receipts, too, are often given, and the amount of the debt has thus to be twice paid. Should a Christian at any time seek redress for continued outrages on person or property, he can appeal only to the local governor or officials, and never to the Sultan, whose time is considered too valuable to be taken up in looking after the welfare of his subjects. The press also is muzzled, as the following rules governing journalism in Constantinople will show:

Art. 5. Avoid personalities. If anybody tells you that a governor or deputy governor has been guilty of embezzlement, maladministration, or of any other blameworthy conduct, treat the charge as not proved, and say nothing about it.

Art. 6. You are forbidden to publish petitions in which individuals or associations complain of acts of mismanagement, or call the Sultan's attention to them.

The Turkish officials, to whom the Christian is supposed to appeal in cases of grievances, are exceeding corrupt, committing even more crimes than their inferior accomplices, whose administration is an abominable scourge. A few years ago one of the missionaries in Erzeroum told me that while he was on one of his mission tours he came across a poor Christian shepherd who had just been attacked by the Kurds and despoiled of thirty sheep from his flock. The next day, upon the missionary's return to Erzeroum, he called upon the commander of the army to complain of the outrage, and discovered fifteen of the thirty sheep in his yard!

Under the ruinous management of these mercenary officials, the country which God made so rich in resources has become poor. These men have transformed their official privileges into prerogatives of tyranny, and there is no bound to their avarice. Such is the system of political economy practiced in the internal affairs of the provinces in the name of Padishah by officials who are "lofty in adulations and calumny, perfidy and treason." In the eyes of the Turkish government, suspicion of her non-Mussulman subjects is equal to proof, intention to mischief, and the intention is not less criminal than the act. This was the attitude of the government in relation to the recent Sassoun massacre. As soon as the Pasha of Bitlis sent word to Constantinople that the Armenians were in rebellion, without waiting for proof, the Turkish troops were sent to the scene with orders to suppress the revolt—orders which they knew they must interpret as

A TURKISH CAWAS.

meaning the extermination of whole villages if they would please the Sultan. After wholesale butchery, Zeki Pasha reported that, "not finding any rebellion, we cleared the country so that none should occur in the future." This stroke of policy was afterwards praised in the Court as an act of patriotism.

Why has the Sultan failed to perform his obligations as pledged in the Berlin Treaty? Because, according to Mohammedanism, "no promise can bind the faithful against the interest and duty of their religion." For nearly twenty years he has occupied the throne, but all the justice which he has shown, and the peace that he has been able to maintain, must be ascribed to the pressure brought upon him by the Treaty Powers. Take, for instance, the case of Mussa Bey. When all Europe demanded an investigation, the Sultan bestirred himself to a pretense of political reformation, but it was short-lived. Duplicity, shiftlessness and deceit are his great characteristics.

No pledge made in the Berlin Treaty has been respected. According to that, there was to be religious toleration in Turkey. Has there been? Far from it. The Sultan has scarcely lived up to the injunction of Mohammed, who said, "Christians and Jews may have their churches or synagogues, repair or rebuild them; but no new churches or synagogues shall be built."

It is the delight of the Turks to profane and pillage Christian churches, and in this sacrilege they are upheld by the weakness of the Sultan.

Who is this man? Well may one ask,

> Upon what meat doth this our Caesar feed,
> That he has grown so great?

He is the son of a slave of obscure parentage, with no endowments of mind or heart that should fit him for the responsible position of sovereign and pontiff. He is utterly incompetent to remedy official vices, and leaves the affairs of the country to adjust themselves while he busies himself in deciding what shall be the costume of the comedians and actresses in the French opera, for which he has a great fondness. His palaces and kiosks exceed all former examples of royal luxury. His domestics number 6000, and $11,000,000 is required to cover the annual expenses of his royal house and table. Nothing arouses his lethargy save the sound of pleasure or music or the talk of his concubines, wives and comedians, who are really his ministers. While 6000 courtiers (who are the mercenaries of many fragmental tribes) wait on his holy person daily, the Christians are supporting his tottering throne; yet the whole policy of the government of the officials of the Kurds and Circassians is the extermination of the Armenians. This is all in accordance with Said Pasha's policy, who said: "The solution of the Armenian question consists in the annihilation of the Armenian race." Will the following well-authenticated instance, which is but one of hundreds, be a surprise to you? During the spring of 1889, in the Armenian town of Zeitune, consisting of about 20,000 inhabitants, 600 boys alone were poisoned by the doctors, who were bribed by the government to use impure vaccine matter; while individual cases of murder of noted Armenians are of daily occurrence all around the empire.

Although the Kurds and Circassians are by no means the only agents in satisfying Said Pasha's craving for Armenian blood, they are very powerful factors in carrying on the work of destruction. When Sultan Medjid was talking of driving them out of the country, the cunning advice of his counsel was: "Let them alone to exterminate the non-Mussulmans, or to keep them subject to your throne."

Ever since they have been the favorites of the Sultan and government, who have equipped them with modern rifles in defiance of Article LXI of the Berlin Treaty, to assist them in their work of rapine, confiscation and depredation. Yet, lawless and barbarous, they are not only tolerated by the government, but upheld. A numerous swarm of these mercenaries assisted Zeki Pasha in the recent massacre, led either by bribes or by the hope of spoil or by the threats of fanatic mufti, whose cry echoed far above the groans of the dying, "Fight, fight! Paradise, paradise!"

Today Turkey presents an awful picture of death and ruin. War, pestilence and famine press their rival claims, and we cry from a full heart, "How long, O Lord, how long?"

What, then, is left to us? The sad experience of five hundred years has shown that neither obedience nor submission can secure to us the safety of our mothers, sisters, wives and property. These many years we have submitted our bodies to the Turk; but patience is no more a virtue. It is an evil and unjust government that forces us to raise the voice of righteous indignation. If a government is a divine appointment, then its mission should be to work for the welfare of the nation, holding its interests in trust. Since the Berlin treaty, intoleration by ruler and officials has gone from bad to worse. While subjects to the Sultan, we are considered as strangers and treated like enemies. The Turks claim that the recent troubles came from organized revolutionary societies among the Christians. Were the Armenians organized in societies when the massacres of 1835, 1860, 1876 and 1878 took place? Nay! Yet Armenian mothers were torn from their children, wives from their husbands, daughters from their parents, and given over to a fate more horrible than death. Is it necessary, then, in order to justify our claim and secure the intervention of Europe, that the Turks should massacre twice or three times more than 15,000 Armenians? The present existing struggle resolves itself into a conflict between Christianity and Mohammedanism, between Christian civilization and the effete civilization of Islam, between aggressive Christian progress and the indolence of the fatalistic Turk. Instead of being allowed to develop the industries of the country, we have been oppressed for five centuries by the iron hand of tyranny. We have been obliged to abandon agriculture, our farms being usurped by the officials for the support of Turkish mosques. Misfortune after misfortune, however, has but intensified national love, and we would fain be prepared to support our own autonomy. Should not Christian nations feel an interest in our country and in our struggle for life and liberty, and appoint a European governor, vested with full power of governing the country?

CHAPTER III.

ABDUL HAMID, SULTAN OF TURKEY.
A Character Sketch. By W. T. Stead.

[The Finest Pearl of the Age, and the esteemed Centre of the Universe; at whose grand portals stand the camels of justice and mercy, and to whom the eyes of the kings and people in the West have been drawn; the rulers there finding an example of political prowess and the classes a model of mercy and kindness; our Lord and Master the Sultan of the two Shores and the High King of the two Seas; the Crown of Ages and the Pride of all Countries, the greatest of all Khalifs; the Shadow of God on Earth; the successor of the Apostles of the Lord of the Universe, the Victorious Conqueror (Al-Ghazi) Sultan Abdul Hamid Khan.

May God protect his Kingdom and place his glory above the Sun and the Moon, and may the Lord supply all the world with the goodness which proceeds from his Holy Majesty's good intentions.—Turkish newspaper quoted by Mr. H. Anthony Salmone, Nineteenth Century, November, 1894.]

Amen and Amen! But if the stock of goodness at the disposal of the Lord does not exceed that which proceeds from His Holy Majesty's good intentions, it is to be feared the rest of the world will be put on short rations. Not that His Holy Majesty, the Shadow of God on earth, is lacking in the material with which on classic authority it is understood that hell is paved. He means well, his intentions are excellent. Where he fails is in the execution. It is this trifling detail that at present stands in the way of the elevation of Abdul Hamid's glory above that of the sun and the moon, and, indeed, it is to be feared, has consigned it to the nethermost depths—which, however, is unjust.

Abdul Hamid is, of all men, one of those most to be pitied, but at the present moment there is but little pity or compassion shown him. The custom of punishing the Pope for Caesar's crimes is still fashionable among mankind, and Abdul Hamid is being made the scapegoat for all the atrocities of all the Ottomans. Not that he is without crimes of his own—black and bloody crimes, according to our Western ideas; but, in the eyes of the Oriental, their only criminality consists in that they are not black and bloody enough to achieve their end. For the government of Osmanli has always been, since the days when the Tartar horsemen first taught Asia how terrible was their wrath, a government of terror. By terror, the Sultans climbed to supreme power; by terror, they have maintained themselves on the throne of the Caesars for five centuries, and it is only because they can no longer inspire sufficient terror that the Ottoman Empire is crumbling into ruin. Abdul Hamid, no doubt, resorted to massacre as a British Prime Minister attempts to renew his power by a dissolution. Atrocities are as natural to the Turk as the general elections to a Parliamentarian. They are the traditional Ottoman method of renewing the mandate of the ruler. No doubt this is offensive to Western civilization. The Sultan is an anachronism in the last decade of the nineteenth century, and those who have been trying to make believe that he was a civilized sovereign are no doubt experiencing the revulsion natural to disappointed hope. But those of us who have never for one moment forgotten that the Turk is simply the aboriginal savage encamped on the ruins of a civilization which he destroyed, can afford to be more mild and just in our estimate of the character of the last of the line of Othman.

In this article I shall not depart from the rule governing all these character sketches. I shall try to represent Abdul Hamid as he appears to himself at his best, rather than as he appears to his victims at his worst. It is of course impossible to write entirely from his standpoint. But it is possible to avoid the habit of judging the Sultan of Stamboul as if he were a smug citizen of a London suburb. And if we can but start from the point of realizing that it is as natural and as habitual to a Sultan to massacre as it is to a redskin to scalp, we shall at least avoid one element that would be utterly fatal to any realization of Abdul Hamid's position.

I. BEFORE HIS ACCESSION.

Put yourself in his place! Abdul Hamid, the nephew of Abdul Aziz, was reared in the seclusion of the seraglio. Forbidden to take any part in public affairs, he was flung in his earliest manhood into the midst of that debauchery which makes Constantinople the cesspool of the world. For some years he spent his life in riot and excess. Then he suddenly reformed. From a progligate he became an ascetic. Like Prince Hal, he banished Jack Falstaff and all his companions of the wine cup, and set himself, with the zeal of a convert, to live a higher and a purer life. His enemies impute it to calculation. But it would be more charitable to believe that the young man had passed through the experience of conversion—a phenomenon fortunately by no means peculiar to the Christian faith. The penitent prodigal is not the less welcome because he goes to a mosque rather than to a church, and there seems to be no doubt that long before there was any prospect of his succeeding to the throne Abdul Hamid reformed his mode of life and became, according to his lights, a pious and devout disciple of the Prophet. This was the more remarkable, as his conversion took place while Turkish society was still reveling in the false security and fictitious wealth that resulted from the loans which his uncle contracted with reckless prodigality. The latter part of the reign of Abdul Aziz was for the East what the closing years of the Second Empire was for France. Constantinople, like Paris, had its vulgar orgie of splendid debauchery—modern versions of Belshazzar's feast, in which the handwriting on the wall was hardly discerned before the avenger was at the gates.

THE FALL OF ABDUL AZIZ.

The French Empire went down in the earthquake of Sedan in 1870. It was not till five years later that that Nemesis overtook Abdul Aziz. The treasury, emptied by the Sultan's extravagance, could no longer pay the interest on the coupon, and when Abdul Aziz could no longer borrow, his end was at hand. After a brief pause, during which the storm clouds gathered and broke in insurrection in the extreme western province of the Herzegovina, the conspirators prepared to depose the Sultan. Then events followed each other with the rapidity of the swiftest tragedy. Abdul Hamid, from his retreat among the mollahs and imams, was

BEGGARS.

startled by the news, first of the deposition of his uncle, then of the proclamation of his brother, Murad as Sultan. Fast on the heels of this came the suicide of the deposed Sultan. Then like a thunderclap came the assassination of the ministers who had deposed Abdul Aziz, and the summary execution of their murderer. Meanwhile, the war clouds were gathering black and heavy on the Russian frontier. Massacres and atrocities in Bulgaria had filled Europe with shuddering horror. Montenegro and Servia had gone to war; Russian volunteers were flocking to the Servian camp; the capital was seething with excitement. There was the underswell of a revolution in Stamboul, the menace of a Russian invasion in Europe and in Asia. In the midst of all these portents of doom, the pious recluse was suddenly confounded by the announcement that his brother Murad had gone mad, and that he must ascend the throne of Othman.

THE DEPOSITION OF MURAD.

It is difficult to imagine a more trying ordeal than that through which Abdul Hamid had passed between the deposition of his uncle and the removal of his brother. It would have severely tested the nerves of the most experienced politician in the most stormy of South American republics. What it must have been to the inexperienced and devout Hamid no one can quite realize. What is clear is that he shrank timidly from the perilous dignity of the tottering throne. He refused to consent to the deposition of his brother. He was reluctant to credit the reports of the physicians. He insisted upon foreign advice. But Midhat had decided that Murad must be removed. According to the statements made in the recently published book about Murad, the unfortunate Sultan might easily have recovered had he been allowed to rest. As it was, the conspirators purposely rendered his recovery impossible. The moment the foreign physician's back was turned, they succeeded in driving their unfortunate victim into a condition of imbecility which justified, if it did not even necessitate, his deposition. Abdul Hamid persisted to the last in deprecating his brother's removal. He objected strenuously to his own elevation to the Sultanate. Only when it was made clear to him that Murad would be deposed in any case, and that he had only to choose between being Sultan himself or being put out of the way by the Sultan whom Midhat would instal in his stead did he yield and consent to accept the thorny crown of the Ottoman Empire. So it came to pass that Murad was formally deposed and Abdul Hamid reigned in his stead.

II. SULTAN.

"Yildiz, the palace of the Sultan," says a recent writer, "like the seraglio of the 'good old times,' contains all the dramatis personae of the tales of the Scheherazaide, the eunuchs, mollahs, pashas, beys, astrologers, slaves, sultanas, kadines, dancing women, Circassian and Georgian odalisques, whose main object in existence is their own self-advancement. Above this ant-hill of picturesque folk the interesting figure of the Sultan stands out in striking relief."

When Abdul Hamid was installed as Sultan of Turkey above this picturesque ant-hill, the situation was such as might well have appalled the stoutest heart. Possibly the Sultan's ignorance—for although he is no fool, he, like all the other Turks, has never quite grasped the elementary facts which underlie the modern world—may have helped him. If he had had a wider range of knowledge or a more vivid imagination he might have gone the way of Murad.

ALONE.

Without training, without preparation, without a single friend whom he could trust, Abdul Hamid was suddenly brought forth from his seclusion by the men who had deposed his uncle and his brother, and established on a throne reeling from the blows of domestic insurrection and foreign war. The last days of the Ottoman Empire seemed to have come. Among all the Powers, not one would promise him any help. Among all his pashas there was not one whom he did not believe would depose him tomorrow if private gain or public policy appeared to demand such a step. The treasury was empty. The credit of the empire was at such a low ebb that no new loan was possible, yet armies had to be retained in the field to keep Servia and Montenegro in check. Preparations had to be pushed forward to prevent the threatened Russian invasion. Greece was threatening in the south, Russia in the north and east, while Austria was suspected of aggressive designs in the west. There was hardly a single province which was not threatening revolt.

The Powers were clamoring for reforms, the first condition of which was lacking. What and where and whom was he to trust?

KISMET.

Now, Abdul Hamid was not learned, nor clever, nor heroic, nor indeed anything in particular. But he was born of the house of Othman, and he was a devout disciple of Mohammed. For five centuries it had been the will of Allah that there should never be lacking a member of the House of Othman to reign as the Shadow of God among men. Therefore he might not unreasonably conclude it was the will of Allah that he, the rightful representative of that great house, should deliver Islam from the ruin which menaced it. But if it was the will of Allah that such a deliverance should be wrought, then it was not for him, Abdul Hamid, to tremble or to escape from the task laid upon him by providence. Years before, when he was still a young man, he had accompanied his uncle on the famous European tour, in the course of which Abdul Aziz visited London and was banqueted by the Lord Mayor. In those days it was noted that Abdul Hamid was of a very shy and retiring disposition. It was reported that when he was in the gardens at Buckingham Palace he would always slink behind the bushes and conceal himself if he saw anyone approaching. By constitution he was not self-assertive, and, like Hamlet, he regarded it as a cursed spite that he was told off to put to right times so cruelly out of joint. But, unlike Hamlet, Abdul Hamid is a Moslem, and a prince of the house which genera-

KHALIL RIFAAT PASHA, THE NEW GRAND VIZIER, ON HIS WAY TO TAKE UP HIS POST.

tion after generation produced warriors and statesmen who were the terror of Christendom and the object of the envious admiration of the Eastern world. Hence he did not hesitate, when the call came, to fairly shoulder his burden and to undertake the task of saving the empire with qualifications almost as scanty as those of Tommy Atkins for commanding an army corps.

MIDHAT AND HIS CONSTITUTION.

When he became Sultan, Midhat had conceived the idea of throwing dust in the eyes of Europe by proclaiming a constitution. The Sultan assented to it as he would probably have assented to any other expedient which the Grand Vizier proposed at that time. But he never liked it, and took the first opportunity of dissolving the Parliament and putting the constitution on the shelf. Parliaments indeed were not in his line. The House of Othman has many virtues, but those of constitutional kingship were not of them. The founder of the dynasty and all his most famous descendants had been men of personal initiative. They not only reigned, but ruled. They first carved out their realms for themselves with their own scimiters, and then governed it by their own autocratic, theocratic will. To Abdul Hamid, who believed only in two things—in God and in his house—the very idea of a parliament or of any limitation on the sovereign power of the Sultan partook of the nature of a blasphemy. Not by such means would Allah deliver the faithful. Abdul Hamid would stand in the ancient ways, walk by the ancient light, and trust in the God of his fathers to deliver him from the perils that encompassed him round about. For a time, in deference to Midhat, he tolerated the theatricality of the constitution, hoping that it might delude the infidel and deliver Turkey from war. But when it failed, and the infidel would not be deluded, and the Russian armies crossed the Danube and invaded Armenia, then the time for such fooling was past. Midhat was banished to Arabia, where he shortly afterward died, the parliament was dissolved, and the constitution vanished in thin air.

THE ONE MAN POWER.

Henceforth the Sultan was to be the Sultan. And for nearly twenty years Abdul Hamid has been the Sultan and no mistake. Believing in no one but himself, he trusted no one but himself. Surrounded by men who had betrayed his uncle and his brother, living in an atmosphere malarious with corruption and saturated with intrigue, he early decided to trust no one, and to govern single-handed. And hopeless though the enterprise appeared, Abdul Hamid may at least claim that whatever may be said in criticism of his policy, it has at least achieved one great and indisputable success. It has enabled him to survive. And that is more than most people believed possible. Not only has he survived for twenty years, but he has, until quite recently, been regarded as one of the ablest and most successful rulers of our time.

The worst enemy of Abdul Hamid cannot deny that he is one of the most industrious of sovereigns. He toils early and late, seventeen and eighteen hours a day. Neither can it be imputed to him that he has not always labored for what he believed to be the real interest of the great trust which Allah has committed to his hands. He has worked like a galley slave in the peopled solitude of his palace. An imperial convict sentenced to hard labor for life, with constant liability to capital punishment, he has scorned delights and lived laborious days. He is not a genius, but he has held his own; not a hero, but he has borne the heat and burden of a long and toilsome day without complaining, and if he were gathered to his fathers tomorrow, he would have a record of which, when due allowance is made for his environment, no Sultan of his line need be ashamed.

COURAGE WITH SELF-RELIANCE.

It is the fashion nowadays to denounce Abdul Hamid as an abject coward. Cowardice has never been a note of the House of Othman. The breed is brave by heredity, and Abdul Hamid has given enough proof of his courage to show that he belongs to the imperial line. Almost immediately after his accession, he had to face the Russian invasion. On both eastern and western frontiers burst the storm of Russian war. His arsenals were almost empty; his treasury was bankrupt. Even the rifles for his legions had to be bought in hot haste across the Atlantic. Of his pashas, some of the most highly placed were believed to be in Russian pay. There was no one in camp or cabinet who was of proved genius and who could command the confidence either of his sovereign or of Europe. Among the great Powers there was not one which could be relied upon for a cartridge or a sou. England, which in olden days had been the sworn ally of his predecessors, had taken offense about the suppression of the Bulgarian insurrection, an inscrutable piece of squeamishness on her part which Abdul Hamid to this day finds impossible to understand. As if the Ottoman Empire could exist without such suppression of rebellions! For the Turk without atrocities is as the leopard without his spots, and a sudden qualm of conscience as to the existence of spots cannot be understood by the leopard with whom we had been in alliance, spots and all, for more than the lifetime of a generation. France, prostrate after the German conquest, was useless. Abdul Hamid had to depend on himself alone, as his ancestors had done before him—on himself, on the swords of the faithful, and on Allah, the all-powerful, who at the eleventh hour might make bare his arm and overwhelm the hosts of the infidel.

THE DEFENSE OF CONSTANTINOPLE.

So argued the forlorn Sultan, and without more ado he set himself to beat back the tide of Russian war. The terrible year that followed added its deep impress to those of the tragedies which had preceded it. The heroic defense of Plevna by Osman Pasha was a solitary gleam of light amidst the ever-deepening gloom of military defeat. Alike in Europe and in Asia, the crusading Russians pressed slowly but steadily onward. Kars fell in Armenia. Plevna at last sur-

MOSQUE OF THE SULTAN AT SWEET WATERS OF EUROPE

rendered in Europe, and then the Russian army, like a long dammed-up flood, surged irresistibly over the Balkans, and rushed foaming up to the very gates of Stamboul. Then it was that the Sultan showed that he possessed some of the old military instincts and the fighting spirit of his race. Panic reigned at the Porte, and the pashas, appalled by the sudden collapse of their armies, were counseling a hasty retreat to Broussa, on the other side of the Sea of Marmora. Abdul Hamid, calm and undismayed, concentrated all his energies upon the preparations for the defense of Constantinople. Mouktar Pasha was placed in command of the lines, behind which the wreck of the Ottoman armies was mustered for a last stand.

HE VETOES THE FLIGHT TO BROUSSA.

While still absorbed in the preparations for the defense of his capital against the Russians, Abdul Hamid was suddenly startled by an intimation that the British fleet, which all the autumn had lain sullenly vigilant in Besika bay, was about to force the passage of the Dardenelles. Orders were given to the forts to resist the naval invasion, and the gunners in the forts that command the Straits made ready to try conclusions with Admiral Hornby's ironclads. At the last moment, however, the ships were allowed to pass.

Lord Beaconsfield undoubtedly intended the advance of the fleet to be a demonstation against the Russians. But it so happened that it created more consternation among the Turks, who seemed to feel themselves suddenly assailed in front and rear by a fresh enemy. It was just about the time when the British fleet had forced the Dardenelles and anchored at Prince's Islands, within a day's steaming of Stamboul, that a council was held in the capital to consider the Grand Vizier's proposal for an immediate retreat to Asia. The assembly of ministers and pashas was numerous and influential. The prevailing opinion was that as the capital lay now between the Russians at San Stefano and the British fleet at Prince's Islands, nothing remained but flight into Asia. Then it was found that the Sultan showed himself a true descendant of Othman. Confronted by the craven crew of his own council, urging instant flight, Abdul Hamid calmly, but resolutely, refused to abandon the capital. Come what might, he would remain in Constantinople, and share the fate of the city that for four hundred years had been the throne of his dynasty. The word of the Sultan prevailed. The flight to Broussa was countermanded, and Abdul Hamid, amid his craven councillors, kept the Crescent above the Cross on the great cathedral of St. Sophia.

AND SAVES THE TURKISH FLEET.

Nor was this the only trial of his nerve. When the negotiations were going on between General Ignatieff and the Turkish plenipotentiaries at San Stefano, the Russians demanded as one of the prizes of war the whole Turkish fleet. Achmet, Vefyk and Safvet Pashas, the strongest members of the ministry, urged compliance with the Russian demands. Turkey, they held, was powerless to resist. To refuse the Russian terms would be to renew the war. If the war was renewed the Cossacks would canter almost unopposed to the palace of the Sultan, and the Ottoman Empire would not survive the capture of its capital. But here again the indomitable spirit of Abdul Hamid burst out. "Never," he exclaimed—"never," and with his own hand he wrote a letter to the Grand Duke Nicholas, declaring it was impossible to give up the fleet. He added, with an emphasis unusual to him, that he would prefer to see the vessels blown up with himself on board rather than that they should fall into the hands of Russia. This might be bluff, but it was bluff of the supreme sort, the bluff of a monarch on the edge of the abyss, and above all it was bluff that succeeded. The Russians waved their demand: the Turkish fleet, like the Turkish capital, was saved by the Sultan, and the Sultan alone.

It is enough to recall these two severe crises to understand how it is that the Sultan feels that it is he and no other, he, the Commander of the Faithful, to whom Allah has intrusted the responsibility of government. And so it has come to pass that ever since that time Abdul Hamid has insisted upon governing himself alone. In small things, as in great, in the appointment of a policeman in Erzeroum, or in the regulation of a theatre in Stamboul, equally as in the great affairs of State, the Sultan is supreme. He alone must order everything, sanction everything, superintend everything. As in the eyes of Allah there is nothing great or nothing small, but all things are of equal importance, so it is with the chosen of Allah who reigns and rules at Stamboul.

III. WHAT HE HAS DONE OF GOOD.

What has Abdul Hamid done for the empire over which he reigns? First and foremost, he has kept it in existence for twenty years. He has survived war, insurrection, treason, attempted assassination, bankruptcy. And that in itself is no mean achievement. There seemed but a forlorn hope that he would succeed. But he has succeeded—so far at least as a man may be said to succeed who succeeds in evading the continual menace of annihilation.

HIS FOREIGN POLICY.

Secondly, he has, on the whole, been more reasonable and practical in his dealings with the Powers than he might have been. He was slow to give up Dulcigno to Montenegro and Epirus to Greece. His resolution needed to be quickened by a naval demonstration in the Adriatic and a threatened descent on the custom-houses of Smyrna; but in the end he gave way. In his dealings with Bulgaria he was more reasonable than anyone anticipated. When Eastern Roumelia tore up the Berlin Treaty and adjoined herself to the principality of Bulgaria, the Sultan would have been within his treaty rights, and he would probably have had, to say the least, no opposition from Russia, if he had invaded the rebellious province and re-established his authority at Philippopolis. But he refrained from interfering, and as the net result of twenty years' diplomacy he is probably on better terms with the Bulgarians than are the Russians, to whom they owe their emancipation. Thirdly, he has not done any-

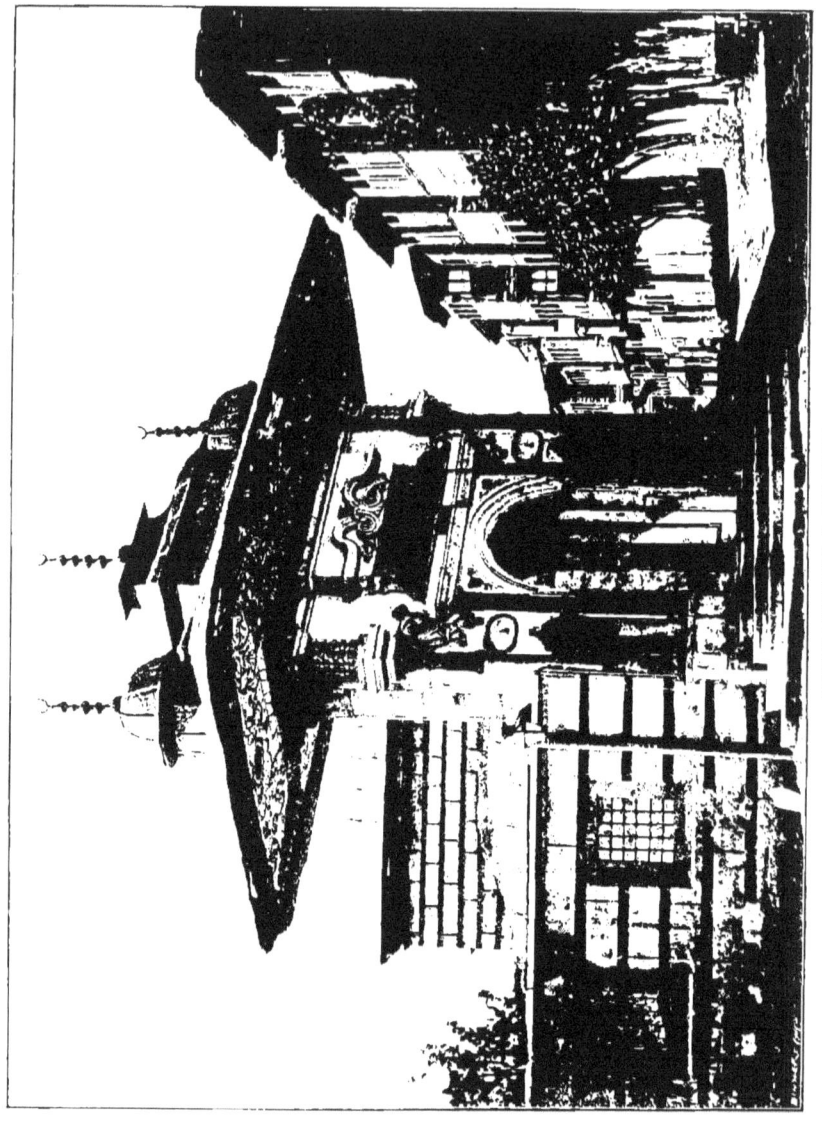

ENTRANCE TO A MOSQUE.

thing like the mischief he might have done in Egypt. He might have complicated things terribly if he had accepted our proposal for a joint occupation. He refused, and although he may have been regretting it ever since, he has in reality contributed mightily to establish English authority in Cairo. Rumor says that he encouraged Arabi to revolt. If so, we owe him only one more good turn. For if Arabi had not revolted, the British redcoat would never have been established in the barracks at Cairo. Fourthly, he has had to face a very dangerous revolt in Arabia. He quelled it by a policy of concession, which warded off a serious peril to the empire and gave to the Arabs securities against oppression.

RESTORATION OF FINANCES AND ARMY REFORM.

Fifthly, he established an International Commission for the payment of the interest on the debt. This required considerable nerve. He had seen in Egypt what international commissions came to. He naturally shrank from establishing an imperium in imperio at his own door. But when convinced that it was necessary, he bowed to the will of Allah, and was rewarded for his self-sacrifice by the re-establishment of the credit of the empire in the stock exchanges of Europe. When he came to the throne, Turkey was bankrupt. Her last loan had been floated at 12 per cent. Today the treasury, although not overflowing, is able to meet its obligations, and with such punctuality and dispatch as to enable a Turkish loan to be floated at 5 per cent. Sixthly, he has done a great deal for the improvement of the discipline and the equipment of the army. He placed it under German direction, and, according to Captain Norman, who recently wrote on the subject in the United Service Magazine, he has done a great deal toward making it a valuable fighting force. He has replenished the batteries of artillery, provided his troops with magazine rifles, and can now, it is said, put 500,000 men into the field.

EDUCATION AND ART.

Seventhly, Abdul Hamid has shown a praiseworthy appreciation of the importance of education. When the Russians were in full march upon Adrianople, he was busily engaged in founding the Mulkieh school, a preparatory college for the civil service. After the war was over he founded a school of law at the capital. Many other special schools have been founded by him, and more than 2000 elementary schools, attended by 100,000 scholars, have been opened since he ascended the throne. Eighthly, Abdul Hamid deserves credit for his interest in the education of women. He has taken a notable step in advance by establishing various girls' schools in Constantinople and other towns. Ninthly, Abdul Hamid has taken a new departure in bestowing some attention on art. There is more treasure-trove within his empire than exists elsewhere on the world's surface. But hitherto sultans have concerned themselves as much with the priceless remains of Greek art as an Ashantee concerns himself about the higher mathematics. Abdul Hamid has broken with this barbarous tradition. Mr. Shaw Lefevre, who visited Turkey in 1890, says:

For the first time the interesting contents of his treasury have been arranged, and, under special permits, are open to inspection. He has also established a museum of antiquities, under the care of Hamdi Bey, a very competent antiquarian, a Moslem by religion, but the son of a Greek who was stolen as a boy from Scio. There has been a recent find of three splendid sarcophagi at Sidon, one of which is believed to have contained the remains either of Alexander or one of his generals; it has bas-reliefs of the very best period of Grecian art—equal in merit, in the opinion of many, to the Elgin marbles, and far more perfect in preservation. This alone makes the fortunes of the museum, and must attract every sculptor in Europe. He has formed a school of art.

ADMINISTRATIVE REFORM.

Tenthly, he has busied himself very much about the reorganization of the judicial administration. As to the value of this I am skeptical. But it is probable that the Sultan means to do the best he can. He has certainly taken no end of trouble about it. According to Hakki Bey, the reign of the Sultan has witnessed the most effective improvements in this respect. The reorganization of provincial tribunals, the nomination of procurators and advocates-general, the establishment of a regular system of advancement for judges, and a firm guarantee insuring their trustworthiness and impartiality, the institution of criminal and civil procedures, are samples of this reforming policy applied to the administration of justice, besides the creation of a law school destined to furnish the department of justice with able and well-instructed functionaries. The reorganization of the police took place during this reign, which has witnessed so many acts for the welfare of the Ottoman people. The ancient confusion between the duties of the police, gendarmerie and department of penal jurisdiction ceased, and the gendarmerie as an armed force being attached to the War Department, the ministry of police remained with its essential attributes with regard to public safety.

Eleventhly, he has paid some attention to the construction of railways, the making of roads, and the supply of the necessary appliances of civilization to the cities of his empire. It is true that all these are but mere fragmentary trifles. Still, such as they are, they must be taken into account.

SISYPHUS ON THE BOSPHORUS.

Abdul Hamid has at least maintained his empire in peace. He might so easily have involved it in war. He has remained proof against all temptations of a warlike nature. He was not responsible for the Russian war. He inherited it, and he did the best he could. Since then he has succeeded in avoiding all armed collision with his neighbors, and has devoted his whole energies to what he regards as the true welfare of his people. Arminius Vambery, who recently paid a visit to the Sultan, bears emphatic testimony to the zeal with which he labors in the public service. He says:

The Sultan has got hardly the time to undertake a walk in his garden; how could he allow to himself the luxury of a longer holiday? To Sultan Abdul Hamid the throne is not at all a resting-place, and, having the honor to be his guest a few weeks ago, I can state from what I see that there has never been an Asiatic prince who devoted all his energies to the welfare of his country like the present ruler of Turkey.

IMPERIAL KIOSK OF SWEET WATERS OF ASIA, CONSTANTINOPLE.

IV. WHAT HE HAS DONE OF ILL.

If these be the good deeds of Abdul Hamid, what are his evil deeds? From the point of view of the House of Othman his evil deeds are two, neither of which count for much with his most acrimonious critics, and both of which can be explained and excused as the natural result of the circumstances under which he came to the throne.

HIS NEGLECT OF THE FLEET.

First and foremost, and worst of all, he has neglected the fleet. He imperiled his empire in order to prevent it passing into the hands of the Russians. He has allowed it to perish of red rust and decay. The ironclads are still anchored in the Bosphorus, but they can neither fight nor steam. When the Kiel canal was opened and the warships of all nations were assembled in honor of the new international highway, the Sultan found that in all his navy there was only one ironclad whose boilers could be trusted to hold out for so long a voyage as that from Constantinople to Kiel and back. As the result of this neglect of the navy, his capital is today at the mercy of the Czar. The Russian Black Sea fleet could any night force the entrance to the Bosphorus, and place Constantinople under the fire of their guns. Constantinople is now to all intents and purposes the fief of Russia. The Sultan, as the Russians say, is the Czar's keeper of the back door of the Russian Empire. The Sultan has to pay Russia for seventy years to come a tribute of £350,000 per annum. Whenever he fails to pay up, Russia can levy execution.

Even Greece is able nowadays to hold her own against the once puissant Ottoman. Turkey, once one of the greatest of sea powers, has now ceased to be a power at all, even in her own waters. To allow the fleet to moulder down in rusty ruin, that is the worst offense to be alleged against the Sultan from the point of view of an Ottoman.

PARALYSIS FROM OVERCENTRALIZATION.

The second great fault of Abdul Hamid has been the paralysis of his administration due to the congested centralization of his empire. As he persists in doing everything himself, things don't get done. There is a vast accumulation of arrears of work always before him. It used to be said of our Lords of the Admiralty that they were kept so busy signing papers all day they had no time left in which to think of the fleet at all. So it is with the Sultan. Mr. Shaw Lefevre says:

> There is no detail of administration of his government so small or trivial that it does not come before him personally for his approval and signature. The British Ambassador, as an illustration of this, told me that he could not get his steam launch repaired in the Turkish dock-yard, at his own expense, without the matter going before the Sultan for his approval. Another ex-ambassador said that in an interview at the palace the Sultan complained of overwork, and pointed to a great heap of papers on his table on which his decision was required. The ambassador, glancing his eye at the papers, observed that the first of them consisted of proposed regulations for a cafe chantant in Pera.

The result is paralysis, nothing is attended to in the right time, and everything gets out of joint.

CIVILIZATION TOO COMPLEX FOR THE SULTAN.

It is easy to see how this has arisen; it is even easier to see how it must work out. The Sultan, believing only in himself, will do everything himself. He and no other is the chosen of God. He therefore, and no other, must decide everything; sign everything. He is the delegate of Omnipotence, without permission to redelegate his supreme power. This was possible when sultans had little or nothing to do in the government of the provinces which they conquered. In the primitive barbarism of the Ottoman there was little trouble taken about the civic government. The cadi sat under the palm tree administering justice; the Sultan lived in his tent in the midst of his soldiers, leading them on to battle. Bajazet knew nothing of the endless minutiae of administrative details which harass Abdul Hamid. Amurath did not concern himself with regulating cafe chantants. A multiplex civilization, with innumerable wants, has invaded the primitive Ottoman State, and the Sultan who tries to deal with it single-handed is about as helpless as the baggage master of Julius Caesar would have been if he had been suddenly called upon to handle with his old ox-carts the goods traffic of the London and Northwestern Railway.

HIS INTERVIEW WITH MR. HEWITT.

The Sultan would be omnipotent, but he is not omniscient; and it is impossible, imprisoned in the Yildiz Kiosk, to know what is going own in his distant provinces. Mr. Hewitt, one time mayor of New York, told me of an interesting conversation which he once had with Abdul Hamid at Constantinople. Mr. Hewitt, who is a shrewd and observant American, had been much impressed during his travels in Asia Minor by seeing a peasant cut down a fine date tree that grew at his door, because he was unable to pay the taxes. He was driven permanently to impoverish himself in order to escape a levy which he had not means to meet. When he returned to Constantinople he told the Sultan what he had seen, and laid great stress upon the folly of killing the goose which laid the golden eggs. Abdul Hamid was most sympathetic, thanked him cordially, and dismissed the official responsible for collecting the taxes in that particular district. But he lamented the impossibility of keeping an eye on all parts of his empire, and he begged Mr. Hewitt, with an effusiveness that rather touched the New Yorker, to write to him whenever he saw anything or heard of anything which he, the Sultan ought to know.

I rallied Mr. Hewitt for not embracing this opportunity of becoming the eyes and ears of the Sultan, for he had not availed himself of the advantage. Mr. Hewitt was, however, much impressed with the sincerity of the Sultan's anxiety to do right, and the bitter sense of impotence under which he labored.

THE POVERTY OF THE PEASANTS.

The financial condition of the empire is much improved from the point of view of the stock exchange. But there is reason to fear that the improvement in Ottoman credit has been achieved by levying taxes with a severity which has

INTERIOR OF MOSQUE OF ST. SOPHIA, CONSTANTINOPLE.

dried up the sources of the prosperity of the peasants. Mr. Caillard, the English member of the International Commission of the Public Debt, reported as long ago as 1889 that the condition of things in the provinces was growing desperate.

The peasant in the interior has reduced his wants to their simplest expression, and signs are to hand which show him to be less and less able to purchase the few necessaries he requires. For instance, a few years ago in any decent peasant household copper cooking utensils were to be seen. Now they are scarcely to be found, and they have been sold to meet the pressing needs of the moment. Their place has been taken by clay utensils, and, in the case of the more affluent, by iron. The peasant's chief expenses lie in his women-folk, who require print stuffs for their dresses and linen for their underclothing; but of these he gets as little as possible, since, as often as not, he cannot pay for them. This smallness of margin is one of the reasons why the amount of importations increases so slowly. The peasant hardly ever pays for his purchases in cash; what little he has goes in taxes. He effects his purchases by barter. Another significant sign is the increase of brigandage which has taken place. New bands of brigands are continually springing up; reports from the interior are ever bringing to our knowledge some fresh acts of violent robbery. This simply means that men desperately poor, and refusing to starve, take to brigandage as a means of living.

THE WEALTH OF THE SULTAN.

At the same time the peasants are growing poor, the Sultan is growing rich. He has by one means and another acquired immense estates. According to an American antiquarian who has spent some years in Bagdad and Syria:

More than half of the landed property of the province of Bagdad has passed into the hand of the Sultan, and he has possessed himself of the whole of the valley of the Jordan. One effect of this was that the province no longer paid its way in the sense of returning a surplus income to the treasury, as the Sultan's land and those cultivating it were not subject to taxation.

V. THE SULTAN AT HOME.

No one knows really how the Sultan lives. A recent visitor at Yildiz received three different accounts of how he spends his day from three different pashas, each of whom ought to have been in a position to know the truth. What is known is that Abdul Hamid lives very simply in the comparative retirement of the Yildiz Kiosk. Frances Elliott, in her "Diary of an Idle Woman in Constantinople," gives an account of his daily life, which is probably as authentic as any that can be discovered in the press of Europe:

YILDIZ KIOSK.

Abdul Hamid is a nervous man. Even since the tragic death of his uncle he has obstinately refused to move from the small kiosk or palazzetto called Yildiz, about three miles from the city, on the European range of hills bordering the Bosphorus. The way to Yildiz lies through the draggle-tailed streets of Pera, into comparative country. After going up and down hill at a breakneck gallop, the outline of a palace kiosk, modern and small, reveals itself rising out of a cincture of dark groves. This is Yildiz Kiosk, where lives the Commander of the Faithful. It is not a palace at all, but originally was a summer villa. The park, which is well wooded, is spacious, with grassy slopes, diversified with other kiosks, also shaded with groves, descending to a quay on the Bosphorus. It has most charming views over land and sea, Europe and Asia. Near at hand is the broad channel of the deep blue Bosphorus, with its frieze of white palaces, steamers, caiques and vessels, with sails set, gliding by every instant.

HIS DAILY LIFE.

No Sultan has mounted the throne of Mohammed II more blameless in private life or endowed with more sentiments of general humanity. The hideous custom of the murder of infant nephews has ceased under his reign. He is modest in the requirements of his harem. Like the Pope, the Sultan eats alone, seated near a window overlooking the Bosphorus, except on special occasions when he receives with the most finished courtesy royal visitors, ambassadors and their wives, every European luxury being understood and served upon the board. Habitually he drinks only water, brought to the palace in casks under special precautions. His food is extremely plain, consisting chiefly of vegetables, served in silver saucepans, presented to him at table sealed. No one works harder than Hamid. He takes but few hours of sleep, and sometimes passes the entire night, pen in hand, signing every document himself, from the appointment of a governor to the lowest officer at the palace.

FROM DAWN TO SUNSET.

Like most Orientals, he is an early riser. After the prayers and ablutions enjoined by his religion—and he is eminently a pious Turk—he drinks a cup of coffee, and then begins smoking cigarettes, which (as was the case with Louis Napoleon) he continues all day. At 10 A. M. he receives the reports of his ministers, works alone or with his secretaries till 1, when he eats; then he drives in the grounds or floats in a gilded caique on a lake for a couple of hours, never leaving the park of Yildiz except to go to the mosque, after which he returns to preside at the Council of State, or to receive ambassadors or ministers. His dinner is at sunset, when the national pillaf of rice and sweets are served with sherbet and ices. After this he betakes himself to the Selaulek to receive pashas and generals of high rank, such as

Osman Ghazi, or oftener he disappears into the harem to pass the evening hours with wives, mother and children. Music is his delight, and in private he himself takes his place at the piano.

Turk and Ottoman to the backbone, he is convinced that his soldiers are the best in the world, the most enduring and amenable to discipline. In speech he is a purist, speaking well in a slow monotonous voice, but sometimes the flood of expression is let loose, and he is said to burst into something like eloquence. The mollahs and dervishes find in him a ready listener and a liberal protector; indeed, he is liberal, and takes pleasure in rewarding those who serve him well. His gifts to European ladies are especially magnificent in gems and pearls, of which he has drawersful in the old seraglio.

AT THE SELAULEK.

It is only on Friday, when the Sultan goes to the mosque, that he ever leaves the shelter of the park. All the troops are turned out, the ministers are in attendance, an immense crowd gathers to catch a glimpse of the Shadow of God. A newspaper correspondent thus describes the scene when the Sultan appears:

The silence suddenly becomes absolute as the Sultan leaves the apartments, and then, as he appears, it is simply broken by the equivalent to a Turkish "hurrah" from the Marine Guard, given from hundreds of throats as with one voice, in three or four ringing syllables. At a gentle trot the open barouche slips past. On the right sits a small bowed figure, with eyes cast down and hands clasped on his knees. The beard is a dusky gray and the skin sallow and earthy. The Sultan looks ten years more than his age, one might say ten years older almost than he did in 1892. On his left is Ghazi Osman Pasha, who is growing old by the side of his great master. Under the windows, filled with foreign spectators, amidst a curious hush, under the fire of every eye, passes the carriage with its terrible freight, the

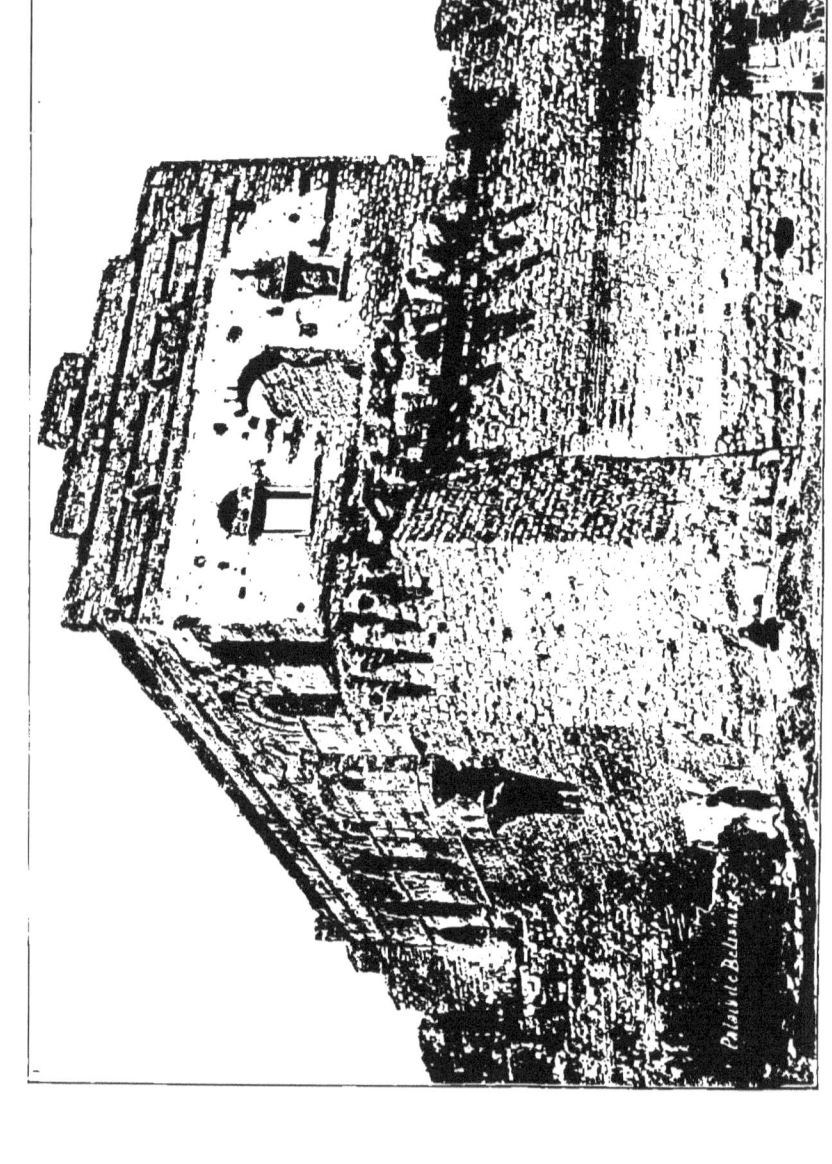

PALACE OF BALARIUS, CONSTANTINOPLE

inscrutable will on which depend the lives of millions. As Abdul Hamid Khan II is assisted up the steps of the mosque, the shrill cry of the muezzin cleaves the blue stillness as he stands out a mere speck on the minaret rail against the sky.

Then the doors close and the act is over. The curtain figuratively falls, and tongues are loosed. An American remarks that the Sultan looks so like the late Mr. Jay Gould that if the latter could have been placed by the side of Ghazi Osman, as he then was, and were so to drive back, not one in the crowd would detect the difference.

In half an hour he comes out again, enters a victoria, takes the reins of the two gray horses, and drives away at a walking pace.

THE SULTAN AS HE LOOKS.

Miss Elliott, when she saw him, remarked:

The Sultan is the most wretched, pinched-up little sovereign I ever saw. A most unhappy-looking man, of dark complexion, with a look of absolute terror in his large Eastern eyes. People say he is nervous, and no wonder, considering the fate of his predecessor. Yet this is to be regretted, for if he could surmount these fears, his would be an agreeable and refined countenance, eminently Asiatic in type, and with a certain charm of expression. All I can say is that his eyes haunted me for days, as of one gazing at some unknown horror; so emaciated and unnatural is his appearance that were he a European we should pronounce him in a swift decline. I hear that his greatest friend and favorite is his physician. And no wonder, for he must need his constant care, considering the life he leads. How all the fabled state of the Oriental potentate palls before such a lesson in royal misery! The poorest beggar in his dominions is happier than he!

HIS DREAD OF ASSASSINATION.

It is not surprising that Abdul Hamid should fear assassination. Abdul Aziz was so afraid of being poisoned that he lived chiefly on hard-boiled eggs. Abdul Hamid never stirs outside his park. He refused to accompany the German Emperor to Sophia.

Some grand duchess whom he received at his court, on his complaining that his health was indifferent, advised him to take more exercise and change of air, and to drive about the country. On her departure, he is reported to have said: "What harm have I done that this woman should desire my death? Why does she advise me to run into such dangers?"

ESPIONAGE UNIVERSAL.

He lives, like Domitian, in constant suspicion of all around him; and all who surround him are believed to live in imminent peril of their lives, should their imperial master suspect they meditate designs against his life. He changes his bodyguard every week, and never allows his ministers to go out of his palace without a written permission. Everywhere he has his spies—in the Ministry, in the harem, in the street. Brother can hardly speak to brother without one suspecting the other to be a spy. The Sultan lives in the midst of this atmosphere of suspicion. It is to him the breath of life. If the butler could but trust the cook, the Sultan's life might be taken in the night. He distrusts everyone. He once put Osman Pasha—Osman the Victorious, Osman the hero of Plevna—under arrest for three days, owing to a false report that he had saluted Reschad, heir apparent to the throne. No one is to be anybody but Abdul Hamid.

The press is gagged. Ministers are reduced to the position of mere puppets. If anyone distinguishes himself in any way, his very distinction is his doom. He is banished, lest the discontented should rally round him. No one must be conspicuous. Everyone must be reduced to the universal dead-level of abject mediocrity.

THE TELEGRAM TO LORD SALISBURY.

But while he thus silences criticism within his dominions, he is tremblingly alive to the comments of the press outside Turkey. He is as sensitive as Lord Rosebery was to the printed criticism of anonymous and insignificant journalists. Instead of letting the scribblers of Little Pedlington rave to the desert air, he has their leaders carefully translated for his special benefit. The world was astonished, and not a little amused, by the Sultan's pathetic appeal to Lord Salisbury. The Sultan said he had been very much pained by Lord Salisbury's incredulity, and that he was resolved to execute what he had undertaken. "I have already told my ministers so. The only reason why Lord Salisbury should thus throw doubt upon my good intentions must be the intrigues of certain persons here, or else false statements have been made to cause such opinion." After some intermediate observations which Lord Salisbury did not quote (at the Brighton meeting), where he read this historic document, the message went on: "I repeat, I will execute the reforms. I will take the paper containing them, place it before me, and see myself that every article is put in force. This is my earnest determination, and I give him my word of honor. I wish Lord Salisbury to know this, and I beg and desire that his lordship, having confidence in these declarations, will make another speech by virtue of the friendly feeling and disposition he has for me and for my country. I shall await the result of this message with the greatest anxiety." So ran the famous message from Abdul Hamid to Lord Salisbury—a significant indication of the decadence of the Sultanate. Imagine the descendant of the fierce warrior who swore he would feed his horse with oats on the altar of St. Peter's in Rome, telegraphing to the Prime Minister of the infidels, begging him to "make another speech by virtue of the friendly feeling and disposition he has for me and for my country!"

THE STORY OF A "P. M. G." TELEGRAM.

Mr. Cust, the brilliant and successful editor of the Pall Mall Gazette, who visited the Sultan this year, told me a curious story of his own experience, which better than anything else illustrates the present position of affairs at Yildiz. Mr. Cust saw a good deal of the Sultan, and at one of his interviews Abdul Hamid informed him that it was his intention to carry out some reforms which the Powers had not even asked for. He was going to do this, he said, as a proof of his good will and his anxious desire to meet the wishes of the Powers. Mr. Cust, thinking that it might please the Sultan, decided to send a telegram to the Pall Mall Gazette embodying the substance of the Sultan's message. He drafted the telegram and sent it in to the telegraph office.

Next morning a mounted messenger galloped in with a message from the Sultan summoning Mr. Cust at once to

A MOUNTAIN CAMP OF SALMON RIVER UTES.

Yildiz. When he arrived there he found the Sultan in deep cogitation over the telegram, which had not been dispatched pending the imperial pleasure. Would Mr. Cust consent to some alteration in the telegram? "That depends," said Mr. Cust, "upon what the alteration is."

So the Sultan and his ministers set to work to redraft the telegram. After a time it was brought out. Would Mr. Cust object to this form? He glanced at it. The amended imperially edited message began somewhat like this: "Another proof of the beneficent goodness of His Imperial Majesty is," etc. "Nonsense!" said Mr. Cust; "it would only make the Sultan ridiculous to publish such a telegram in London." So the message went back to the Sultan. The poor man tried again; then came another draft. It was equally impossible. A third time his advisers labored over the redrafting of this telegram. A third time their efforts were abortive. At it they went again, until at last, after seven mortal hours of incessant lucubration, the message came out in a form which, although perfectly inane, was not positively ludicrous. All the compliments were dropped, and the announcement which was made of his good intentions in the original telegram was toned down to nothing. Mr. Cust, who had only written the telegram at first thinking it would please the Sultan, consented to dispatch the finally revised version, which represented the net result of seven hours' deliberation. So he took it to the telegraph office and thought no more about it.

Next morning, however, came another messenger from the Sultan. Again he had to go to Yildiz, this time to learn that the Sultan had delayed the dispatch of the telegram in order that he might sleep upon it. He had slept upon it, and the result of his meditations was that he thought on the whole the telegram had better not be sent! Into the waste paper basket therefore it went, and there was an end of it.

REDUCTIO AD ABSURDUM.

But what a picture we have here of the irresolute fumbler who occupies the throne of Mohammed! For these seven long hours the whole administrative machine of the Ottoman Empire was at a standstill, while Abdul Hamid and his Grand Vizier, with the aid of Osman the Victorious, and I know not how many pashas besides, concentrated their brains upon the momentous task of redrafting a trumpery telegram which was to be dispatched to the Pall Mall Gazette as a mere matter of courtesy to the Sultan! This is surely the ultimate of irrational centralization and imbecile vacillation.

"THE DEVIL'S CHARIOT."

The Sultan has not the gift of administrative perspective. He bothers himself about the veriest trifles, prohibiting bicycling in and near Constantinople as immoral and "dangerous to the State," and an officer of an Italian corvette was taken into custody for having been found riding a bicycle, or a "devil's chariot," as the Turks name it. No dictionary is allowed to circulate containing such words as evolution, equality, liberty, insurrection, as such words are likely to "excite the minds" of people. Again, theatrical pieces, such as "Hamlet," "Macbeth," Victor Hugo's "Le Roi s'Amuse" ("Rigoletto") cannot be acted on any stage. "Othello" is allowed, but in a mutilated form.

Even the Bible must be expurgated to please his censors. The passages which are particularly objected to are those relating to the restoration of the Jews to Palestine, and to the Kingdom of Christ. The phrases "Kingdom of Heaven," "of God," or "of Christ" must be omitted. The words "Jew" and "Hebrew" must be left out. The words "According to the law of the Jews" cannot be admitted, because the Jews have no laws separate from that of other rayahs in the Ottoman Empire. The reference to the "Queen of the South," contained in Matthews xii, 42, is for some reason ordered to be left out altogether. And all the time when these momentous trivialities are being discussed, whole provinces are being desolated, and the great empire is settling down to ruin.

VI. WHAT IS TO BE DONE.

The atrocities which have recently startled the world in Armenia are nothing new. I doubt whether they should be regarded as a count in the indictment against Abdul Hamid. He is simply doing as Turks always do, and always will do as long as the Ottoman Empire exists. It would be as absurd to complain of a dog for biting or of a cat for mewing as to arraign the Grand Turk for resorting to that which has been for centuries the recognized method of maintaining the State.

"LET DOGS DELIGHT, ETC., FOR 'TIS THEIR NATURE TO."

No one knows this better than the Rev. Canon MacColl, who in his latest article expressly admits and asserts it in the following passages, which is as true as it is vivid and powerful. After referring to the saturnalia of horrors reported from Asia, the Canon says:

There is, however, nothing new in this exhibition of Turkish policy. These massacres of Christians are periodical in Turkey; and they are never the result of local fanaticism; they are invariably organized and ordered by the Sultan and his ministers, for the purpose of keeping down the Christian population. Abject cowardice has made this Sultan more recklessly ferocious than his predecessors; that is all. The policy is the same, having at one time Greece for its theatre; then Syria; then Bulgaria and the Herzegovina; then Armenia. It is a deliberate system of pollarding the various Christian communities as each threatens to overtop its Mussulman neighbors in population and prosperity.

THE SULTAN'S SHARE IN THE ATROCITIES.

I am not wishing to defend the atrocities. They are damnable enough in all conscience. Nor do I for a moment wish to imply that Abdul Hamid is not responsible for them. He is as responsible for them as a tiger is for its stripes and its carnivorous appetite. These things are of the essence of Turkish rule. Mr. MacColl believes that the Sultan is directly responsible for the massacres. He says:

In my pamphlet on "England's Responsibility Toward Armenia," and in an article in this month's Contemporary

GATE TO A PALACE.

INTERIOR OF MOSQUE OF ST. SOPHIA.

Review, I have proved, by an overwhelming mass of official evidence, that Abdul Hamid has been engaged for four years in carefully maturing his plans for the perpetration of the horrors which have lately roused the indignation of the civilized world. He it is who is responsible, not the Kurds and Turks, who have only been the instruments of his cruelty.

Possibly in the inner arcanum of his own conscience I doubt whether Abdul Hamid would even desire to repel this accusation. Probably he feels more chagrined at the incompleteness of his work than grieved because of the blood already shed.

THE ARMING OF THE KURDS.

There is little doubt but that in many cases the orders to kill emanated from the Sultan. But the worst sufferings inflicted upon the Armenians were due to the arming of the Kurds. Mr. Richard Davey, writing before the present outbreak, said of the Hamedieh, as the Kurdish irregulars are named after the Sultan, their enrolment was one of the greatest mistakes ever made:

The Sultan doubtless had in his mind the success of the Russian Emperor with his Cossack regiments, when he gave permission for these barbarians to be supplied with uniforms and arms. The only distinction they obtained in the war of 1877 was for their blood-curdling atrocities on the poor wretches who fell into their hands, and their diabolical mutilation of the dead. Their headquarters are at Melaigerd, on the Eastern Euphrates, and there are about thirty regiments of them registered in the area of the plateau, each regiment consisting of from 500 to 600 men. They will not, and possibly cannot, accept discipline, and their natural savageness is rendered ten times more dreadful when they are provided with modern arms and ammunition and taught how to use them.

THE ACTION OF THE TURKISH SOLDIERY.

These gentry are responsible for much. But some of the later massacres were the work of the Turkish soldiers. The Times correspondent in Erzeroum, writing after the Armenians had been slaughtered in that city, gave a very vivid account of the matter-of-fact way in which the massacre had been ordered and executed. He says:

The following is a conversation I had with the Turkish soldier who was one of the three guarding our door after the affair: "Where were you when this thing commenced?"

Answer—"In the barracks, playing cards. We were all called out by a signal from the bugle and drawn up in line. Our officer then said to us, 'Sharpen your swords; today you are to kill Armenians wherever you find them for six hours; after that you are to stop, and the blood of any Armenian you kill after this is my blood; the Armenians have broken into the Serai.' At the given signal, which was just after noon," he said, "the troops started for the Serai. We wondered how the Armenians could get into the Serai. When we arrived there we did not find any Armenians with arms, and I saw only one shot fired at us by an Armenian. We were ordered to kill every Armenian we saw, just as it was at Sasun," continued this soldier, who had been at Sasun; "if we tried to save any Armenian friend, our commanding officer ordered us to kill him; we were to spare no one." Other soldiers told pretty much the same story. The soldiers evidently had no great relish for their horrible work, but once begun they did it thoroughly and brutally.

S. S. Cox, late Minister to Turkey, in his "Diversions of a Diplomat," published about ten years ago, gives some interesting reminiscences of the Sultan. He describes his reception and a State dinner:

THE RECEPTION.

The Sultan receives us, standing on a rug of camel-hair

felt, covered with embroidered flowers in different colored silk braid of Turkish work.

As we are ushered into the presence, we make three bows: one at the door on entering, the second half-way and the last when we stop, a few feet from his person. We do not bow as low as the Turkish Ministers, but we do our best. The Sultan is standing at the far end of the room, in front of a table.

The Sultan is middle-sized and of the Turkish type. He wears a full black beard, is of dark complexion and has very expressive eyes. His forehead is large, indicative of intellectual power. He is very gracious in his manner, though at times seemingly a little embarrassed. He wears the following decorations: The Grand Cordon of the Osmanli, which is a green scarf worn across the breast; the first class of the Medjidie, in diamonds; the Nichan Imtiaz, an order instituted by his grandfather, Sultan Mahmoud, and the Nichan Iftihar. The insignia and medals are inlaid with precious stones. The green sash or scarf is of a rich color and texture. No person was ever decorated in more gorgeous array, and yet in his bearing and demeanor he is unostentatious. Notwithstanding the prejudice of the Ottoman against images, his photograph has been permitted.

There is an etiquette which Turkish officials observe in the Sultan's presence. It has been much modified by time, and since the Crimean war greatly modified, like other old habits here, especially as they affect strangers. On approaching the Sultan, the officials, when about ten yards distant, make a salaam. This consists in bending the body till the right hand touches the ground. The hand is then brought to the heart, the mouth, and then to the forehead. What does this mean? Its idea is, that you take the earth from the ground as a symbol of lowliness. Then you carry the hand to your heart and head. The lips approve your regard. After the first salaam, you advance five or six yards and repeat. If you are an official, again and again you repeat until you are a yard and one-half from the Sultan. Then a third salaam is made. Then the person stops. He crosses his hands on the lower part of his stomach. This is said to be a relic of Persian usage. It has a meaning. It is intended to show that the servant has no concealed weapon in his hand. These officials never address the Sultan. Every time he looks towards them they repeat the salaam. After much genuflexion they are asked what their business is. They tell their story, and bow lowly and bow out.

A STATE DINNER.

When we arrive at the gate of Yildiz, the Kavass dismounts. He is no longer wanted, and he retires to the legation. The soldiers on guard escort us up the drive, and the coachman, conscious of the presence of royalty, lashes his horses into a gallop.

"Are we late?" I ask, tremulously.

"About five minutes," responds the dragoman. We breathe freely.

In the gloaming of the evening I only notice that the garden wall is a mass of Bankshire roses and the palace a wilder-

GATE OF SERASKIERAT, CONSTANTINOPLE

ness of lights. The carriage stops. We alight. We are met at the vestibule by a grand Pasha in uniform and decorations. We walk upon carpets, ascend and descend steps into the marble entrance, and there are invited to take off our wraps. We are ushered into a small side room. In a few minutes the master of ceremonies leads the way to the upper salon. He is followed by the Ministers and the rest of the company. Each is presented in turn to the Sultan. We are in the presence of the Sultan. If I were to give the opinion of the female portion of the company, I should say that he has large, fine eyes and a most gracious manner. The latter is illustrated by his cordial shaking of the hand with all. On his motioning to the ladies, they are seated on the divan. He then calls up the three princes: his son, who is seventeen years old, and his two nephews. These youths wear military suits, epaulettes, spurs and swords. They are each presented in their turn. How the company is disposed, with the view to a movement towards the dining saloon and table, it is unnecessary to state; except this, that the Sultan accompanies his guests to the door of the grand salon, with a parting salutation, and remarks that he will continue the reception after dinner.

The table is a picture. It is wide and long, with a gorgeous display of flowers, fruits, light and crystal shades. We enter at the end of the room and are tendered our respective seats. Our little ministerial family are placed among the princes. One of the nephews, Tewfik, is about ten years of age. He is a meek, quiet, subdued-looking child. When the dinner begins, although they do not drink wine, there is much geniality. Meanwhile, the Sultan's band plays rare music from the adjoining room, and the dinner goes on very much like a French or Russian dinner. I find that the princes are anxious about geography. They inquire about Egypt. They ask about America. We explain much of the recondite history of Egypt, including incidental remarks about the mummies, temples and tombs. Although they only drink water, we drank their health, and they enjoy it. Asking after their amusements, we do not receive much information. I imagine that the princes are more or less restricted by their exalted position. The menu is tempting. The wines are good. The service, in silver at first, and then in gold, winds up with the finest crystal for finger-bowls. Dainty little gold shells hold the ices. Ten servants, in gold-trimmed uniforms and fez caps, serve the table.

The dinner is not tedious, for it is not long. The bonbons are passed about, the princes being always first served. Each takes one and passes it to my wife, with a quaint courtesy. After arising from the table, we march down the line of Pashas, aides and servants, all of whom bow, after the Oriental method. Then, passing through a corridor, we enter a polished green and black-tiled coffee-room, which has a dais railed off at one end. How rare and beautiful are the Turkish carpets and divans here! How tempting for a siesta, after dinner! How exquisite the chairs and the malachite tables!

After being seated, the dragoman surprises my wife and the company. He approaches her with a box.

"I have something to show you, madam," he says.

"Yes," she responds. "It is lovely outside. What is in it?"

He opens it, remarking: "Shall I put it on you?"

"What do you mean?" she inquires.

"I have the pleasure of decorating you, at the Sultan's wish, with the Grand Order of the Chefekat."

Thereupon he throws the Cordon over her head, and, with the aid of the German Ambassadress, who is familiar with the decorations, it is decorously arranged. It is a surprise as well as an honor, coming as it does almost within one year of our service with the American legation. It is a star in brown, gold and green enamel, with diamond brilliants. It has five points, and twenty-six diamonds on each point. Surely no woman of good training would refuse such a gift! It is fastened upon the front of the corsage, and, with the Cordon, it serves as an ornament to the dress. The pashas, the aides and the officers make their felicitations on the happy event.

After the presentation of the decoration to my wife, on this occasion, and after other courtesies, the ladies enter the carriage. They are driven toward but not to the harem. They are not invited to see the domesticities. The gentlemen follow upon foot. The beautiful lights in the gardens and from the windows make the scene like one from the Arabian Nights. The plashing fountains and the fragrance of the air produce the impression of something magical and marvelous.

Then we enter a grand salon, with a parquetes floor, covered with rugs, divans, chairs and tables, where a rare library, a white porcelain stove and numerous secretaries fill the side walls, from which depend red satin hangings. Here the Sultan receives us again. A beautiful table occupies the centre. Upon it are some American photographs. It happened on that very morning that another box of American photographs was received through the Porte, and not through myself as Minister. His Majesty sits in an armchair at the head of this table, dressed, as usual, in his dark-blue frock coat, suit, sword and fez cap. His black whiskers and large eyes produce a picturesque effect. He seems more at ease than any of his company. He chats with each and all, and always on appropriate subjects, and with musical, subdued tones and fluent language. Every sentence is received by the interpreter with a profound bow, carrying his right hand from near the floor to his heart and head. The sentences are passed through our own dragoman to the ministerial ear with equal grace.

These courtesies ending, the violinist Wilhelmj is ushered in. He has a large forehead and the air of a man of genius. He makes a graceful bow at the door, and seems relieved when he reaches the piano stool, where an accomplished pasha awaits and afterwards accompanies him in some rare and rich music. The national air of Germany is given, on the rendering of which the Sultan and all of us rise. Then, as a tribute to Germany, or to the unseen goddess of Metaphysics, he asks each of us to smoke. The ladies, of course, decline, but the American Minister is not in that mood. The Sultan lights his own cigarette from a silver match-box, and, pointing to it, says:

A SCENE IN TURKEY.

"Tell my friend, Mr. Hewitt, that I keep his gift by me, as a pleasant souvenir."

When we retire to the library, the Sultan shows his guests the elegant specimens of American art and scenery which he had received in the morning. He had selected a few from the new lot. He also shows me a letter in Turkish from his Minister, which informs him of the arrival of the package. He states that he has directed the Minister to telegraph the President his grateful regard and thanks for these interesting gifts. He also requests me to send a similar message.

The tea is then served in gold cups and saucers. The music is concluded. Thanks are sent to the musician, along with a pretty decoration. Then the Sultan rises, takes little Tewfik, his nephew, by the hand, and leads him to the piano, saying, apologetically:

"The boy will give us some music, although he has only learned by the ear."

The quiet little prince plays a spirited march. It is a national air. Then he plays from "Norma." After that he leaves the piano and stands in his place meekly, till the Sultan indicates for him to sit. The Sultan kindly explains that he is a child of one of his brothers, who has died when Tewfik was but a few months old, and that he was educating him, as well as his other nephew, as companions to his son.

The Sultan now arises. He will detain us no longer. It is etiquette at the palace to remain until the Sultan gives the signal to leave. This he generally does by a glance at his watch, saying:

"I fear you will be late," or, "Perhaps I am detaining you."

He shakes hands with the ladies first, and then the gentlemen, with their best grace, back out. The bouquets are distributed to the ladies. A little remark of mine, which was caught as I left the room, caused the Sultan to recall the Minister and the dragoman. I had mentioned that our President was about to be married. He suggests to the dragoman to ask the Minister whether the Ottoman ruler could not in some way honor the expected bride of the President.

As we retire, after many kindly greetings, we look in vain for lattice and curtain to indicate the harem. Every window opens into a beautiful garden, and every garden is filled with flowers and sparkling fountains. It is a fairy scene; but no houri. We enter our carriages at the park gate, take our venerable Kavass along, and, with a cavalry escort behind, we move toward Pera, and thus this Oriental entertainment is ended!

CHAPTER IV.

THE PEOPLE OF TURKEY—THEIR HOME-LIFE AND RELIGION.

THE BIRTH OF A TURKISH CHILD.

As soon as a Turkish child is born, it is enveloped in a tiny chemise and Libarde, or quilted jacket of many colors, bound with a swathe; its limbs are pulled straight down, and then imprisoned in a number of quilted wrappers and tightly bandaged all over by another swathe, giving the unfortunate mummified being the appearance of a Bologna sausage. A red silk cap is placed on the head, ornamented with a pearl tassel, one or two fine gold coins and a number of amulets and charms against the evil eye.

These objects consist of a head of garlic, a piece of alum, a copy of one or two verses of the Koran plaited in little triangles and sewn in bits of blue cloth, and a number of blue glass ornaments in the shape of hands, horseshoes, etc. The baby, thus decked out, is next placed in a fine square-quilted covering, one corner of which forms a hood, the other three being crossed over its body; a red gauze veil thrown over the whole completing its toilet. After the child's birth, a state couch is prepared on a bedstead used for the occasion, decorated with the richest silks, the heaviest gold embroideries and the finest gauzes of the East. The bed is first covered with a gauze sheet, worked with gold threads; five or six long pillows of various colored silks, covered with richly-embroidered pillow-cases, open at the ends, occupy the head and one side of the couch, one or two yorgans, or quilted coverlets, heavily laden with gold embroidery, occasionally mixed with pearls and precious stones, and the under-sides lined with gauze sheets, are thrown over it. On this bed of state the happy mother is placed, at no small sacrifice of ease and comfort. Her head is encircled with a red Fotoz, or scarf, ornamented with a bunch of charms similar to that placed on the head of the child, the garlic insinuating its head through the red veil that falls on the temples. A stick, surmounted by an onion, is placed in one corner of the room, against the wall.

When these preliminary arrangements have been made, the husband is admitted, who, after felicitating his wife on the happy event, has his offspring put into his arms; he at once carries it behind the door, and, after muttering a short prayer, shouts three times into the baby's ear the name chosen for it. He then gives back the infant to its mother and quits the room.

For several days (the exact time depending upon the mother's health) water, either for drinking or ablutionary purposes, is not comprised in the regime imposed upon the invalid, whose lips may be parched with thirst, but not a drop of water is given to her. Sherbet, made from a kind of candied sugar and spices, varied by a tisane extracted from the maiden-hair fern, is the only drink administered. Turkish ladies, after confinement, get little rest; the moment the event is known, relations, friends and neighbors crowd in,

ROBERTS COLLEGE, CONSTANTINOPLE. FOUNDED BY REV. CYRUS HAMLIN, D. D.

and are at once permitted to enter the chamber and partake of sherbet, sweets and coffee, not even abstaining from their inveterate habit of smoking cigarettes.

On the second day, a great quantity of this sherbet is prepared, and bottles of it sent to friends and acquaintances by Musdadjis, also an invitation to the Djemiet, or reception held on the third day. The house on this occasion is thrown open to visitors, invited or uninvited. Dinner is served to the former and sherbet to the latter. Bands of music are in attendance to receive and accompany upstairs the most distinguished guests, who arrive in groups, preceded by servants bearing baskets of sweets, prettily got up with flowers and gilt paper and enveloped in gauze tied up with ribbons.

The guests are first conducted into an antechamber, where they are divested of their Yashmaks and Feridjes (veils and cloaks), previous to being introduced to the presence of the invalid. The latter kisses the hands of all the elderly hanoums, who say to her, "Mashallah, ermuli kadunli olsoun" (Wonderful! Let it be long-lived and happy!). Very little notice is taken of the baby, and even then only disparaging remarks are made about it, both by relatives and guests, such as Murdar (dirty), Chirkin (ugly), Yaramaz (naughty). If looked at it is immediately spat upon, and then left to slumber in innocent unconsciousness of the undeserved abuse it has received.

As soon as the visitors have departed, a few cloves are thrown into the brazier, to test whether any ill effects of the evil eye have been left behind. Should the cloves happen to burst in burning, the inference is drawn that the evil eye has exerted its influence; the consequences of which can only be averted by some hair from the heads of the mother and child being cut off and burnt with the view of fumigating the unfortunate victims with the noxious vapor. Prayers and sundry incantations, intermingled with blowings and spittings, are made over the heads of the stricken creatures, and only desisted from when a fit of yawning proclaims that the ill-effects of the Nazar (evil eye) have been finally banished. The party suspected of having given the Nazar is next surreptitiously visited by some old woman, who manages to possess herself of a scrap of some part of the suspected person's dress, with which a second fumigation is made.

Among the lower orders, coffee, sugar and other provisions frequently replace the baskets of sweets; and if the father of the child is an official, his superior and subordinates may accompany these with gifts of value. The poor, who cannot afford to give dinners, content themselves with offering sherbet and coffee to their visitors. With the poor, the third, and with the rich the eighth, day is appointed for the bathing of the mother and child. There is a curious, but deeply-rooted superstition, accepted by all Turkish women, which imposes upon them the necessity of never leaving the mother and child alone, for fear they should become Albalghan mish, possessed by the Peris. The red scarfs and veils are also used as preservatives against this imaginary evil. When a poor person is unavoidably left alone, a broom is placed by the bedside to mount guard over her and her child.

If the ceremony of the bath takes place in the house, the

Ebe Kadin and a number of friends are invited to join the bathers and partake of luncheon or some other refreshments. When the ceremony is carried out at the public bath, the company march there in procession, headed by the Ebe Kadin carrying the baby. Each family sends a carpet and the bathing linen tied up in a bundle, covered with the embroidery and pearls sometimes amounting in value to $150 or $200. The mother and child are naturally the chief objects of attention. The former, divested of her clothing, is wrapped in her silk scarf offered to her by the Hammamji Hanoun (mistress of the bath), puts on a pair of high pattens worked with silver, and is led into the inner bath, supported on one side by the Hammamji and on the other by some friend, the baby in charge of the Ebe Kadin bringing up the rear. Hot water is thrown over it, and it is rubbed and scrubbed, keeping the company alive with its screams of distress. This concluded, the infant is carried out, and its mother taken in hand by her Ebe Kadin, who, before commencing operations, throws a bunch of keys into the basin, muttering some prayers, and then blows three times into it. A few pails of water are thrown over the bather, and after the washing of the head and sundry manipulations have been performed, she is led to the centre platform, where she is placed in a reclining position, with her head resting on a silver bowl. A mixture of honey, spices and aromatics, forming a brownish mess, is thickly besmeared all over her body, and allowed to remain about an hour. Her friends surround her during this tedious process, and amuse her with songs and lively conversation, every now and then transferring some of this composition from her body to their mouths with their fingers. The spicy coating thus fingered gives to the lady a singular zebra-like appearance; but though not becoming, it is believed to possess very strengthening and reviving powers, and it is considered a good augury even to get only a taste of it. What remains of this mixture after the friends have been sufficiently regaled is washed off.

The lady, no doubt greatly benefited by this application, is then wrapped in her bathing-dress, the borders of which are worked with gold, and is ready to leave the bath. Previous to doing so, she must make a round of the baths, and kiss the hands of all the elderly ladies, who say to her in return, "shifalou olsoun." Refreshments are offered in abundance to the guests during the ceremony, which lasts the greater part of the day. These formalities are only required at the birth of the first child; at other times they are optional.

The cradle plays a great part in the first stage of baby existence. It is a very strange arrangement, and, like many Turkish things and customs, not very easy to describe. It is a long, narrow wooden box fixed upon two rockers, the ends of which rise a foot and one-half above the sides, and are connected at their summits by a strong rail, which serves as a support to the nurse when giving nourishment to the child. The mattress is hard and no pillow is allowed. The baby lies on its back, with its arms straight down by its sides, its legs drawn down, and toes turned in.

It is kept in this position by a swathe, which bandages the child all over to the cradle. A small cushion is placed on

IMPERIAL PALACE OF DOLMA BAYTCHE, CONSTANTINOPLE.

the chest and another on the knees of the child, to keep it in position and prevent the bandage from hurting it. The infant thus secured becomes a perfect fixture, the head being the only member allowed the liberty of moving from side to side. This strange contrivance (called the kundak) has a very distorting effect, and is one of the principal causes of the want of symmetry in the lower limbs of the Turks and of the Armenians (who are reared in the same fashion), who are, as a rule, bow-legged and turn their toes in. The kundak system is going out of fashion among the higher classes, but it is still resorted to by the lower, who find it extremely convenient on account of the leisure it affords to the mother. The child thus disposed of, is left in the cradle for five or six hours at a time; it is occasionally nursed, and in the intervals sucks an emsik, composed of masticated bread and sugar, or some Rahat Lakoum (Turkish delight) tied up in a piece of muslin.

All Turkish mothers and many Armenians of the lower orders administer strong sleeping draughts, generally of opium, poppy-head or theriac, to their infants; some carry the abuse of these to such an extent that the children appear always in a drowsy state, the countenance pale, the eyelids half-closed, the pupils of the eyes contracted, the lips parched and dry, and a peculiar hazy expression fixed upon the face; all the movements are lethargic, in marked contrast to the sprightly motion of a healthy American child. The natural baby cry is replaced by a low moan, and no eagerness is shown for the mother's milk, only an inclination to remain listless and inactive. Besides the stupefying effect of these opiates on the brain, they are highly injurious to the digestive organs, occasioning constipation, which, treated under the designation of sangyu (colic), is increased by frequent employment of heating medicines, such as spirits of mint, camomile or aniseed. A Turkish mother never thinks of giving her child an aperient; almond oil is the nearest approach to a remedy of this kind.

Sleeplessness, uneasiness or slight indisposition in babies are generally put down to the effects of the evil eye. Any old woman, whose breath is considered most efficacious, is called in. She takes hold of the child, mutters prayers over it, exercising a sort of mesmeric influence, and blowing it at intervals, a remedy that results in soothing the child to sleep for awhile. Should her breathing powers prove inefficacious, the Sheikh (whose breath is held in the highest esteem) is called in. The magnetizing powers of the latter are increased by the addition of a muska (amulet) hung around the neck of the child, for which a shilling is paid. When all these remedies prove unavailing, the doctor is applied to; but his advice, generally little understood and less credited, is never thoroughly carried out. The Turks have no faith in medicine or doctors—"kismet" overrides all such human efforts.

No regime is followed with regard to the food of a child. It is allowed to eat whatever it can get hold of, and digest it as best it can.

CIRCUMCISION.

A rite of childhood, which must not be passed over, since it is accompanied by curious ceremonies, is circumcision.

The obligatory duty of parents in this matter falls heavily on the middle classes and entails great expense upon the budget of the wealthy. When a Turk of some standing is expected to have a Sunnet Duhun, the coming event is watched for by a number of persons who cannot afford individually to undertake the responsibility of the outlay the ceremony would involve. All such individuals send in the names of their children, begging that they might be allowed to participate in the ceremonial rite. The grandee appealed to fixes the number of these according to his means or his generosity. When the ceremony takes place in the imperial palace, the Sultans have not the liberty of limiting the number of applicants, which sometimes amounts to thousands, and occasions a very heavy drain upon the treasury.

The Sunnet Duhun begins on a Monday and lasts a whole week. The ages of the candidates range from four to ten years. The boys are sent to the bath, where the uncropped tufts of hair left on the crown of their heads are plaited with gold threads, allowed to hang down their backs up to the moment of initiation. The chief candidate is provided with a suit of clothes richly worked with gold and ornamented on the breast with jewels in the shape of a shield; his fez is also entirely covered with jewels. The number of precious ornaments necessary for the ceremony is so great that they have in part to be borrowed from relatives and friends, who are in duty bound to lend them. The caps and coats of all the minor aspirants are equally studded with gems. They are provided with complete suits of clothes by the family in whose house the Sunnet Duhun is held, by whom also all other expenses connected with the ceremony are defrayed.

On the Monday, the youths, decked out in their parade costumes, and led by some old ladies, make a round of calls at the harems and invite their friends for the coming events, Monday and Tuesday being dedicated to a series of entertainments given in the Selamlik, whose hospitality is largely extended to the poor as well as the rich. Wednesday and Thursday are reserved to the Haremlik, where great rejoicings take place, enlivened by bands of music and dancing girls. On the morning of the latter day the ladies busy themselves in arranging the state bed, as well as a number of others of more modest appearance. The boys, in the meantime, mounted upon richly-caparisoned steeds and accompanied by their Hodjas, the family barber and some friends, and preceded by music, pass in procession through the town. On returning home, the party is received at the door by the parents of the boys. The father of the principal candidate takes the lead and stands by the side of the stepping-block, the barber and Hodja taking their places at his side. The horse of the young boy is brought round, and the hand of the father, extended to help him to dismount, is stayed for a moment by that of the Hodja, who solemnly asks him, "With what gift hast thou endowed thy son?" The parent then declares the present intended for his son, which may consist of landed property or any object of value, according to his means, and then assists him to dismount. The other boys follow, each claiming and receiving a gift from his father or nearest of kin. Should any of the boys be des-

GREAT MOSQUE—TOMB OF JOHN THE BAPTIST, DAMASCUS.

TOMB OF SULTAN MAHMAUD.

titute of relatives, the owner of the house takes the father's place and portions him.

The children are then taken to the Haremlik, where they remain until evening, when they return to the Selamlik and do not again see their mothers till the morning of the completion of the ceremony, when they are carried to the Haremlik and placed upon the beds prepared for them. The entertainments this day are carried on in both departments. The children are visited by all their friends and relations, who offer them money and other presents, the ladies every now and then disappearing, in order to allow the gentlemen to enter and bring their offerings. The money and gifts collected on these occasions sometimes amount to considerable sums. The Hodja and barber are equally favored. The Musdadji receives a gold piece from the mother on announcing to her the completion of the sacred rite.

Every effort is made in the harem to amuse and please the children and beguile the time for them till evening, when the fatigue and feverish excitement of the day begin to tell upon them, and they show signs of weariness, the signal for the break-up of the party. On the next day the boys are taken home by their relatives, but the entertainments are continued in the principal house till the following Monday.

The Turks, hospitable on all occasions, are particularly so on this, and consider it a religious duty to show special regard and attention to the poor and destitute.

CHILDREN IN THE HOME.

Both at home and at school the Moslem learns almost

nothing that will serve him in good stead in after life. Worse than this: in those early years spent at home, when the child ought to have instilled into him some germ of those principles of conduct by which men must walk in the world if they are to hold up their heads among civilized nations, the Turkish child is only taught the first steps toward those vicious habits of mind and body which have made his race what it is. The root of the evil is partly found in the harem system. So long as that system keeps Turkish women in their present degraded state, so long will Turkish boys and girls be vicious and ignorant. Turkish mothers have not the slightest control over their children. They are left to do very much as they like, become wayward, disobedient and unbearably tyrannical. As a general rule, the manner in which children treat their mothers among the lower classes is still worse and quite painful to witness.

Should their requests meet with the slightest resistance, they will sit stamping with their feet, pounding with their hands, clamoring and screaming, till they obtain the desired object. The mothers, who have as little control over themselves as over their children, quickly lose their temper, and begin vituperating their children in language of which a very mild, but general form, is, Yerin dibine batasen ("May you sink under the earth!").

They are not favored with the possession of the instructive books, toy tools, games, etc.

A Turkish child is never known to take a cold bath in the morning; is never made to take a constitutional walk, or have his limbs developed by the healthy exercise of gymnastics. No children's libraries exist to stimulate the desire for study, for which, it is true, little taste is displayed.

No regular hours are kept for getting up and going to bed. The children, even when sleepy, obstinately refuse to go to their beds, and prefer to stretch themselves on a sofa, whence they are carried fast asleep. On rising, no systematic attention is paid either to their food, ablutions or dressing. A wash is given to their faces and hands, but their heads, not regularly or daily combed, generally afford shelter to creeping guests, that can only be partially dislodged at the Hammam. Children are allowed to breakfast on anything they find in the larder or buy from the hawkers of cakes in the streets. There is no reserve of language observed before young girls, who are allowed to listen to conversations in which spades are very decidedly called spades.

The girls are allowed free access into the selamlik up to the time they are considered old enough to wear the veil; which, once adopted, must exclude a female from further intercourse with the men's side of the house. The shameful neglect girls experience during childhood leaves them alone to follow their own instincts; alternately spoiled and rudely chastened by uneducated mothers, they grow up in hopeless ignorance of every branch of study that might develop their mental or moral faculties and fit them to fulfill the duties that must in time devolve upon them. In this respect, a change for the better is taking place at Constantinople; the education of the girls among the higher classes is much improved.

TURKISH WEDDINGS.

The Turks generally marry early, from seventeen for the men, and from eleven for the girls, who all marry, so that an old maid is absolutely unknown in Turky. This custom of early marriages is encouraged by parents as a check upon their sons contracting wild habits.

The Nekyah, or betrothal, comprises the fiancailles as well as the matrimonial contract. The preliminaries of the engagement are undertaken by the parents of the contracting parties. The mother or some near relative of the young man, in company with a few of her friends and the Koulavouz, starts on a tour of inspection, visiting families known to possess marriageable daughters. The object of the visit being made known, they are admitted, and the eldest girl presents herself, offers coffee, kisses hands all round, waits to take the empty cups, and then disappears, her inspectors having to content themselves with the short view they have thus had of her. Should this prove satisfactory, they at once enter into negotiations, make inquiries as to the age and dowry of the girl, answer counter-inquiries on the condition of the youth, and say that, if it be agreeable to both parties and it is Kismet that the marriage should take place, they will come again and make the final arrangements. On the mother's return home, she gives a faithful description of the maiden's appearance to her son, and should this meet with his approval, the intermediaries are commissioned to settle all preliminaries.

The dowry is, of course, among Moslems given by the

MASSACRE IN THE STREETS OF MARASH.

bridegroom; the only dowry Turkish brides are bound to bring consists in a rich trousseau. Should the lady possess any property, the husband cannot assume any right over it, nor over any of the rest of her belongings. The wisdom and generosity of this law cannot be too highly commended; it is an indispensable clause in the canons of polygamy. So easy is it for a Turk to divorce his wife, that he has only to say to her in a moment of anger, "Cover thy face, thy nekyah is in thy hands," and she ceases to be his wife, and must at once leave his abode, carrying with her, luckily for her, "bag and baggage." The privilege of divorce thus indulgently permitted to a man are entirely beyond the reach of a woman, whom no human power can release from her nekyah vows without her husband's free consent. And even if she gain her dowry and trousseau, which she would retain if divorced not of her own motion, this unfair restriction gives rise to many unhappy disputes, issuing in litigation, which ever proves vain and fruitless against the obstinacy of the husband, or, even worse, his helplessness, should he become insane; for a lunatic's word of divorce cannot count before the law. The Turkish husband has the power of divorcing his wife and taking her back twice; but should he send her away for the third time, she must be married to another man before she can again return to her first husband. This strange and disgusting law is meant as a check upon people disposed to abuse too often the privilege of divorce. The person asked to fulfil this strange position of intermediary husband must be advanced in years, generally belongs to the poorer class, and receives a sum of money for his services.

The conditions are that he should enter the abode of the lady for one night only, and quit in the next morning, telling her, "Thy liberty is in thy hands, thou art no longer my wife." Cases have been known when the old gentleman, finding his position pleasant, has refused to give the lady up, and if this should happen, the first husband is wholly without remedy and must forego his desire of reunion with his former wife.

It is customary for the bridegroom to furnish the wedding dress and sundry other accessories, as well as to promise the nekyah money settled upon the wife in case of divorce. These, including the Kaftan (outer wedding dress), are sent with great pomp eight days before the Duhun. The Hodja, priest of the parish in which the parents of the girl reside, is requested to give a declaration that the young lady is free to contract matrimony. This, taken to the Kadi, obtains the marriage license, for which a small fee is paid. A piece of red silk and some sugar-plums are taken by the bridegroom's mother to the house of the bride. The red silk, which later on is made into an under-garment, is spread on this occasion on the floor; upon it the young lady steps to kiss the hand of her future mother-in-law, and receives the gift with her blessing. Half of one of these sugar-plums, bitten in two by her pearly teeth, is taken to the bridegroom as the first love token; literal sweetness in this case making up for any fault in the sentiment. These preliminaries are sealed by the formality performed by the Imam in the presence of witnesses, who are called to the door of the Haremlik, behind which the maiden and her friends stand. The Imam asks the bride if she consents to accept the youth proposed (giving his name) for her husband. The question is repeated three times, the bride answering each time in the affirmative. The Hodja has to declare the amount of the nekyah money promised, and calls three times upon the bystanders to bear witness before God to the contract; a short prayer follows, and the ceremony is concluded. The felicitations are conveyed in the poetical expression of "May Allah grant harmony between their two stars!" The contract, religious as well as civil, is made verbally, and though no other ceremony of importance follows it, the bride and bridegroom do not see each other until the Duhun or wedding festivities have been held. The length of this period may be from a few weeks to a few years, and is a blank which potential love is at liberty to fill with fantastic pictures of coming happiness. No sweet messages, letters or communications of any kind are allowed during the interval to pave the way towards the future binding together of two beings whose common lot is cast, without regard to personal sympathy, into the vague abyss of destiny. Kismet, the supreme ruler of all Turkish events, is left to decide the degree of misery or indifference that marriage, contracted under such unfavorable circumstances, may bring, instead of the looked-for happiness.

THE TROUSSEAU.

The trousseau comprises bedding, sometimes to the amount of fifty sets, each composed of two mattresses, two quilted coverlets, and three cotton bolsters; kitchen utensils, all of copper, very numerous, consisting of two or three immense cauldrons, several large jugs and pans, and a great number of dinner trays with the services belonging to them. Among the wealthy, one of these would be of silver. It also comprises furniture for two rooms of some rich material embroidered with gold, a handsome mangal (brazier), curtains, and a few carpets and rugs, besides the house linen. The wardrobe contains several expensive fur jackets, a shawl or two, some feridjes, and a number of suits of apparel, consisting of undergowns and jackets. The gelinlik or wedding dress, ranging in value from $300 to $500, is embroidered with gold and pearls. The rest are less rich in material, and are of silk and woolen stuffs, and less expensive materials down to print gedjliks. The other articles are chemises, a few pairs of stockings, boots and slippers, some dozens of worked handkerchiefs, head-ties and yashmaks, together with a number of European odds and ends, such as petticoats, gloves and parasols.

The Duhun, like the circumcision ceremony, lasts a whole week, occasioning great expense to the parents, who, however, cannot possibly avoid it, and often incur debts for its celebration that hangs heavily upon them through life.

The bride's face is a mask of gold-dust and gum, worked on the cheeks, forehead and chin with spangles. The eyebrows are thickly painted and meet over the nose, and the teeth are blackened. This hideous disguisement is worn till evening, when the bridegroom, on his first visit to the bride, pours out the water with which she washes it away, in order to give the nuptial kiss.

The wedding festivities begin on Monday. A number of

MOSQUE OF THE SULTAN VALIDE.

BOSPHORUS.

friends and relatives collect at the home of the bride to superintend the final arrangement and expedition of the trousseau to the bridegroom's house.

It is customary for Turkish youths to have homes to take their wives to them on marrying. Should the Konak be too small to accommodate all the married sons, extra wings are added to it. The guests, left to themselves, at once set to work to decorate the bridal chamber, some stretching strings along the walls on which to hang the larger articles of dress, such as furred and embroided jackets, feridjes, cloaks, and intaris, all of bright colors and richly worked and trimmed. The shawls, prayer carpet and bridal boghcha, all objects of value, occupy the centre of these rows, which are successively surmounted by others, consisting of the linen, kerchiefs, towels, head-scarfs and other adjuncts of the toilet, all arranged with great taste. Along the top of the walls run a garland of crape flowers. The bride's corner is richly decorated with these and other artificial flowers, arranged in the form of a bower. This promiscuous exhibition of silk gauze and various stuffs, intermingled with embroidery in variegated silks, gold and silver, is most striking in effect, and forms, with the bridal bower, a sight peculiarly Oriental and gorgeous. The alcove is reserved for the display of jewels and other precious objects placed under glass shades.

When this adornment (which takes up the whole night) is completed, the party goes to the next room and arranges the furniture sent for it, thence proceeding to the hall and unpacking the bedding, which, placed against the walls upon the empty cases, forms a huge mass of colored strata of silk, embroidery and bright cotton print. One or two little stools of walnut wood, inlaid with mother-of-pearl, support the candelabra, and the hochaf tray, with its prettily-cut crystal bowl and ivory spoons, would be placed in front, together with the brooms, dust-pan of walnut wood, inlaid with silver, both patterns of the same materials, and the kitchen utensils, mangals, and all other belongings of the bride.

On Tuesday the bride is taken to the bath with great ceremony, the expenses on this occasion being defrayed by the bridegroom. Before leading to the bath, the bride is led three times round the centre platform, kisses hands all round, and goes out to be dressed. The clothes she wears on this occasion must not belong to her. On Wednesday, the bridegroom's party of lady friends go in a body to the home of the bride, preceded by the Koulavouz, who announce their arrival with an air of great importance. Violent confusion ensues; and mother, followed by her friends, descends the staircase. They form a double row, each couple conducting a visitor between them, beginning with the bridegroom's mother, and proceed upstairs into apartments specially reserved for the friends of the bridegroom, who do not mix with the bride's party on this occasion. When their veils and cloaks have been removed, they seat themselves round the room and partake of bitter coffee and cigarettes, followed half an hour later by sweet coffee. The bride is led into the room by two hanoums, who have only been married once, and kisses the hands of all present, beginning with her future mother-in-law and terminating with the youngest child in the room. She is then seated on a chair near her Kayn Valide, who is allowed on this occasion to take her by her side for a few minutes only, during which masticated sugar is exchanged between them as a token of future harmony. The bride is then taken away, excused by some insipid remarks on the expiring rights of maternal possession over her.

The dancing girls and musicians are now called in and perform before the company, receiving money from each person as they leave the room, in order to entertain the other party of guests. When the bridegroom's friends are about to leave, they throw small coins over the head of the bride, who is led down to the door for the purpose. The scramble that ensues among the hawkers of sweets, fruits, etc., assembled in the court, the children, the beggars and innumerable parasites crowding houses during the celebration of a wedding is beyond description. Before departure, an invitation is given for the evening to take part in the Kena, an entertainment more especially designed for the bride and her maiden friends. When the company is assembled, tapers are handed to each, and a procession formed, headed by the bride and accompanied by the dancing girls and music. They descend the staircase into the garden, and wind among the flower-beds and groves of trees. The lights, the gay dresses, flashing jewels and floating hair of the girls, the bright castanets, and the wild songs and weird music of the accompanists, combine to form a glimpse of fairyland, or a dream of "The Thousand and One Nights."

The ceremony of the Kena consists in the application of the henna mixture, which is prepared toward morning. The bride, after being divested of her wedding finery, enters the presence of her mother-in-law, shading her eyes with her left arm, while she seats herself in the middle of the room. A silk bath scarf is thrown over her outstretched right hand, and is then thickly plastered over with the henna, upon which her mother-in-law sticks a gold coin, her example being followed by the rest of her company. This hand, placed in a silk bag, relieves the other in covering her eyes, and the left hand is in its turn extended and gifted in like manner by the bride's mother and her friends; the feet are also stained with the henna. This is followed by the last dance, called the Sakusum, performed by the Chingis, accompanied by a song and gestures of the most unrestrained and immodest nature, terminating in these dancers taking extraordinary positions before each guest, sometimes even sitting on their knees to receive their reward, which consists of a small gold coin, damped in the mouth and deposited on their unblushing foreheads. In these proceedings the modesty and innocence of the young girls present is never thought about. The bride reposes long enough for the henna to impart its crimson dye, but not to turn black, which would be considered a bad augury.

The only touching scene in the whole course of the wedding ceremonies, the girding of the bride by her father, takes place in the presence of her mother and sisters just before she leaves the home of her childhood. The father enters the room, appearing deeply affected, and sometimes even joining his tears to the weeping of his wife and daughters. The bride, also weeping, falls at his feet, kisses them and kisses his

AN ORIENTAL FUNERAL.

hands, while he presses her to his breast and girds her with the bridal girdle, giving at the same time some good advice and his blessing.

In some district towns the bridegroom's male friends arrive at dawn with torches to take away the bride. She is not, however, seen by her husband until evening, when he is taken to the mosque and accompanies her to the door of his dwelling by the Imam. A short prayer is offered, the company joining in the refrain of Amin, Amin, at the conclusion of which the happy man is pushed into the house, a shower of blows falling on his back; they then partake of sherbet standing, and disperse. The bridegroom, proceeding upstairs, comes upon a bowl of water, which he upsets with his foot, scattering the contents in all directions. The Koulavooz meets and conducts him to the nuptial apartment, where the bride, shy and trembling, awaits the introduction of the complete stranger, in whose hands her destiny for good or for evil is now placed.

She rises as he enters, and kisses his hand; her bridal veil, removed by the Koulavouz, is spread on the floor and knelt on by the bridegroom, who offers a solemn prayer, the bride all the time standing on its edge behind him. The couple then sit side by side, the old lady approaching their heads together, while she shows them the reflection of their united images in a mirror, and expresses her wishes for the continuation of their present harmonious union.

Masticated sugar is exchanged between them as a token of the sweetness that must henceforth flow from their lips. Coffee follows, after which the Koulavouz retires, until her services are again required for bringing in the supper, which consists of sweets and eggs, meat being excluded on the ground that to indulge in it on so solemn an occasion would lead to future bickerings between them. The supper-hour depends upon the shyness, obstinacy or goodwill of the bride, over whom her husband can have no control until he has succeeded in making her respond to his question. Brides are recommended by experienced matrons to remain mute as long as possible, and the husband is sometimes obliged to resort to a stratagem in order to accomplish this. The anxiously looked-for speech is at once echoed by the relieved husband by a knock on the wall, which is the signal for supper. This partaken of, the bride is divested of her finery and the paint and flowers washed off by the Koulavouz, and left to repose after the fatigue and excitement of five successive days of festivity, still to be extended for two days longer. On the morrow she is again decked in her wedding apparel, to receive the crowd of hanoums, invited and uninvited, that flock to the house to gaze upon her.

At Constantinople, the bride is taken on the Thursday morning from the paternal roof and conveyed in a carriage to her new home, followed by a train of other carriages, preceded by music and surrounded by buffons, performing absurd mummeries for the amusement of the party, besides a numerous company of unruly youths, some mounted and others on foot, most of whom get intoxicated and noisy on the occasion. The bride is received by her husband at the door; he offers his arm, and conducts her upstairs through the crowd of hanoums, who are not very careful about hiding their faces, on the plea that the bridegroom being otherwise occupied will not look at them. He leads his wife to the bower prepared for her, but, before taking her seat, a scuffle ensues between them for precedence, each trying to step upon the foot of the other, the successful person being supposed to acquire the right of future supremacy.

FUNERAL CEREMONIES.

According to some verses taken from the Koran, earthly existence is but a fleeting shadow, seen for a moment, then lost sight of for ever; its joys and pleasures all delusion; itself a mere stepping-stone to the celestial life awaiting the true believer.

"Know that this life is but a sport—a pastime—a show—a cause of vainglory among you! And the multiplying of riches and children is like the (plants which spring up after) rain; whose growth rejoices the husbandman; then they wither away, and thou seest them all yellow; then they become stubble."

At the approach of death, the moribund appears resigned to his fate and his friends reconciled to the thought of his approaching end. No Imam or servant of God is called in to soothe the departing spirit or speed its flight by the administration of sacraments. The friends and relatives collected round the couch weep in silence, and if the departing one is able to speak, helal (forgiveness) is requested and given. Prayers are repeated by the pious, to keep away the evil spirits that are supposed to collect in greater force at such moments. Charitable donations are made, and other acts of generosity performed at deathbeds; and frequently at such times slaves are set free by their owners, for it is written: "They who give alms by night and by day, in private and public, shall have their reward with their Lord; no fear shall come upon them, neither shall they grieve."

The moment the soul is believed to have quitted the body, the women begin to utter wailings. Some tear their hair, others beat their breasts, in an outburst of genuine sorrow. A lull soon follows, and, without loss of time, preparations are made for performing the last duties to the corpse; for the Turks do not keep their dead unburied any longer than is necessary for the completion of these preliminaries.

If the death be that of a person of consequence, the Muezzin chants the special cry from the minaret; and invitations are issued to friends and acquaintances for the funeral. Directly after death, the eyelids are pressed down and the chin bandaged; the body is undressed and laid on a bed called rahat yatak (couch of comfort), with the hands stretched by the side, the feet tied together, and the head turned towards the Kibla. A veil is then laid over the body. While the company is gathering in the Selamlik, or in the street, performing the ablution (abtest), and preparing for the prayer (namaz), the corpse, if it be that of a man, is taken into the courtyard on the stretcher, and an Imam, with two subordinates, proceeds to wash it.

The formalities connected with this observance are of strictly religious character, and consequently carried out to the letter. The first condition to be observed is to keep the lower part of the body covered, the next to handle it with great gentleness and attention, lest those engaged in the performance of that duty draw upon them the curse of the dead. Seven small portions of cotton are rolled up in seven small pieces of calico; each of these is successively passed between the limbs by the Imam, while some hot water is poured over the bundles, which are then cast away one after the other. After the rest of the body has been washed, the abtest, or formal religious ablution, is administered to it. This consists in washing the hands, and in bringing water in the hand three times to the nose, three times to the lips, and three times from the crown of the head to the temples; from behind the ears to the neck; from the palm of the hand to the elbow, and then to the feet, first to the right and then to the left. This strange ceremony is performed twice. The tabout (coffin) is then brought in and placed by the side of the stretcher, both of coarse deal, put together with the rudest workmanship. Before laying the body in the coffin, a piece of new calico, double its size, is brought. A strip about two inches in width is torn off the edge, and divided into three pieces, which are placed upon three long scarfs laid across the shell. The calico, serving as a shroud, is next stretched in the coffin, and a thousand and one drachms of cotton, with which to envelop the corpse, are placed upon it. Some of this cotton is used to stop the issues of the body, and is placed under the arm-pits and between the fingers and toes.

The body is then dressed in a sleeveless shirt, called kaflet, and is gently placed in the coffin. Pepper is sifted on the eyes, and a saline powder on the face, to preserve from untimely decay; rose-water is then sprinkled on the face, which is finally enveloped in the remainder of the cotton. The shroud is then drawn over and secured by the three strips of calico, one tied round the head, the other round the waist, and the third round the feet, and the coffin is closed down.

When all is ready, the guests are admitted; and the Imam, turning round, asks the crowd: "O congregation! What do you consider the life of this man to have been?" "Good" is the invariable response. "Then give helal to him." The coffin, covered with shawls, and carrying at the head the turban or fez of the deceased hung on a peg, is then borne on the shoulders of four or more individuals, who are constantly relieved by others; and the funeral procession, composed exclusively of men, headed by the Imam and Hodjas, slowly winds its way in silence through the streets until it arrives at the mosque where the funeral service is to be read. The coffin is deposited on a slab of marble, and a short Namaz, called Mihit Namaz, is performed by the congregation standing. This concluded, the procession resumes its way to the burial-ground, where the coffin is deposited by the side of the grave. A small clod of earth, left at one end of the excavation, in the direction of the Kibla, takes the place of a pillow. The coffin is then uncovered, and the body gently lifted out of it by the ends of the three scarfs, previously placed under it (one supporting the head, another the middle of the body, and the third the feet), and lowered into its last resting-place. A short prayer is then recited, a plank or two laid at a little distance above the body, and the grave is filled up.

At this stage, all the congregation withdraw, and the Imam is left alone by the side of the grave, where he is believed to enter into mysterious communications with the spirit of the departed, who is supposed to answer all the questions of his creed which his priest puts to him. He is prompted in these answers by two spirits, one good and one evil, who are believed to take their places by his side. Should he have been an indifferent follower of the Prophet, and forbidden to enter Paradise, the evil spirit forces him to deny the only true God, and make a profession unto himself. A terrible battle is supposed to ensue in the darkness of the grave between the good and evil spirits called Vanqueur and Veniqueur. The good angel spares not his blows upon the corpse and the evil spirit, until the latter, beaten and disabled, abandons his prey, who, by Allah's mercy, is finally accepted within the fold of the true believers. This scene, however, is revealed to none by the Imam, and remains a secret between Allah, the departed and himself.

It is considered sinful for parents to manifest extreme sorrow for the loss of their children, for it is believed that the children of over-mourning parents are driven out of Paradise and made to wander about in darkness and solitude, weeping and wailing as their parents do on earth. But it is the reverse with the case of children bereaved of their parents; they are expected never to cease sorrowing, and are required to pray night and day for their parents' forgiveness and acceptance into Paradise.

Part of the personal effects of the deceased is given to the poor, and charity distributed, according to the means of the family. On the third day after the funeral, loukmas (doughnuts), covered with sifted sugar, are distributed to the friends of the family and to the poor, for the benefit of the soul of the departed. The ceremony is repeated on the seventh and the fortieth days, when bread is also distributed. These acts of charity are supposed to excite the gratitude of the departed, if already in Paradise, and, if in "another place," to occasion him a moment of rest and comfort.

External marks of mourning are not in usage among the Turks. Nothing is changed in the dress or routine of life in consequence of a death in a family. Visits of condolence are, however, paid by friends, who, on entering, express their sympathy by the saying, "Sis sagh oloun evlatlarounouz sagh olsoun" ("May you live, and may your children live"), with other expressions of a similar nature. Friends and relatives say prayers at stated times for the soul of the departed.

A TURKISH KONAK OR MANSION.

A Turkish Konak is a large building, very irregular in construction and without the slightest approach to European ideas of comfort or convenience. This building is divided into two parts, the haremlik and the selamlik; the former and larger part is allotted to the women, the latter is occupied by the man, and is used for the transaction of business, the purposes of hospitality and formal receptions. The stables are attached to it, forming part of the ground floor, and rendering some of the upper rooms rather unpleasant quarters. A narrow passage leading from the mabeyn (or neutral ground)

TEMPLE OF JUPITER—EAST END OF PERISTYLE, BAALBAK.

BURNED COLUMN OF CONSTANTINE.

to the haremlik joins the two establishments. The materials used for building are wood, lime, mud and stone for the foundations. A konak generally consists of two stories, one as nearly as possible resembling the other, with abundant provision for the entrance of light and air. A large hall, called the devankhane, forms the entrance into the haremlik; it is surrounded by a number of rooms of various sizes. To the right, the largest serves as a sort of ante-chamber; the rest are sleeping apartments for the slaves, with the exception of one called kahve-agak, where an old woman is always found sitting over a charcoal brazier, ready to boil coffee for every visitor. A large double staircase leads to the upper story, on one side of which is the kiler, or storeroom, and on the other the lavatories. The floors are of deal, kept scrupulously clean and white, and in the rooms generally covered with mats and rugs. The furniture is exceedingly poor and scanty; a hard, uncomfortable sofa runs along two and sometimes three sides of the room; a shelte, or small square mattress, occupies each corner, surmounted by a number of cushions piled one upon the other in regular order. The corner of the sofa is the seat of the Hanoum, and by the side of the cushions are placed her mirror and chekmege.

A small European sofa, a few chairs placed stifly against the wall, a console supporting a mirror and decorated with two lamps or candlesticks, together with a few goblets and a small table standing in the centre with cigarettes and tiny ash-trays, complete the furniture of the grandest provincial Buyuk-oda, though some Turks possess many rare and curious objects, such as ancient armor and china, which, if displayed, would greatly add to the elegance and cheerfulness of their apartments. These are always kept packed away in boxes.

Windows are the great inconvenience in Turkish houses; they pierce the walls on every side, with hardly the space of a foot between them. The curtains are usually of coarse printed calico, short and scanty, with the edges pinked out, so that when washed they present a miserably ragged appearance. The innumerable windows render the house ill-adapted either for hot or cold weather; the burning rays of the sun pour in all day in summer, and the frames are so badly constructed that the cold wind enters in all directions in winter.

Bedsteads are not used by the Turks; mattresses are nightly spread on the floor, and removed in the morning into large cupboards, built into the walls of every room.

BATHS.

In a large house or konak this is by far the best-fitted and most useful part of the whole establishment. A Turkish bath comprises a suite of three rooms: the first—the hammam—is a square apartment, chiefly constructed of marble, and terminating in a kind of cupola, studded with a number of glass bells, through which the light enters. A deep reservoir, attached to the outer wall, with an opening into the bath, contains the water, half of which is heated by a furnace built under it. A number of pipes, attached to the furnace, circulate through the walls of the bath and throw great heat into it. One or two graceful fountains conduct the water from the reservoir, and on each side of the fountain is a low wooden platform, which serves as a seat for the bather, who sits cross-legged and undergoes a long and complicated process of washing and scrubbing, with a variety of other toilet arrangements too numerous to mention.

The second room—called the saouklous—is constructed very much in the same style as the first, but is smaller, and has no furniture but a marble platform, upon which mattresses and cushions are placed for the use of those who wish to repose between intervals of bathing, or do not wish to face the cooler temperature of the hammam oda. This room is furnished with sofas, on which the bathers rest and dress after quitting the bath.

Turkish women are very fond of their bath, and are capable of remaining for hours together in that hot and depressing atmosphere. They smoke cigarettes, eat fruits and sweets and drink sherbet, and finally, after all the blood has rushed to their heads, and their faces are crimson, they wrap themselves in soft burnouses, and pass into the third or outer chamber, where they repose on a luxurious couch until their system shakes off part of the heat and languor that the abuse of these baths invariably produces. A bath being an indispensable appendage to every house, one is to be found in even the poorest Turkish dwelling

The public baths, resorted to by all classes, are to be found in numbers in every town. They are fine buildings, exact copies of the Roman baths, many of which are still in existence, defying the march of centuries and the work of decay.

Like the home baths, they consist of three spacious apartments. The outer bathroom is a large stone building lighted by a cupola, but the women, not having the same privileges, are obliged to bring their own rugs, upon which they deposit their clothes, tied up in bundles, when they enter, and repose and dress upon them on coming out of the bath. A fountain of cold water is considered indispensable in this apartment, and in the basin surrounding it may be seen watermelons floating about, placed there to cool while their owners are in the inner bath. The bath itself contains a number of small rooms, each of which can be separately engaged by a party, or used in common with the other bathers.

Turkish women, independently of their home baths, must resort at least once a month to the public hammam. They like it for many reasons, but principally because it is the only place where they can meet to chat over the news of the day and their family affairs.

Some of these baths, especially the mineral ones at Broussa, are of the finest description. Gurgutly, containing the sulphurous springs, is renowned for the remarkable efficacy of its waters, its immense size, and the elegant and curious style of its architecture. It comprises two very large apartments, one for the use of the bathers previous to their entering the bath; the other, the bath itself. This is an immense room, with niches all round containing fountains in the form of shells, which receive part of the running stream; in front of these are wooden platforms, on which the bathers collect for the purpose of washing their heads and scrubbing **their** bodies On the left as you enter stands an immense

KIOSK OF THE REVIEWS.

INTERIOR OF MOSQUE, SOLIMAN.

marble basin, seven feet in length and three in width, into which the mother stream gushes with impetuous force. From this it runs into a large round basin about ten feet in depth, in which dozens of women and children may be seen swimming, an exhausting process, owing to the high temperature of the water and its sulphurous qualities.

COFFEE HOUSES.

Coffee houses are to be met with everywhere, and are very numerous in the towns. The Turks resort to them when they leave their homes early in the morning, to take a cup of coffee and smoke a nargile before going to business. In the evening, too, they step in to have a chat with their neighbors and hear the news of the day. Turkish newspapers have become pretty common of late in these quiet rendezvous, and are to be found in the most unpretending ones. Few of these establishments possess an inviting exterior, or can boast any arrangements with regard to comfort or accommodation; a few mats placed upon benches, and a number of common osier-seated chairs and stools are the seats afforded in them. Small gardens may be found attached to some, while others atone for the deficiencies of their interiors by the lovely situations they occupy.

A KIOSK.

A kiosk is indispensable to the pleasure of a Turk. The imperial and other kiosks on the Bosphorus are miniature palaces, luxuriously furnished, whose elegance and beauty are only equalled by the incomparable advantages of their situation on the richest of soils and beneath the sunniest of skies. Kiosks may be situated anywhere, and may comprise a suit of apartments or be limited to one; they are light and airy in style, generally commanding a fine prospect, often floored with marble, and containing a shadravan or sculptured fountain playing in the midst; a range of sofas runs all round the walls, on which the Turk loves to sit for hours together, lost in meditation, and in the fumes of his inseparable companion, the nargile.

CLUBS.

Clubs, reading-rooms, or other resorts for social and intellectual improvements, are quite unknown among the Turks. Their place is, however, filled to some extent by the old-fashioned cafe for the Osmanli of mature age, and by the casinos and other places of the same doubtful character for "La jeune Turquie," who faute de mieux resort thither to enjoy the delights of taking their raki, or sometimes ruining themselves by indulging in rouge et noir or other games of chance which they do not understand, and, to do them justice, do not, as a rule, largely indulge in.

A TURKISH KITCHEN.

A Turkish kitchen is a spacious building, roughly constructed, and, in the dwellings of the rich, generally detached from the rest of the house. Great attention is paid to keeping the culinary utensils, which are all of copper, clean and bright; but order and neatness in other respects are entirely disregarded, and there are few of those arrangements that render an English kitchen such a pleasant and interesting apartment. A tin lamp, such as has been used from time immemorial, is hung at one side of the chimney, and gives but a very dim light.

MEALS.

The Turks have two meals a day: one, kahvalto, between 10 and 11, and the other, yemek, at sunset. One or two cups of black coffee is all they take in the early morning. The dinner is brought into the dining-room of the haremlik on a large circular copper tray, and deposited on the floor; a similar tray is placed on a stool and covered with a common calico cloth. On this are placed a number of saucers containing hors d'œuvres, a salt cellar, a pepper box and a portion of bread for each person. A leather pad occupies the centre, on which the dishes are placed in succession, and the company sit cross-legged round the tray. Dinner is announced by a slave; the hostess leads the way into the Yemek-oda, or dining-room. Servants approach and pour water over the hands from Ibriks, or curious ewers, holding Leyens, or basins, to catch it as it falls; others offer towels as napkins to use during the meal. As many as eight or ten persons can sit round these trays. The hostess, if she be of higher rank than her guests, is the first to dip her spoon into the soup tureen, politely inviting them to do the same; if her rank be inferior to that of anyone of her guests, they are invited to take precedence.

It is considered a mark of great attention on the part of the hostess to pick up the daintiest bit of food and place it in the mouth of any of her guests. The way in which coffee is served is one of the prettiest of the old Turkish customs. All the slaves and attendants enter the rooms and stand at the lower end with folded arms. The coffee-pot and cup-stands of gold or silver are placed on a tray held by the Kalfa, or head servant; attached to the tray is an oval crimson cloth, richly worked with gold. The coffee is poured out, and the cups offered separately by the other servants, who again retire to the lower end of the room till they are required to take the empty cups.

A SERAGLIO.

A seraglio, like all Moslem dwellings, is divided into haremlik and selamlik. The former is reserved for the family life of the Sultan and his women; the latter is accessible to officials who come to transact State business with his Highness.

It will be of interest to know something about the annual outlay of the Sultan. An account published of the imperial expenditure of the Sultan Abdul-Aziz was $10,000,000. The palace contained 5500 servants of both sexes. The kitchens alone required 300 functionaries, and the stables 400. There were also about 400 caikjis, or boatmen, 400 musicians and 200 attendants who had the charge of the menageries and aviaries. Three hundred guards were employed for the various palaces and kiosks and about 100 porters. The harem, besides this, contained 1200 female slaves.

In the selamlik might be counted from 1000 to 1500 servants of different kinds The Sultan had twenty-five "aides de camp," seven chamberlains, six secretaries, and at least 150 other functionaries, divided into classes, each having its special employment.

One is entrusted with the care of the imperial wardrobe, another with the pantry, a third with the making and serving of the coffee, and a fourth with the pipes and cigarettes.

There were also numberless attendants who carried either a torch, or a jug of perfumed water for ablutions after a repast. There is a chief barber, a superior attendant who has special charge of the games of backgammon and draughts, another superintends the braziers, and there are at least fifty kavasses and 100 eunuchs; and the harem has also at its service a hundred servants for going on errands and doing commissions in Stamboul and Pera.

Altogether, the total number of the employes of the palace is about 5500. But this is not all; these servants employ also other persons beneath them, so that every day 7000 persons are fed at the expense of the palace.

The wages of employes included in the civil list amounted to a total of $1,000,000, exclusive of the salaries of aides de camp, doctors, musicians, etc., which were paid by the Minister of War.

The stables of the palace contained 600 horses, whose provender, according to the estimates of the most reasonable contractors, cost three Turkish liras per month, making a total of about $100,000.

More than 200 carriages of every description were kept in the palace. These were for the most part presents from the

Viceroy of Egypt; but the expenses of the 150 coachmen and footmen, with their rich liveries, are paid by a civil list; also the harness-maker's accounts, and other items of this department.

The annual expenditure for pictures, porcelain, etc., was never less than $700,000; and in one year Sultan Abdul-Aziz spent $600,000 for pictures only. As for jewels, the purchases attained the annual sum of $500,000, and the expenses of the harem for presents, dresses, etc., absorbed $800,000 per annum.

Besides these items, the allowance to the mother and sisters of the Sultan, to his nephews and nieces, and to the heir-apparent amounted to $908,800. This gives a total of at least $6,500,000 annually. To this must be added $400,000 for keeping in repair the existing imperial kiosks and palaces, and $2,900,000 for the construction of new ones. The imperial revenue in the civil list was $6,400,000. The expenditure was really over $10,000,000.

The haremlik of the seraglio contains from 1000 to 1500 women, divided among the Sultan's household; that of his mother, the Valide Sultana, and those of the princes.

This vast host of women of all ranks, ages and conditions are, without exception, of slave extraction, originating from the cargoes of slaves that yearly find their way to Turkey from Circassis, Georgia, Abyssinia and Arabia, in spite of the prohibition of the slave trade. These slaves are sold in their native land by unnatural relations, or torn from their homes by hostile tribes, to be subsequently handed over to the slave dealers, and brought by them into the capital and other large

INTERIOR OF A MOSQUE.

towns. All these women are the offspring of semi-barbarous parents, who seldom scruple to sell their own flesh and blood. Born in the hovel of the peasant, or the hut of the fierce chieftain, their first condition is one of extreme ignorance and barbarism. Possessed with the knowledge of no written language, with a confused idea of religion mixed up with the superstitious practices that ignorance engenders, poorly clad, portionless and unprotected, they are drawn into the seraglio by chains of bondage, and go under the denomination of Adjemis (rustics). No matter how low had been their starting-point, their future career depends solely upon their own good fortune. Their training in the seraglio is regulated by the vocations for which they are destined; those chosen to fulfil domestic positions, such as negresses and others not highly favored by nature, are put under the direction of kalfas, or head servants, and taught their respective duties.

The training they receive depends upon the career to which their age, personal attractions and color entitle them. The young and beautiful, whose lot has a great chance of being connected with that of his Imperial Majesty, or some high dignitary to whom she may be presented by the Valide or the Sultan as odalisk or wife, receives a veneer composed of the formalities of Turkish etiquette, elegance of deportment, the art of beautifying the person, dancing, singing, or playing on some musical instrument. To the young and willing, instruction in the rudiments of the Turkish language are given; they are also initiated in the simpler forms of Mohammedanism taught to women, such as the Namaz and other prayers and the observance of the fasts and feasts.

Ottoman Sultans, with two exceptions, have never been known to marry; the mates of the Sultan, chosen from among the ranks of slaves already mentioned, or from among those that are presented to him, can only be admitted to the honorable title of wife when they have borne children. The first wife is called Bash Kadin Effendi, the second Ikinji Kadin Effendi, and so on in numerical order up to the seventh wife (should there be so many), who would be called Yedinji Kadin Effendi

The slaves that have borne children beyond this number bear the title of Hanoums, and rank after the Kadin Effendis; their children are considered legitimate, and rank with the other princes and princesses. To these two classes must be added a third, that of favorites, who, having no right to the title of Kadin Effendi or Hanoum, are dependent solely upon the caprice of their master or the influence they may have acquired over him for the position they hold in the imperial household.

Under this system every slave in the seraglio, from the scullery maid to the fair and delicate beauty purchased for her personal charms, may aspire to attaining the rank of wife, odalisk, or favorite. The mother of the late Sultan Abdul-Aziz is said to have performed the most menial offices in the establishment. When thus engaged one day she happened to attract the attention of her imperial master, Sultan Mahmoud II, who distinguished her with every mark of attention, and raised her to the rank of Bash Kadin. Generally speaking, however, the wives of sultans are select beauties, who are offered to him yearly by the nation on the feast of Kandil Ghedjessi; others are gifts of the Valide and other persons wishing to make an offering to the Sultan.

When one of these odalisks has succeeded in gaining the good graces of the Sultan and attracted his attention, he calls up the Ikinji Hasnadar Ousta, and notifies to her his desire of receiving the favored beauty into his apartment. The slave being informed of this, is bathed, dressed with great care and elegance, and introduced in the evening to the imperial presence. Should she be so fortunate as to find favor in the eyes of her lord and master, she is on the next morning admitted into a separate room reserved for slaves of this category, which she occupies during the time needful for ascertaining what rank she is in future to take in the seraglio. Should the arrival of a child raise her to that of Kadin Effendi or hanoum, a Daire or special apartment is set apart for her. Those who are admitted to the Sultan's presence, and have no claims to the rights of maternity, do not present themselves a second time, unless requested to do so, nor can they lay claim to any further attention, although their persons, like those of the Kadin Effendi and haroums, become sacred, and the contraction of marriage with another person is unlawful. The distinction between the favored and the discarded favorite is made known by her abstaining from going to the hammam.

TURKISH PEASANTS.

The Turkish peasants inhabiting the rural districts of Bulgaria, Macedonia, Epirus and Thessaly, although the best, most industrious and useful of the Sultan's Mohammedan subjects, everywhere evince signs of poverty, decrease in numbers and general deterioration. This fact is evident even to the mere traveler, from the wretchedness and poverty-stricken appearance of Turkish villages, with their houses mostly tumbling to pieces. The inhabitants, unable to resist the drain upon them in time of war, when the youngest and most vigorous men are taken away for military service, often abandon their dwellings and retire to more populous villages or towns; the property thus abandoned goes to ruin, and the fields in the same manner become waste.

The Turkish peasant is a good, quiet and submissive subject, who refuses neither to furnish his Sultan with troops, nor to pay his taxes, so far as in him lies; but he is poor, ignorant, helpless and improvident to an almost incredible degree. At the time of recruiting, he will complain bitterly of his hard lot, but go all the same to serve his time; he groans under the heavy load of taxation, gets imprisoned, and is not released until he manages to pay his dues.

He is generally discontented with his government, of which he openly complains, and still more with its agents, with whom he is brought into closer contact; but still the idea of rebelling against either, giving any signs of disaffection, or attempting to resist the law, never gets any hold upon him. His relations with his Christian neighbors vary greatly with the locality and the personal character of both. In some places Christian and Turkish peasants, in times of peace, live in tolerable harmony; in others a continual warfare of complaints on one side and acts of oppression on the other is kept up.

The Turkish peasant is well-built and strong, and possesses extraordinary power of endurance. His mode of living is simple, his habits sober; unlike the Christians of his class, he has no dance, no village feast, and no music, but a kind of drum or tambourine, to vary the monotony of his life. His cup of coffee and his chibouk contain for him all the sweets of existence. The coffee is taken before the labors of the day are begun, and again in the evening at the cafine. His work is often interrupted in order to enjoy the chibouk, which he smokes crouched under a tree or wall. His house is clean, but badly built; cold in winter and hot in summer, possessing little in the way of furniture but bedding, mats, rugs and kitchen utensils. He is worse clad than the Christian peasant, and his wife and children still worse; yet the women are content with their lot, and in their ignorance and helplessness do not try, like the Christian women, to better their condition by their individual exertions; they are irreproachable and honest in their conduct, and capable of enduring great trials. Some are very pretty; they keep much at home; the young girls seldom gather together for fun and enjoyment except at a wedding or circumcision ceremony, when they sing and play together, while the matrons gossip over their private affairs and those of their neighbors. The girls are married young to peasants of their own or some neighboring village. Polygamy is rare among Turkish peasants, and they do not often indulge in the luxury of divorce.

On the whole, the Turkish peasant, though not a model of virtue, is a good sort of man, and would be much better if he had not the habit in times of national trouble to take upon him the name of Bashi-Bazouk, and to transform himself into a ruffian.

TURKISH TRADESPEOPLE.

The life led by the Turkish tradespeople is extremely monotonous and brightened by no intellectual pleasures. The shopkeeper, on leaving his house at dawn, goes to the coffee-house, takes his small cup of coffee, smokes his pipe, chats with the habitues of the place, and then proceeds to his business, which is carried on with Oriental languor throughout the day. At sunset he again resorts to the coffee-house to take the same refreshment and enjoy the innovation of having a newspaper read to him—a novelty now much appreciated by the lower classes. He then returns to the bosom of his family in time for the evening meal. His home is clean, though very simple; his wife and daughters are ignorant, and never taught a trade by which they might earn anything. Embroidery, indispensable in a number of useless articles that serve to figure in the trousseau of every Turkish girl, and latterly coarse needle and crochet-work, fill up part of the time, while the mothers attend to their household affairs. The young children are sent to the elementary school, and the boys either go to school or are apprenticed to some trade.

TURKISH LADIES.

A Turkish lady is certainly shut up in a harem, and there

A TURKISH CART.

DAMASCUS—GROUP OF TOMBS OF DAMASQUINS EMIR.

can be no doubt that she is at liberty to indulge in the above-mentioned luxuries should she feel so disposed; she has possibly, at times, to submit to being locked up, but the key is applied to the outer gates, and is left in the keeping of the friendly eunuch. Besides, woman is said to have a will of her own, and "where there is a will there is a way" is a proverb to which Turkish ladies are no strangers. In one sense she may not have so much freedom as American women have, but in many others she possesses more. In her home she is perfect mistress of her time and of her property, which she can dispose of as she thinks proper. Should she have cause of complaint against anyone, she is allowed to be very open-spoken, holds her ground, and fights her own battles with astonishing coolness and decision.

Turkish ladies appreciate to the full as much as their husbands the virtues of the indispensable cup of coffee and cigarette; this is their first item in the day's programme. The hanoums may next take a bath, the young ladies wash at the abtest hours; the slaves when they can find time. The hanoum will then attend to her husband's wants, bring him his pipe and coffee, his slippers and pelisse. While smoking, he will sit on the sofa, whilst his wife occupies a lower position near him, and the slaves roll up the bedding from the floor. If the gentleman be a government functionary, the official bag will be brought in, and he will look over his documents, examining some, affixing his seal to others, saying a few words in the intervals to his wife, who always addresses him in a ceremonious manner with great deference and respect. The children will then trot in in their gedjliks, with their hair uncombed, to be caressed, and ask for money with which to buy sweets and cakes. The custom of giving pence to children daily is so prevalent that it is practiced even by the poor.

The children, after an irregular breakfast, are sent to school or allowed to roam about the house; the effendi proceeds to perform his out-of-door toilet, and leaves the haremlik, when the female portion of the establishment, freed from the pleasure or obligation of attending to his wants, begin the day's occupation. If this should include any special or unusual household work, such as preserve-making, washing or ironing, or general house cleaning, the lady, be she of the highest position, will take part in it with the slaves. This is certainly not necessary, for she has plenty of menials, but is done in order to fill up the day, many hours of which necessarily hang heavily on her hands when not enlivened by visiting or being visited. In the capital, however, less of this kind of employment is indulged in by the fashionable hanoums, who are trying to create a taste for European occupations, by learning music, foreign languages and fine needle work. The time for dressing is irregular. A lady may think proper to do her hair and make herself tidy for luncheon, or she may remain in her gedjlik and slippers all day. This fashion of receiving visitors en neglige is not considered at all peculiar, unless the visit has been announced beforehand.

Visiting and promenading, the principal amusements of Turkish ladies, are both affairs of very great importance. Permission has previously to be asked from the husband, who, if liberally disposed, freely grants it; but if jealous and strict, he will disapprove of seeing his family often out of doors. When a walk or drive is projected, the children all begin to clamor to go with their mother. Scarcely is this question settled by coaxing or giving them money, than another arises, as to which of the slaves are to be allowed to go. Tears, prayers and even little quarrels and disturbances follow, until the mistress finally selects her party. The details of the toilets are very numerous; the face has to be blanched, then rouged, the eyebrows and lashes to be blackened with surme, and a variety of other little coquetries resorted to requiring time and patience before the final adjustment of the yashmak and feridge.

Then comes the scramble for places in the carriage; the hanoums naturally seat themselves first, the rest squeeze themselves in, and sit upon each other's knees. It is wonderful to see how well they manage this close packing, and how long they can endure the uncomfortable postures in which they are fixed.

If the excursion is solely for visiting, the occupants of the carriages make the best of the time and liberty by coquetting with the grooms and agas in attendance, should these be young and handsome, and sending salaams to the passers-by, mingled with laughter and frolic. But when the excursion has a picnic in prospective, or a long drive into the country, the gayety and fun indulged in is bewildering; and the hanoums can only be compared to a flock of strange birds suddenly let loose from their cages, not knowing what to make of their new freedom. Flirting, smoking, eating fruits and sweets, walking about, running, or lounging on the carpets they bring with them, varied by music and singing, fill the day. They usually set out early and return before sunset in time to receive their master on his visit to the harem before dinner. When this meal is over, the company, comfortably dressed in their neglige costume, indulge in coffee and cigarettes, and the events of the day are discussed. The ladies then retire to rest at an early hour, and rise the next day to go through the same routine.

ISLAM IN TURKEY.

The religion of the Turks is properly the orthodox or Sunni form of Islam, the doctrines of which are of special interest, and we describe them here.

MOHAMMEDANISM OR ISLAMISM.

The Mohammedans do not themselves acknowledge the name. They call their religion Islam, which means "full submission to God," and themselves Moslems, or "the people of the Islam." Mohammed designated himself as the restorer of the pure religion revealed by God to Abraham. As the messenger of God, his pagan countrymen to leave their idols and adopt the worship of the one true God; the Jews, to exchange the law of Moses for the new and final revelations given to him; the Christians, to cease worshipping Christ as God, as inconsistent with monotheism and with the true doctrine of Christ himself. The doctrines of Mohammedanism may, in large measure, be traced to the national

religion of the Arabs before Mohammed, to those forms of
Judaism and Christianity which existed in Arabia in his time,
and to those traditions and usages which were the common
heritage of all branches of the Semitic race.

The fundamental doctrine of Islamism, and the only one
which is absolutely necessary to profess in order to be considered a Moslem, is: There is but one God, and Mohammed
is his apostle. The idea of God held by Mohammedans does
not differ essentially from the Christian, except that they reject entirely the doctrine of the Trinity. They believe that a
great number of prophets have been divinely commissioned
at various times, among whom six were sent to proclaim new
laws and dispensations, viz: Adam, Noah, Abraham, Moses,
Jesus and Mohammed. To the prophets were revealed certain scriptures inspired by God. All of these have perished
except four: the Pentateuch, the Psalms, the Gospel, and the
Koran. The first three, they maintain, have been falsified
and mutilated, and the Koran supersedes them all. Mohammed is the last prophet, and the Koran the final revelation. The Mohammedans regard Christ with a reverence
second only to that which they pay to Mohammed, and blasphemy of his name is punishable with death. But they
deny that he is God or the son of Son, though they consider
his birth miraculous. They also deny that he was crucified,
believing that some other person suffered in his place, while
he was taken up to God. He will come again upon the
earth to destroy Antichrist, and his coming will be one of the
signs of the approach of the last judgment. The Moslems
believe in the existence of angels with pure and subtile bodies

created of fire, who have no distinction of sex, neither eat nor drink, and are employed in adoring and praising God, interceding for mankind, keeping a record of human actions, and performing various other services. Four are held by God in peculiar favor: Gabriel, who is employed in writing down the divine decrees, and by whom the Koran was revealed at various times to Mohammed; Michael, the especial guardian of the Jews; Azrael, the "angel of death," who separates the souls of men from their bodies, and Israfil, who will sound the trumpet at the resurrection. There is also a lower class of beings than the angels, like them made of fire, but of a coarser nature, called jinns (generally rendered genii), who eat and drink, and are subject to death. Some of these are good, some evil. The chief of the latter is Eblis, or "despair," who was once an angel named Azazel, but who, having refused to pay homage to Adam, was rejected by God, and wanders over the earth until the resurrection. These genii have various names, as peri (fairies), div (giants), fates, etc. In regard to the state of man during the time between death and the resurrection, many different opinions prevail. There are also different views as to the last judgment; but the essential point agreed upon by all is that men will have awarded to them that condition of happiness or misery to which God shall judge them entitled by their conduct and belief during this life. The time of the resurrection is known only to God; its approach will be indicated by certain signs, among which will be the decay of faith among men, wars, seditions, tumults, the advancement of the meanest men to the highest dignities, an eclipse, the rising of the sun in the west, and numerous

MOSQUE OF SULTAN AHMED, CONSTANTINOPLE.

other portents. After the judgment all must pass over the bridge Al-Sirat, which is finer than a hair, sharper than a sword, and beset on either sides with thorns. The good will pass over easily and speedily; the wicked will fall headlong into hell. The delights of heaven are for the most part sensual, made up of pleasures especially suited to each of the senses, while the torments of hell consist chiefly in the extremes of heat and cold. The Moslems hold that all who believe in the unity of God will finally be released from punishment and enter Paradise. Those who deny the absolute unity of God, idolators and hypocrites, will suffer eternally. To hypocrites they assign the lowest place in hell. They believe in the absolute foreknowledge and predestination of all things by God, and, at the same time, in the responsibility of man for his conduct and belief. Their practical religion, which they call din, chiefly insists upon four things: 1st, purification and prayer, which they regard as together making one rite; 2d, almsgiving; 3d, fasting; 4th, the pilgrimage to Mecca. Prayer must be preceded by ablution; cleanliness is regarded as a religious duty, without which prayer would be ineffectual. The Moslems pray five times each day: soon after sunset (not exactly at sunset, for fear they should be considered sun-worshippers), at nightfall (generally about an hour and one-quarter after sunset), at daybreak, near noon, and in the afternoon. The times of prayer are announced by the muezzins (mueddzins) from the minarets of the mosques. In praying, the believer must turn his face toward Mecca, and the wall of the mosque nearest that city is marked by a niche. Twice during the night the muezzins also call to prayer for those who wish to perform extra devotions. Prayer may be said in any clean place, but on Friday they must be said in the mosque. Women are not forbidden to enter the mosque, but they never do so when the men are at their devotions. Before prayer all costly and sumptuous apparel must be laid aside. Almsgiving was formerly of two kinds: legal, called tzekah, and voluntary, called sadakah. The former was in reality a tax paid to the sovereign, and by him distributed as he saw fit; it has long since fallen into disuse. The sadakah consists of cattle, money, corn, fruits and wares sold. It is given once a year, and generally amounts to about $2\frac{1}{2}$ per cent. of the stock on hand; but no alms are due unless the stock amounts to a certain quantity, nor unless the articles have been in the owner's possession for eleven months. At the end of the fast of Ramadan every Moslem is expected to give alms if he is able for himself and each member of his family—a measure of wheat, rice or other provisions. The Moslems also lay great stress upon fasting. During the whole of the month Ramadan they fast from the rising to the setting of the sun; they neither eat nor drink nor indulge in any other physical gratification. They observe this fast with great rigor, but certain classes of persons to whom the fast would be physically injurious are excused from its observance. There are other days during which fasting is regarded as specially meritorious though not obligatory, and fasting at any time is regarded as peculiarly acceptable to God. The pilgrimage to Mecca, called hadji, is a relic of the ancient idolatrous religion which Mohammed desired to do away with, but which was too deeply rooted in the habits and interests of the people to be abolished. Hence he sanctioned it, and made it obligatory, having first destroyed the idols in the temple and introduced new regulations. All Moslems, men or women, should at least once during their lives, provided they are able, make the pilgrimage to Mecca. The duty may be performed by a substitute, in which case the whole merit redounds to the principal. He who has performed this pilgrimage is entitled to prefix to his name the word hadji. Of late years the number of pilgrims has greatly fallen off. The Moslems regard the Koran not only as the rule of their religious, but also of their civil and social life. Before the time of Mohammed, it was not uncommon among the Arabs to put to death their female children. This practice was forbidden by him. The following things are also forbidden in the Koran: eating of blood, or the flesh of swine, or of any animal that dies of itself, or has been strangled or killed by accident or by another beast, or has been slain as a sacrifice to an idol; playing games of chance, whether with or without a wager; the drinking of wine or of any inebriating liquor (but some construe this prohibition as only applicable to their excessive use, while a few of the very strict construe it as applying to opium, bang and even coffee and tobacco); the taking of interest upon money lent, even when the loan is made to a person of different religion; divination and various other superstitious practices. Murder seems to be regarded by the Koran as a crime against individuals rather than against society; hence it was punishable with death or a pecuniary fine, at the option of the family of the murdered man. But at present in the Turkish Empire murder is punished with death, and commutation by fine is not permitted. If a believer kills another accidentally, the slayer must pay a fine, and redeem a believer from slavery. The punishment for theft is cutting off the hand, but in modern times this has generally fallen into disuse, and the bastinado or imprisonment has been substituted. Polygamy existed among all the Semitic nations previous to the time of Mohammed, and he restricted rather than extended it. While claiming for himself special privileges in regard to his domestic relations, asserting that they were allowed him by the direct permission of God, he limited the number of wives which a true believer might take to four.

Aside from the domestic relations, the ethics of the Mohammedan religion are of the highest order. Pride, calumny, revengefulness, avarice, prodigality and debauchery are condemned throughout the Koran; while trust in God and submission to His will, patience, modesty, forebearance, love of peace, sincerity, truthfulness, frugality, benevolence, liberality—indeed, aside from the differences of opinion in regard to theological subjects, all those qualities which the Anglo-Saxon race have idealized under the term "Christian gentleman" are everywhere insisted upon.

The inquiry has often been made, "What part of the Koran promises Paradise to the triumphant Mohammedan?" I make the best quotation possible as an answer:

"The whole earth will be as one loaf of bread, which God will reach to them like a cake; for meat they will have the ox, Balam, and the fish, Nun, the lobes of whose livers will suffice 70,000 men. Every believer will have 80,000 servants and seventy-two girls of Paradise, besides his own former wives, if he should wish for them, and a large tent of pearls, jacinths and emeralds; 300 dishes of gold shall be set before each guest at once, and the last morsel shall be as grateful as the first. Wine will be permitted, and will flow copiously, without inebriating. The righteous will be clothed in the most precious silks and gold, and will be crowned with crowns of the most resplendent pearls and jewels. If they desire children, they shall beget them, and see them grow up within an hour. Besides the ravishing songs of the angel Israfil, and the daughters of Paradise, the very trees will, by the rustling of their boughs, the clanging of bells suspended from them, and the clashing of their fruits, which are pearls and emeralds, make sweetest music."

The Ordinances of the Mohammedan faith are strictly observed wherever the Prophet is accepted. A Mohammedan, when the time arrives for his prayer, has no business with worldly affairs until his prayer is ended. To him no earthly business can compare with the duty of prayer.

The first chapter of the Koran is a prayer. It is a prayer which is held in great veneration by the Mohammedans. It is considered the quintessence of the Koran. It is often repeated. It is the Lord's Prayer of the Moslem. There has been much discussion as to its recondite meaning, for, be it known, that there have been many contentious theologians in the Orient ever since the time of the early fathers. The fathers defined closely the true meaning of certain words and phrases upon which an eternity of happiness or misery depended. This prayer is a sample of the very best meaning of this wonderful Mahomet: .

"Praise be to God, the Lord of all creatures! The most merciful, the King of the Day of Judgment! Thee do we worship, and of Thee do we beg assistance. Direct us in the right way, in the way of those to whom Thou hast been gracious, not of those against whom Thou art incensed nor of those who go astray."

The foregoing are the words of the Moslem common prayer, without any of its wearisome repetitions, which protract it to a great length. Some portions are repeated three, six and even nine times at each course. The same repetitions are to be found in our Christian Litanies.

The prayer will remind the reader of the Psalms of David: "O God most high, there is no God but God. Praises belong unto God. Let Thy name be exalted, O great God. I sanctify Thy name, O my God. I praise Thee; Thy name is blessed, Thy grandeur is exalted, there is no other God but Thee. I flee to Thee against the stoned demon, in the name of God clement and merciful. Praise belongs to God, most clement and merciful. He is Sovereign of the Day of Judgment. We adore Thee, Lord, and we implore Thy assistance. Direct us in the path of salvation, in the path of those whom Thou loadest with Thy favors, of those who have not deserved Thine anger, and who are not of those who go astray. O God, hear him who praises Thee. O God, praises wait for Thee. O God, bestow Thy salutation of peace upon Mahomet, as Thou didst upon Ibrahim and the race of Ibrahim, and bless Mahomet and the race of Mahomet, as Thou didst bless Ibrahim and the race of Ibrahim. Praise, grandeur and exaltation are in Thee and to Thee."

The most solemn sight connected with any religious ceremony that I have ever witnessed was the one upon which I looked from the gallery of St. Sophia. Below me were thousands of human beings in regular lines, all looking toward Mecca while they prayed. Not a single suppliant connected with this devotion failed to bow his head to the floor, as by one impulse, when the shrill chant of the priests died away among the pillars and in the dome of the vast temple.

DANCING DERVISHES.

TURKISH LADIES.

Occasionally there was a pause, as between the summons and the judgment.

The Turk has at least an outward show of piety. If he be a good Moslem, his life is regulated by his faith. He moves with a humility which belongs to a reflective mind. He may be rich and live in luxury within his konak or palace, but when he enters the mosque there is for him no worldly pomp. He is in the presence of the unseen God. He prays without ceasing, aligned with others, some of whom may be beggars, water-carriers or charcoal venders. Here he feels that he is but one of the atoms among the many which make up a remarkable and infinite congregation of souls. Certainly such humility is in strange contrast with the complacent luxury of Western churches, with their richly-cushioned pews, their carved pulpits, their gilt-edged hymn-books and their sometimes pompous clergy.

The call to prayer is a picturesque feature of this remarkable faith. Morning, noon and night that shrill cry echoes over these wonderful cities and waters:

"Most High! There is no God but the one God. Mahomet is the Prophet of God! Come to prayer! Come to the Temple of Life!"

"Fasting also is an observance of the Mohammedan. His Lent, from one moon to another, is kept with religious regard while the sun is above the horizon. "How often have I looked over and seen the wonderful beauty of Stamboul in that Ramazab season, when the mosques are burning their countless lamps, and from minaret to minaret there is a profusion of brilliant lights! It is during this month that the worship of the Prophet is celebrated with a splendor only limited by Moslem skill in illumination. When the electric light shall appear in the East, to penetrate the dark places of

Stamboul and shed its refulgence through St. Sophia, Suleiman and the other grand mosques and structures of the capital—with their immense interiors filled with surging and kneeling forms and bowing foreheads—the splendors of the Roman ritual in St. Peter's and the glories of Westminster Abbey and St. Isaacs will be eclipsed before those of Islam."

The established church, so to speak, of Turkey is governed by the Ulema, or learned men trained in the mosques, often supported by pious endowments. The popular faith, on the other hand, is led by the various sects of dervishes, between whom and the Ulema there exists an unconquerable rivalry. Some accounts of these two parties is essential to any description of the people of Turkey.

The Ulema are the hereditary expounders of the Koran, to the traditional interpretation of which they rigidly adhere. They have nothing to say to the many innovations that time has shown to be needful in the religion of Mohammed, and they brand as heretics all who differ a hair's-breadth from the old established line. The result of this uncompromising orthodoxy has been that the Ulema, together with their subordinates the Softas (a sort of Moslem undergraduates), have managed to preserve an esprit de corps and a firm collected line of action that is without a parallel in Turkish parties.

The order of Ulema is divided into three classes: the Imama, or ministers of religion; the Muftis, doctors of the law, and the Kadis or Mollahs, judges. Each of these classes is subdivided into a number of others, according to the rank and functions of those that compose it.

The imams, after passing an examination, are appointed by the Sheikh ul Islam to the office of priests in the mosques.

The fixed pay they receive is small, about $35 or $40 per annum. Some mosques have several imams. Their functions are to pronounce the prayer aloud and guide the ceremonies. The chief imam has precedence over the other imams, the muezzins (callers to prayer), the khatibs, hodjas and other servants of the mosque.

A strange license of the Turkish law is that crime is not punished unless its actual commission is certified by eyewitnesses; this is the reason that evidence of crime committed during the night is not admitted as valid by the laws of the country. The imams, under the pressure of this law, think twice before they give evidence; nor do they much like the unpleasant duty of accompanying police inspections, from which they generally excuse themselves.

The muftis, or doctors of the law, rank next; seated in the courts of justice, they receive the pleas, examine into the cases and explain them to the mollah, according to their merits or the turn they may wish to give to them.

The mollahs or kadis form the next grade in the Ulema hierarchy. They are appointed by the Sheikh ul Islam, and are assisted in their functions by the muftis and other officials. The avarice and venality of this body of men are among the worst features of Turkish legislature. Few judges are free from the reproach of partiality and corruption.

DERVISHES.

Notwithstanding their vices, nothing can exceed the veneration in which the dervishes are held by the public, over whom they exercise an irresistible influence. This influence is especially made use of in time of war, when a motley company of sheikhs and fanatical dervishes join the army, and encourage the officers and men by rehearsing the benefits promised by the Prophet to all who fight or die for the true faith. The voices of these excited devotees may be heard crying, "O ye victorious!" "O ye martyrs!" or "Ya-llah!" Some of these men are fearful fanatics, who endeavor by every means in their power to stimulate the religious zeal of the troops and of the nation. Every word they utter is poison to public peace.

It is impossible here to enter into details as to the constitution of the various dervish orders (of which there are many) or the tenets held by them, or the ceremonies of initiation and of worship. Still, a few words are necessary about the two or three leading orders of dervishes in Turkey. The most graceful are the Mevlevi, or revolving dervishes, with their sugar-loaf hats, long skirts and loose jubbes. Once or twice a week public service is performed at the Mevlevi Khane, to which spectators are admitted. The devotions begin by the recital of the usual namaz, after which the sheikh proceeds to his pistiki, or sheepskin mat, and, raising his hands, offers, with great earnestness, the prayer to the Pir, or spirit of the founder of the order, asking his intercession with God on behalf of the order. He then steps off his pistiki and bows his head with deep humility towards it, as if it were now occupied by his Pir; then, in slow and measured step, he walks three times round the Semar Khane, bowing to the right and left with crossed toes as he passes his seat, his subordinates following and doing the same. This part of the ceremony (called the Sultan Veled Devri) over, the sheikh stands on the pistiki with bowed head, while the brethren in the mutrib, or orchestra, chant a hymn in honor of the Prophet, followed by a sweet and harmonious performance on the flute.

The Semar Zan, director of the performance, proceeds to the sheikh, who stands on the edge of his pistiki, and, after making a deep obeisance, walks to the centre of the hall, and gives a signal to the other brethren, who let fall their tennouris, take off their jubbes, and proceed in single file, with folded arms, to the sheikh, kiss his hand, receive in return a kiss on their hats, and there begin whirling round, using the left foot as a pivot while they push themselves round with the right. Gradually the arms are raised upwards and then extended outwards, the palm of the right hand being turned up and the left bent towards the floor. With closed eyes and heads reclining towards the right shoulder, they continue turning, muttering the inaudible zihr, saying, "Allah, Allah!" to the sound of the orchestra and the chant that accompanies it, ending with the exclamation, "O friend!" when the dancers suddenly cease to turn. The sheikh, still standing, again receives the obeisance of the brethren as they pass his pistiki, and the dance is renewed. When it is over, they resume their seats on the floor and are covered with their jubbes. The service ends with a prayer for the Sultan. The whole of the ceremony is extremely harmonious and interesting; the bright and variegated colors of the dresses, the expert and graceful way in which the dervishes spin round, bearing on their faces at the same time a look of deep humility and devotion, together with the dignified attitude and movements of the sheikh, combine to form a most impressive sight.

HOWLING DERVISHES.

Equally curious are the Rifai, or howling dervishes. They wear a mantle edged with green, a belt in which are lodged one or three big stones, to compress the hunger to which a dervish is liable, and a white felt hat, marked with eight grooves (terks), each denoting the renunciation of a cardinal sin. In their devotions, they become strangely excited, their limbs become frightfully contorted, their faces deadly pale; then they dance in the most grotesque manner, howling meanwhile; cut themselves with knives, swallow fire and swords, burn their bodies, pierce their ears, and finally swoon. A sacred word whispered by two elders of the order brings the unconscious men round, and their wounds are healed by the touch of the sheikh's hand, moistened from his mouth. It is strange and horrible to witness the ceremonies of this order; but in these barbarous performances the devout recognize the working of the Divine Spirit.

PRAYERS.

You can give no higher praise to a Turk than saying that he performs his five prayers a day. In right of this qualification, young men of no position and as little merit are often chosen as sons-in-law by pious people. A Turk of the old school is proud of his religion, and is never ashamed of letting you see it. So long as he can turn his face towards

A TURKISH LADY OF WEALTH.

HOWLING DERVISH.

Mecca, he will say his prayers anywhere. The Turks like to say their namaz in public, that they may have praise of men; and it is to be feared that a good deal of hypocrisy goes on in this matter. This, however, is on the decrease, because fewer Turks in all classes say their prayers or observe the outward forms of religion than formerly. This is no doubt partly due to the influence of "Young Turkey," though other causes are also at work.

But the orthodox Turk must do more than observe the prayers. The fast of Ramazan is a very important part of his religious routine. Everyone knows this terrible month of day-fasting and night-fasting. It tells most severely on the poor, who keep it strictly, and are compelled to work during the day exactly as when not fasting. Women also of all classes observe the fast religiously. But there are very few among the higher officials, or the gentlemen who have enrolled themselves under the banner of La Jeune Turquie, who take any notice of it, except in public, where they are obliged to show outward respect to the prejudices of the people.

This fast-month is a sort of revival-time to the Moslems. They are supposed to devote more time to the careful study of the Koran and to the minute practice of its ordinances. Charity, peacefulness, hospitality, almsgiving are among the virtues which they specially cultivate at this time, and though the theory is not put in practice to the letter, and hospitality not carried out as originally intended—the rich man standing at his door at sunset, bringing in and setting at his table all the poor that happened to pass by, and sending them away with presents of money—it is still very largely practiced.

THE SULTAN AT PRAYERS.

The ceremony of attending mosque is never omitted, if the Sultan be alive. It matters not whether it hails or rains, whether there be an earthquake, a plague or a pestilence or personal sickness, this observance is one of the scrupulous duties of the Sultan, who is at the same time the absolute Caliph of the Faith. The prayer which he offers cannot be said by anyone else for him. It is a religious duty to be done by him in person. It is reckoned the most honorable of his functions and the greatest of all his privileges. To omit his appearance on that day would almost provoke a riot.

This custom came into use in the year A. D. 1361. Then the reigning Sultan, Murad I, having offered to give evidence before the Mufti in a case in which one of his favorites was concerned, his testimony was rejected on the ground that, according to the law of the Koran, no person can be admitted as a witness in a religious court of justice who has not joined in common prayer in the mosque. In acknowledgment of the justice of this decision, Murad proceeded, on the following Friday, in great state, to the mosque. He joined with the other worshippers, and performed his devotions as one of their own number. The custom has since been observed with the utmost strictness and regularity. Sultan Mahmoud I, though very ill, insisted on going to the mosque, with the result that on his return to the palace he fell down dead at the entrance as he was dismounting from his horse. The same fatality happened to the Sultan Osman II, who, heedless of the advice of his physicians, left his sick-bed in order to attend the usual Friday prayers. He returned safely to the palace, but expired on the following night.

The ceremony is not now attended with as much eclat as in the early days, when the Sultan's servitors were dressed in velvet and gold, and scattered handfuls of gold and silver along his path as he passed on his way to the mosque of St. Sofia.

In those early days, when Turkish power was literally sublime, the far-famed carpets of the East were spread over the ground, upon which pranced the Sultan's steed. The Oriental escort, with its flowing robes, immense turbans, military music and official retinue, has been more or less discarded by the fashions of the present day and by the advancement of the Turk himself in European customs.

When the Sultan attends prayers at the mosque the time is fixed by the Turkish clock at 7. This means about 2 o'clock in the afternoon, European time. He generally comes in a large and elegant open carriage. He is accompanied by a trusted friend, the aged Namyk Pasha, who is the very pink of courtesy, and Osman Pasha, the hero of Plevna. From 5000 to 7000 troops usually keep the way on these occasions. They come in with bands of music from all parts of the city, bearing their sacred banners of green, inscribed with Koranic texts and their own regimental flags. They are in line before the Sultan appears. Some of the battalions or regiments appear in fanciful uniform, such as the Albanian. They had a corps of stalwart sappers and miners, in leathern aprons and huge battle-axes. Every part of the dominion is represented by the troops. They are a strong body of soldiers, well officered. They have a variety of uniform. Their fine music and the esprit du corps of the escort give something more than a religious aspect to the occasion.

Those who would see the "Salemlik" or the Sultan as he enters the mosque and comes from it should take their stand about noon either at the guardhouse or at the new quarters. "In the multitude of the people is the King's honor." The population turns out en masse on these occasions. The black-tasseled, bright-red fez cap gives its color to the scene. The general tone of the uniform, however, is that of the zouave, whose scarlet trousers reach to the knee. The soldiers are olive-colored, and bronzed with many a sun, and are of splendid physique. As the Sultan enters the mosque, he is surrounded by dozens of his officers, whose uniforms glitter with a profusion of gold lace and decorative orders. He is met by the Imam, or Moslem priest, at the door. There is no special order about the crowd, except that they are kept more or less in check by the soldiery. Carriages, horses and people mingle together in confusion. Many of the carriages contain the wives of the Sultan, his children, cousins and nieces and his mother and aunt. Diamonds shine with unusual profusion upon the veiled beauties.

The Sultan enters the mosque. All is quietude without, until he has finished his prayers. Then is heard a bugle-note; a carpet is laid down, and the officers, who are his adjutants, ministers and others, mount their horses. They are ready for the movement. The soldiers "present arms!" the iron gate opens, and the shout goes up, "Padisha! Chok Yasha!" (the Sultan! Let him live forever!). Sometimes the Sultan is mounted on a white steed, which is appareled for the occasion; but generally, amid salutation, he comes and returns in his carriage, takes the reins himself, and drives to and from the palace. His people close about him, and the spectacle is over.

You may ask how he is dressed. I have generally seen him in a blue-black frock coat, closely buttoned, edged with red cord. The present Sultan is a graceful rider, and, when on horseback, like his fellow-countrymen, he shows to advantage. His title as Sultan does not signify all the power which he possesses as an absolute ruler, but yet it signifies much. Padisha signified most. It is the chief and favorite title. It signified Father of all the Sovereigns of the Earth. He has other titles, such as Imam-ul-Muslemin (Pontiff of Mussulmans), Alem Penah (Refuge of the World). Any more? Yes. Other titles are that of "Lord of Two Continents and Two Seas, King of Kings, High and Mighty Lord, Servant of the Two Holy Cities, Shadow of God upon Earth, Hunkiar, or Man-Slayer." Any more? Yes; more still. He is called Ali-Osman Padishahi (King of the Descendants of Osman), Shahin Shahi Alem (King of the Sovereigns of the Universe), Hudavendighar (Attached to God), Shabin Shahi Movezem ve Hilloulah (High King of Kings and Shadow of God; and, to illustrate the theocratic democracy which pervades the civil order and the Mohammedan religion, he also bears the title of "The Son of a Slave." He thus combines with the highest human exaltation the lowest humiliation. It is the law of the Koran. He is the son of a slave-mother, and, therefore, should he not be humble? He is the Divine representative of Mahomet, and the father of his people, and, therefore, should he not be exalted? His family line runs back with unbroken links to the middle of the thirteenth century, and, though he may not be as great in war and as rugged in manner as Orchan or Sulieman, or as stately and tall as his brother, Abdul Aziz, or perhaps as kingly in theatric style as his father, Abdul Medjid, he has a splendid eye and a royal mien, becoming the lineage of Osman. His face is pale, and its general contour and features indicate a man who is amiable, shrewd, vigilant and able.

THE OFFICIAL PRAYER OF ISLAM.

The official prayer of Islam, which is used throughout Turkey, and daily repeated in the Cairo "Azhar" University by 10,000 Mohammedan students from all lands, throws a flood of light on the subject. The following translation is from the Arabic:

"I seek refuge with Allah from Satan, the rejeem (the accursed). In the name of Allah the Compassionate, the Merciful! O Lord of all Creatures! O Allah! Destroy the infidels and polytheists, Thine enemies, the enemies of the religion! O Allah! Make their children orphans, and defile their abodes, and cause their feet to slip; and give them, and their families, and their households, and their women, and their children, and their relatives by marriage, and their

MOHAMMEDANS AT PRAYER.

brothers, and their friends, and their possessions, and their race, and their wealth, and their lands, as booty to the Moslems, O Lord of all Creatures!"

All who do not accept Mohammed are included among "the infidels" referred to in the prayer.

SUPERSTITION.

There are few people so superstitious as the people of Turkey All nations have their traditions and fancies; but in Turkey every action, every ceremony, every relation, is hedged round with fears and omens and forebodings. Whatever happens to you is the work of supernatural agencies, and can only be remedied by the nostrums of some disreputable hag or some equally suspicious quack diviner. If you lose anything, it is the evil eye of some kind friend that has done it. If you look fixedly at anybody or anything, it is you who are trying to cast the evil eye.

They make periodical visits to the graves of their dead to discover whether the soul is at peace. If the body is not fully decomposed at the end of the year, they believe that their relation has become a Vrykolakas, and use every means to lay the spirit. But the Vrykolakas, though the most ghastly of spirits, is not alone. There are invisible influences everywhere in Turkey. If the Vrykolakas haunts the graveyards, old Konaks have their edjinlis, fountains their peris, public baths their peculiar genii.

All these imaginary beings, whose existence is implicitly believed in, are expected to be encountered by the persons upon whom they may choose to cast their baneful or good influence. Their dreaded hostility is combatted by the Christians by religious faith, such as an earnest appeal to Christ and the Virgin, by repeatedly crossing themselves in the name of both, or by taking hold of any sacred amulet they may have on their persons. These amulets consist of small portions of the "true cross," enshrined in crosses of silver, a crucifix, or an image of the Virgin, which, trustingly held and shown to the apparitions, have the effect of rendering them impotent and causing them to vanish. The Turks have recourse to the repetition of a certain form of prayer, and to their maskas or amulets, in which they place as much faith as the Christians do in theirs.

The spirits that have their abodes in mineral baths are especially courted by the sick, who are taken to the establishments and left under the beneficent care of these beings. The mineral bath of Kainadjah, near Broussa, is a dark dungeon-like place, extremely old, and much famed in the district for its healing powers. Its waters, strongly impregnated with sulphur, are boiling hot, rendering the atmosphere of the bath intolerable to any but the credulous.

MAGIC.

Magic plays a great part in Turkish affairs. Christians and Moslems, Greeks and Bulgarians, Turks and Albanians, implicitly believe in the power possessed by evil-minded persons of casting spells upon their enemies or rivals, and extraordinary means are resorted to with a view to removing the baneful influence.

Most of the spells cast upon persons are aimed at life, beauty, wealth and the affections. They are much dreaded, and the events connected with this subject that daily occur are often of a fatal character. A Turkish lady, however high her position, invariably attributes to the influence of magic the neglect she experiences from her husband, or the bestowal of his favor on other wives. Every Hanoum goes down to the laundry regularly and rinses with her own hands her husband's clothes after the wash, fearing that if any of her slaves performed this duty she would have the power of casting spells to supplant her in her husband's good graces. Worried and tormented by these fears, she is never allowed the comfort of enjoying in peace that conjugal happiness which mutual confidence alone can give. A buyu boghcha (or magic bundle) may at any time be cast upon her, cooling her affection for her husband, or turning his love away from her. The blow may come from an envious mother-in-law, a scheming rival, or from the very slaves of whose services the couple stand daily in need.

The buyu boghcha is composed of a number of incongruous objects, such as human bones, hair, charcoal, earth, besides a portion of the intended victim's garment, etc., tied up in a rag. When it is aimed at the life of a person, it is supposed to represent his heart, and is studded with forty-one needles, intended to act in a direct manner and finally cause his death. The advice of magicians, fortune-tellers, dream-expounders and quack astrologers is always consulted by persons desirous of being enlightened upon any subject. Stolen property is believed to be recoverable through their instrumentality, and the same faith is placed in them as a victim of some wrong would put in the intelligence and experience of a clever detective.

THE EVIL EYE.

Belief in the evil eye is perhaps more deeply rooted in the mind of the Turk than in that of any other nation, though Christians, Jews and even some Franks regard it as a real misfortune. It is supposed to be cast by some envious or malicious person, and sickness, death and loss of beauty, affection and wealth are ascribed to it. Should you happen to fix your gaze on a person or object in the presence of ill-disposed Turks, you are liable to receive rude remarks from them under the idea that you are casting the evil eye. The preservatives employed against the power of this evil are as numerous as the means used to dissipate its effects. The principal preventives and antidotes are garlic, cheriot, wild thyme, boars' tusks, hares' heads, terebinth, alum, blue glass, torquoise, pearls, the bloodstone, carnelian, eggs (principally those of the ostrich), a gland extracted from the neck of the ass, written amulets, and a thousand other objects. The upper classes of the Christians try to avert its effect by sprinkling the afflicted persons with cold water, fumigating them with the burning branches of the palms used on Palm Sunday, and by hanging amulets round their necks; as preservatives, coral, blue glass ornaments and crosses are worn. The common people of all denominations resort to other means in addition to these. On the last day of February they take the heads of forty small fish, and string and hang them up to dry. When a child is found ailing from the supposed effects of the evil eye, the heads are soaked in water, and the horrible liquid given to it to drink. It is considered a good test of the presence of the evil eye to place cloves on burning coals and carry them round the room. Should many of these explode, some malicious person is supposed to have left the mischievous effects of the Nazar behind him. Blue or gray eyes are more dreaded than dark ones, and red-haired persons are particularly suspected.

DREAMS.

Dreams play a great part in Eastern life. The young girl, early taught to believe in them, hopes to perceive in these transient visions a glimpse of the realities that are awaiting her; the married woman seeks, in their shadowy illusions, the promise of the continuation of the poetry of life, and firmly believes in the coming realities they are supposed to foreshadow; while the ambitious man tries to expound them in favor of his hopes and prospects, often guiding his actions by some indistinct suggestion they convey to his mind.

CHAPTER V.

CONSTANTINOPLE.

The city of Constantinople is distinguished for its situation, history, trade and political importance.
Situated on a series of hills which rise from the shores of the Marmora, the Bosphorus and the Golden Horn, with a water frontage of fifteen miles, every hill and conspicuous site crowned by stately mosque or by imperial palace, grand public edifice or noble private residence, the approach to the city is truly enchanting. Situated on the European side of the Bosphorus, the city is divided into two parts by a deep inlet, which by reason of its horn-shape and fine harbor is called the Golden Horn. On the south side of the Golden Horn, of triangular shape, with a circumference of twelve miles, is Constantinople proper, called by the Turks, according to their custom of changing proper names, Istambol, or Stamboul. The apex of the triangle is the Seraglio Point, where the waters of the Marmora, the Bosphorus and the Golden Horn meet; the two sides of the triangle are the shores of the Marmora and of the Golden Horn, and the base is the land intervening between the sea and the inner extremity of the Horn. On the north side of the Golden Horn, directly opposite Stamboul, is the quarter called Galata, with a water frontage of several miles, the seat of the banks and chief commercial houses, and on the hills above Galata, partly facing

toward the Golden Horn and partly toward the Bosphorus, is Pera, largely a European city, the site of the foreign embassies and the great hotels.

Directly opposite Constantinople, on the Asiatic shore, are the cities of Scutari, the ancient Chrysolis, and Kadikeuy, the ancient Chalcedon. The swift and dark-blue Bosphorus, a mile wide and twelve miles long, with high banks lined on both sides with picturesque villages and beautiful mansions and gardens, separates Asia from Europe and conects the Black sea and the Marmora.

During the past sixty years the widening, straightening and lighting of the streets; the construction of buildings of stone and brick instead of wood; the increased supply of water, and the organization of a fire department; the formation of a disciplined and fairly serviceable body of police in the place of the janissaries, and the vastly improved means of communication, by the multiplication of carriages, by numerous steamboats, by the Roumelian Railroad, by three lines of tramway, and by the tunnel between Galata and Pera, have greatly helped to make life in the city and suburb secure and agreeable.

To say nothing of the fine anchorage afforded by the shores of the Marmora and of the Bosphorus, the harbor of the Golden Horn, half a mile wide, five miles long, and deep enough for the largest man-of-war, with no tide and protected from every wind, offers ample room and perfect security for 1200 ships.

Situated on the forty-first parallel of north latitude—the same as New York—the winters are yet neither so cold nor the summers so hot as those of the commercial capital of America. The very situation of the city affords an easy drainage, while the winds and the rains aid greatly to keep the air sweet and pure.

Supplied with every variety of flesh, fish, vegetable and fruit, the market lacks naught which health or the palate demands.

From its earliest years Constantinople has been the natural centre of the grain trade between the countries bordering on the Black Sea and those bordering on the Mediterranean, and hither in modern times have been brought for sale and exchange the manufactured goods of the West and the handmade carpets, the embroideries, perfumes, drugs, silk, wool and mohair of the East. Some 25,000 sailing-vessels and 1500 steamers enter annually the port of Constantinople. The foreign commerce as well as almost every work of public utility is in the hands of foreigners and native Christians, while the Turks are engaged in the civil and military service and in certain local trades.

During the past half-century the Turkish government has established not only military and naval schools exclusively for Mussulman youth, but also civil, art and medical schools for the youth of every nationality. Every community provides, at its own expense, for the common-school education of its own children. The literary works published in Constantinople in various languages, many of them being translations of European works, are numerous. The different communities have many collections of books in their mosques and churches, but there are no public libraries in the European sense. There are also published nineteen daily newspapers and thirty-four other periodicals; of the former five are Turkish, five Armenian, four French, three Greek, and two English.

Including the inhabitants of the cities and suburbs on both sides of the Bosphorus, the population of Constantinople is fairly estimated at 1,000,000, of whom 500,000 are Mohammedan Turks, Arabs, Persians and Ethiopians; 250,000 are Greeks, 150,000 Armenians, 70,000 Jews, 25,000 Europeans and 5000 of various other nationalities. The Turks have never made a serious attempt to weld into one body the various races, and to this day they remain separate and distinct in nationality, language, religion and custom. At the same time it is apparent to all that for many years there has been going on a gradual but sure diminution of the Turkish population and an increase of the other races, and natural causes will, of themselves, in time settle the Eastern question.

Constantinople proper was the ancient city of Byzantium, founded by a colony from Megara, Greece, about 650 B. C. Rebuilt and renamed by Constantine the Great (330 A. D.), the city was protected by strong walls, which up to 1204 resisted seventeen attempts to capture it; it was supplied with underground cisterns sufficient to supply with water a million men for four months; it was adorned with many of the masterpieces of ancient art brought from Egypt, Greece and Italy; before its capture by the Latin crusaders, it is said to have had 500 churches, of which fifty have been identified in recent times, the most of these being in the hands of the Turks, five in the hands of the Greeks and one in the hands of the Armenians. The most beautiful edifice—used by the Turks as a mosque since 1453—was the renowned church of Justinian, built 632-638 A. D., at an estimated cost of $5,000,000, and dedicated to Holy Wisdom (Agia Sophia), unhappily called by Europeans Saint Sophia. For 900 years from the time of Constantine the city was the chief seat of European civilization, art, learning, commerce and wealth, and for centuries it successfully resisted the advance into Europe of the barbarous and multitudinous Asiatic tribes. The cruel capture and spoiling of the city in 1204 by the Latin crusaders prepared the way for its subsequent capture by the Ottoman Turks, in 1453.

THE HELLESPONT OF TODAY.

The Strait of the Dardanelles, to which numerous references are now being made in the papers, is, as many know, a narrow and tortuous waterway of no great length leading in from the north Ægean to the inland Sea of Marmora. But what many do not know is that the Turkish fortifications of the Dardanelles—at least those of any importance—are situated in a single locality in the vicinity of the squatty little Turkish town of Chanak-Kalesi (or the "Pottery Castle") which lies on the Asiatic shore a few miles in from the mouth of the strait. One of these batteries—a low-lying fortification constructed of mud, or, rather, clay walls, faced here and there with stone—is situated at Chanak-Kalesi itself. Another is planted about two miles further northeast on the same shore, while immediately across the strait from Chanak-

Kalesi other battlements have been reared on somewhat higher ground. None of these defences are especially formidable, as modern fortifications go, although it must be admitted that, inferior as they are in many respects, they do mount some heavy Krupp guns of modern construction and undoubted power, while torpedoes, it is said, have lately been sunk in the channel. Every now and then the Turkish government buys a new gun and sets it up at the Dardanelles with a sublime confidence that thereby the integrity of the empire will be effectually secured.

But the Turks understand little about the handling of these great guns, although the Osmanli soldiers are brave when well officered, and it is probable that in the event of actual hostilities the gunners would soon be driven from these defences, and many of the guns themselves be dismounted (by the skilful fire at long range of a fleet lying just inside the lower strait) before the Osmanli garrison could discharge more than a few wild shots with their intricate but poorly managed ballistic apparatus. What really adds more to the strength of these doorway defences of Turkey, so to speak, than any qualities of the garrison in these forts, is the swiftness of the currents and the tortuous character of the ship channel of the Dardanelles. Yet it is not improbable that once crippled by a fire at long range, a nervy and resolute captain of a modern battleship could run the gauntlet of the upper batteries before the bewildered gunners could adjust their artillery to the warship's varying range, or succeed in accomplishing more than a smashing of some of the vessel's upper works. Out of a fleet of half a dozen vessels endeavoring to force the passage of the Dardanelles, two would probably be disabled or would helplessly ground in manœuvring, while the balance would steam triumphantly past Gallipoli, at the upper end of the Dardanelles, and thereafter have absolutely free course directly to the Golden Horn and that part of the pretty Bosphorus overlooked by the windows and modest facades of the Yildiz palace.

It is said that in the old days of three-deckers, an American frigate, whose right of entrance had been challenged by the Turks, hove to opposite Chanak (as the Orientals familiarly and almost affectionately term the palace), fired a salute and then, under the cover of the smoke thus raised—for that was before the days of "smokeless powder"—made boldly up the strait for the Sea of Marmora before the Turks could recover from the astonishment or interpose any forcible remonstrance. Another American naval officer tells an amusing story of an experience that befell him when his ship was anchored off Chanak awaiting the reception of "pratique." After some delay, a boat was observed putting off from shore in the direction of the United States corvette. As the boat came alongside, a dirty Turkish officer stood up in the stern-sheets, and pointing with his thumb in the general direction of Constantinople, exclaimed: "Stamboula git!" The officer of the deck did not understand the whole force of the expression (Go to Constantinople!), but with the quick wit of a Yankee he instinctively divined the significance of the "git" (an imperative from the Turkish verb gitmek), which seemed to possess a certain resemblance to Yankee slang, and immediately gave orders to get the anchor aboard and

bear away up the strait toward Stamboul as fast as the slow American tub could travel. Outgoing (that is, westward-bound) vessels stop their engines abreast of a Turkish guard ship no bigger than a North river tug, anchored about two miles above Chanak-Kalesi, and there the permission in documentary form which they had received authorizing the navigation of the Turkish waters by them they deliver up before steaming past Chanak out among the Greek islands of the Ægean. If a venturesome or ignorant merchant steamer on entering the strait presumes to pass on beyond a certain point, a shot is fired across her bow, and the cost of the powder thus burned is collected scrupulously from the owners or agents of the vessel on her arrival at Stamboul, as Oriental logic fails to comprehend why poor Turkey should pay for any foreign disregard of her rules!

The Dardanelles practically constitute the front door of the Turkish empire (at least as regards its westward exposure), whereat many would-be visitors are now ringing the bell. But the Turk is not at home to all callers, and just now is especially shy of such observers as foreign men-of-war that may be hanging around Besica Bay—a piece of water just off the famous plain of Troy, where Dr. Schliemann made his much-discussed discoveries, which is readily reached by a few hours' ride from Chanak-Kalesi along the southern shore of the Dardanelles and thence up and over a fine range of hills that affords a magnificent view of Samothrace, Imbros and other historic islets of the blue Ægean.

CHAPTER VI.

THE ARMENIANS—WHO ARE THEY?

Their Religion, Occupation, Habits of Life, Intelligence, Strength and Weakness.

By James D. Barton, D. D., Secretary of the American Board.

According to Armenian histories, the first chief of the Armenians was Haik, the son of Togarmah, the son of Gomar, the son of Jahpeth, the son of Noah. It is an interesting fact that the Armenians to this day call themselves Haik, their language "Haiaren," and their country "Haiasdan." "Armenia" and "Armenian" are words which cannot be spelled with Armenian characters or easily pronounced by that people. That name was given them and their country by outside nations because of the prowess of one of their kings, Aram, the seventh from Haik.

Probably this people is composed of the resultant of strong Aryan tribes overrunning and conquering the country now occupied by the Armenians, and which was then possessed by primitive Turanian populations. Subject to the vicissitudes of conquest and invasion, the borders of Armenia have fluctuated. Lake Van has always been within the kingdom, and the capital has usually remained during their highest prosperity at the city of Van. They have had a long line of kings of valor and renown. They were an independent nation, but with varying degrees of power, until A. D. 1375, when they became completely a subject people. Since that time their country has been under the governments of Russia, Persia and Turkey, far the larger portion being in Turkey. During the years of their greatest prosperity, from 600 B. C. to about 400 A. D., this nation played a prominent part in the wars of the Assyrians, Medes, Persians, Greeks and Romans.

There are perhaps, from 2,500,000 to 3,000,000 Armenians in Turkey, Russia and Persia. In the absence of accurate records we must be content with a mere estimate, based upon observations and inadequate government returns. In no extended district do they comprise a majority of the inhabitants. They are everywhere mingled with and surrounded by Kurds and Turks. The Armenians are forbidden to carry or possess arms under severe penalties, while the other races are armed, many of them, by the government.

Armenian histories relate that, soon after the resurrection of Christ, Abgar, the King of Armenia, with his court, accepted Christianity. This was short-lived, however; but in the third century A. D., under the leadership of Gregory the Illuminator, the Armenian people, as a nation, became Christian. This was the first nation to adopt Christianity as a national religion. The Church was called "Gregorian" by those outside, but "Loosavochagan" by the Armenians, the word meaning "Illuminator," the name given to Gregory. The Gregorians and Greeks worked in harmony in the great councils of the Church until 451. At the fourth Ecumenical Council, which met at Chalcedon that year, the Gregorian

Church separated from the Greek upon the so-called Monophysite doctrine, the former accepting and the latter rejecting it. Since then the Gregorian Church has been distinctly and exclusively an Armenian national Church.

The organization and control of the Church is essentially Episcopal. The spiritual head is a Catholicos; but in addition to him there is a Patriarch, whose office bears largely upon the political side of the national life as related to the Ottoman government. There are three of the former residing in the order of their importance at Echmiadzin, in Russia, Aghtamar, on an island in Lake Van, and at Sis in Cilicia, each with his own diocese. There are two of the latter residing at Constantinople and Jerusalem. There are nine grades of Armenian clergy.

The Bible was translated into their language in the middle of the fifth century. Owing to a change in the spoken tongue the Bible became a dead book to the people, although it was constantly read at their church services. As the priests scarcely ever understood the scripture which they read, Christian doctrines were kept alive by oral teachings; but the restraint upon life which pure Christianity exercises was largely removed. They blindly accepted the Bible as the Word of God. They have many large, fine churches, some of which are several hundred years old.

This nation has suffered great persecutions for its faith during the last eleven centuries, but with wonderful patience and endurance has clung to the old beliefs and forms of worship. Mission work was begun among them for the purpose of introducing into the Church the Bible in the spoken language of the people, in order that its teachings might reform the Church and the nation.

The Armenian nature is essentially religious. Born into the Church, its customs, traditions and teachings have large influence over the life. Although much of their teachings and many of their customs are based upon mere traditions and are not in accord with the enlightened, educated Christianity of the West, nevertheless the fact that during the last few months thousands among them have deliberately chosen death, with terrible torture, to life and Islam, shows that among them there exists much essential Christian faith. It must not be overlooked that the old Church has been greatly enlightened and elevated by the mission schools and colleges planted in their country and the evangelistic work carried on among them. They, too, in imitation of the evangelical branch of their nation, have organized schools, accepted the Bible in the spoken language, and introduced into their church worship many of the methods of Christian instruction used by the Christian Church all over the world.

The Armenians' greatest enemy outside of Islam is their incompatibility of character. They cannot agree among themselves. "Haik voch miapan" ("Armenians cannot agree") is one of their many proverbs. This is their national weakness. Owing to this fact, which led to internal jealousies and bickerings and strife, during the period of their most successful national life, they were weakened, then disrupted and finally completely subjugated. This characteristic has constantly appeared in the management of their ecclesiastical affairs; and the Turks, in order to control them, have made great use of this weakness, playing one party off against another. The source of this national weakness lies in their jealousy of imagined or actual rivals. Suspicious of each other and jealous of competition, the race has been broken up into factions which has rendered impossible anything like a national growth or unity, and has made it easy for the ruling Turk to keep them in complete subjection. Many times the Armenians themselves have been the most effective instrument in the hands of their diplomatic rulers in checking national progress.

Owing to this fact, if for no other reason, a plan for a general revolution upon the part of the Armenians could lead only to exposure and failure. The most intelligent have from the first fully understood this, and have deprecated any agitation which must necessarily end in disaster. The advocates of revolution have almost invariably been men of narrow views and no leadership in the nation at large, who have, outside of Turkey, organized rival societies to collect money from credulous Armenians to the credit of their own personal bank account and for the injury of their protesting people in Turkey. This same characteristic would make it impossible today for the Armenians to be self-governing.

The Armenians are the most intelligent of all the peoples of Eastern Turkey. In Western Turkey their only rivals are the Greeks. They far outclass their Mohammedan rulers in the desire for general and liberal education and in their ability to attain to genuine scholarship. During the last twenty years few institutions of higher education in the United States and in England have failed to have Armenians

ARMENIAN WOMEN IN WORKING COSTUME.

among their pupils, and the rank which they have usually taken is most creditable to the race.

The popularity of Euphrates College, in Harpoot, and of Central Turkey College, at Aintab, whose students are almost exclusively Armenians, as well as Anatolia College, at Marsovan, and Robert College, at Constantinople, which have many Armenians among their students, taken together with the fact that large sums are paid each year by the people for the education of their sons and daughters, all proves that in addition to the ability to advance mentally there is a strong desire upon the part of the Armenians for general enlightenment. Bilingual from childhood, and many of them trilingual, they learn languages easily. Their general tendency is to prefer metaphysical studies, being inclined rather to the speculative in their manner of thought. They have taken readily to the idea of female education, and the three colleges for girls in Turkey are among the most popular evangelical institutions. These are largely patronized by the Armenians. This nation has produced many well-known scholars, which fact, taken together with the general high standard of scholarship among her students, and the eager desire prevalent among the people for a liberal education, shows that the race intellectually compares favorably with the most favored nations of the world.

The Armenians are the farmers, artisans, tradesmen and bankers of Eastern Turkey. They have strong commercial instincts and mature ability, and, being industrious withal, have made much progress in all these lines. In spite of the heavy restrictions placed upon them by the Turkish government, in the form of general regulations and excessive taxes, in some parts of Turkey the leading business operations are largely in their hands. In some sections of the vilayets of Harpoot and Diarbekir, twenty-five years ago, the land was owned almost entirely by Moslems, but rented and farmed by the Armenians. At that time the Armenians were not permitted to possess, to any extent, the soil. Lack of industry upon the part of the Mohammedans and the acquirement of property upon the part of the Armenians, largely by emigration to the United States, have led the Turks to sell their ancient estates to Armenians, who are supplied with funds from their friends who are working in this country. The careful management of the property thus acquired led to the advancement of the proprietor farmer, while the one from whom the land was purchased was left without an income.

While the Turks in many of the principal cities where Armenians dwell own most of the shops, the renters are largely Armenians. An intelligent Turkish governor once told the writer that if the Armenians should suddenly emigrate or be expelled from Eastern Turkey, the Moslem would necessarily follow soon, as there was not enough commercial enterprise and ability coupled with industry in the Turkish population to meet the absolute needs of the people.

The Armenian, while industrious and naturally inclined to follow in the footsteps of his father, takes very readily to a new trade. When emigrating to foreign countries, he easily adapts himself to his new surroundings and does creditable service in almost any line of work. This adaptability, together with a tendency to hold on to a line once begun, has given a stable character to the nation.

The Armenian is domestic in his habits and aspirations, and not military. In the early history of the race we do not find much written of their conquests. They did not go outside of their borders, as a general thing, to conquer their neighbors. While not lacking in physical courage and prowess in war, when called to defend their country against invasion, they did not seek to conquer. Sometimes in driving back an aggressive foe they carried the war into his territory and levied upon it for injuries received; yet it never seems to have been their ambition to be a great nation ruling over conquered races. Their chief ambition appears to have been to possess in quiet their beloved fatherland, "hairenik," where they might worship God according to the demands of their own national Church. Today they have no desire of conquest or ambition to rule. Their greatest wish is to be permitted to enjoy without fear the blessing of their simple domestic life, together with the privileges of worship and education and the opportunity to possess in peace the fruits of their frugal industry. The Armenian loves his children and is most closely attached to his home. When he emigrates it is only for the purpose of trade and gain. His heart's affection centres in the old rude home to which he, if unprevented, will return to rejoin his loved ones. In all his native land the city or village of his birth is the dearest spot on earth.

The Armenians are most simple and frugal in their manner of life. Uncomplaining and generally cheerful, they continue their occupations, following in the footsteps of their fathers without desire for change. The son of the carpenter is a carpenter content with the adz and saw, and the shoemaker sticks to his last without a thought of being anything else so long as that trade serves him. The home life is patriarchal, the father ruling the household, and the sons bringing their wives to the paternal roof. In the event of the death of the father, the oldest son takes his place at the head of the family. The aged are held in high esteem, and their counsel sought and honored. The women occupy inferior positions, the nation copying many customs in regard to them from the Turks among whom they live. They are not an immoral race, but are inclined to drink wine, which is a cheap product of their country.

Thus we have a race old in national history when Alexander invaded the East; and with its star of empire turning toward decline when the Cæsars were at the height of their power; a nation not mingling in marriage with men and women of another faith and blood now as pure in its descent from the undiscovered ancestors of nearly three decades of centuries ago as the Hebrews stand unmixed with Gentile blood; with a language, a literature, a national Church, distinctively its own, and yet a nation without a country, without a government, without a protector or a friend in all God's world. This is not because it has sinned, but because it has been terribly sinned against; not because of its intellectual or moral or physical weakness, but because it has little to offer in return for the service, which the common botherhood of man among nations should prompt the Christian nations of the world to render.

CHAPTER VII.

THE ARMENIAN CHURCH.

By Herant Mesrob Kiretchjian, General Secretary the Armenian Relief Association.

From the earliest day when the human family began to dwell in groups of clans and nations upon the face of the earth, there dwelt upon the highlands of Mount Ararat in Asia a people in partriarchal simplicity and vigor. The fertile earth, watered by the rivers of Paradise, nourished them, and honest toil, that held commerce with nature and coped with the elements, developed in them human virtues which have been treasured through the storms of ages in the impregnable fortress of a pure and normal family life. In the annals of history they are known as the Armenian nation, and their country, the ancient Ararat, as the Land of Armenia.

The ceaseless floods of war and devastation that make up the history of the ancient world, all passed over Armenia or drew her into the torrents of fire and blood. But the awful conflicts with great barbaric nations again and again laid the nation low and brought her into subjection, only to see her rise once more with undaunted courage in defense of home and country.

You will at once seek an explanation of this power of endurance of ancient Armenia when you remember all that history has to tell us concerning those great military nations who were the neighbors of Armenia from the very outset—Assyria, Babylon, the mighty Persian Empire, and, later, Rome, that held in her sway continents and empires and massed them against one another for cruel destruction; when you remember that the wars that these nations waged were wars of extermination and of such efficiency that they themselves, ultimately, disappeared from the face of the earth. Armenia stood upon her highland home of Ararat and faced these barbaric hordes, one after the other, and at times more than one together; now conquering them and now falling under their assaults; now using their language and literature and then again having kings and princes in numbers who came under her sway and under the influence of her language and literature; and yet today, after the map of Asia has been cast and recast again and again with mighty upheavals that sealed the doom of nations, Armenia stands in the nineteenth century, still upon the soil of ancient Ararat and presents the same national characteristics that distinguished her as a nation in the beginning of days. That which was most interesting, and at the same time most touching to me, at the British Museum, was a long bronze tablet, dark with the rust of centuries, but showing clearly an Assyrian king sitting upon his throne, and Armenian kings and princes bringing him tribute.

If anything is needed at this time to move the hearts of men toward Armenia, over and above the fact that they are human beings subjected to the greatest injustice and tyranny ever known, it will be found in this fact, that the Armenian

OBELISK, CONSTANTINOPLE.

nation has stood up for an idea and a principle, and has proven certain national, social and spiritual facts which she can present to the Western world today as her share of the priceless inheritance of human experience that is to be left for the coming generations of men.

And this is the story of the nation:

Haig was the leader of that highland clan which founded the Armenian nation. The historian describes him as handsome and noble in stature, with magnificent curls and strong brawny arms. Those were days of mighty men upon earth. They went about proudly, holding captive whole families of men over the earth. The mad lust of conquest was then born, and drove these men of the plains so that the "sword of each man was thrust into the side of his neighbor in the attempt of ruling over one another." Among these strong men was one Belus (or Pel in Armenian), who carried his depredations as far as the land of Ararat, where the hero Haig had taken refuge with his whole clan, numbering about 300. There were valiant men also among the lovers of home and peace, of whom was Haig. He believed in God and refused to submit to Pel or to worship him as others did; and on the plains beneath mighty Ararat this little band of highlanders, led by the fearless Haig, with the motto "Let us die or conquer," plunged into the heart of the vast horde of thousands of wild warriors led by Pel. Haig himself slew Pel in the fight, and the first battle for independence on record was fought successfully on the side of right against might; and from that day the Armenian kingdom was established and grew apace. This is but a sketch of the interesting story as Moses of Khoren, the father of Armenian history, in the fifth century, gives us. Even if regarded as a legend, it certainly was a story of the beginning of a nation, full of inspiration to make the succeeding generations stand up for home and liberty.

It was the great King Aram, the sixth after Haig, who first won fame by conquests far and wide among the surrounding nations, and we have thus been called "Armenians," while in the Armenian language we are called Haik, or Hayer, after the name of Haig. Thenceforward, the story of our people is like that of other Oriental nations: they conquered and were conquered; they built cities and established dominion over the land. Then came wars and disasters, and ruins were left for monuments of past glory. The Armenian kingdom, with a population of some 50,000,000, once extended far into Asia Minor, and almost to the Ægean, and from the Black Sea down to the coast of the Mediterranean. Four dynasties of kings ruled the land, besides princes and governors innumerable, until the sceptre departed from the nation in the year 1375, and the last king, Levon VI, being taken captive by the Arabs, was ultimately released, and took refuge in France, where he died in 1393, and was buried in the Chapel of St. Denis. There Armenians gathered in 1893 to commemorate the 500th anniversary of his death, and once more to revive the hope of the nation that the tomb of Levon VI was a token that the salvation of our people was to come from the West.

But, magnificent as are the ruins of ancient Armenia, and interesting as are her national life and traditions, her poetry and her architecture and the achievements of her kings among those of other Oriental rulers, they all fail in importance before this one supreme fact of the preservation of the Armenian home upon the highlands of Ararat, generation after generation, until the coming of Christ, when it found a sure refuge in the Christian Church. It is true that the salvation of the Armenian nation, out of the disasters of the Assyrian, Babylonian, Parthian, Persian and Roman invasions, was wonderful and unique; and yet for those who have had even a glimpse of the life of these nations, no words are necessary to emphasize the fact that the salvation of the Armenian family out of the unutterable corruption of the life of these Oriental nations, with whom they were in contact for centuries, and were even in subjection under the heavy yoke of their tyranny, was a far greater miracle, and so far as human knowledge can go, must ever stand as a testimony that the promises of God are sure, and that for those that love Him and keep His commandments, the blessing goes down to a thousand generations; that from the simple faith and pure life of the father and hero, Haig, there went out a momentum of spiritual potency that carried the nation safely through those floods of Oriental corruption whose power for destruction the Western mind can hardly conceive. And it may be stated here that, horrible as the butchery of Mohammedan massacres have been, the corrupting influence of the foul sensuality that has pressed upon the Christians in Turkey for five hundred years is the far greater evil, and that it is a curse to know the Turkish language, as we all come to know in the cities of Turkey, and go about and daily hear the talk of all classes of the Turkish population, since the human mind and heart receive and carry lasting impressions.

Through all those thousands of years the Armenian nation clung to the integrity and purity of the family, even in the days of idolatry, and, as a consequence, the intelligence and the vitality of the nation were kept and developed as the centuries rolled by. There was the Prince Ara, the son of the great Aram. Of such noble mien and form he was that he is known in our history as "Ara the Beautiful." Of him Moses of Khoren tells us that, when urged by the licentious Queen Semiramis of Babylon to become her husband, he chose to go into war and lose his life in unequal combat with the might of Babylon rather than desecrate the sanctity of the Armenian family; for, although the queen had given orders to her generals that they should capture Ara the Beautiful alive, he went into the thick of the fight and was slain. And in his memory, perhaps with a pang of tardy repentance, this heathen queen, Semiramis, built the city of Van and its impregnable citadel, rising there by our beautiful Armenian lake, as an everlasting testimony that even in the days of idolatry, according to the traditions of Armenia, the chastity of man and woman was to be held at par, even by her princes.

No wonder Christianity found a ready acceptance in Armenia when at its very dawn the light of the Christ shone upon our land through the preaching of the apostles Thaddeus and Bartholomew. It brought with the gift of spiritual life a greater appreciation of true freedom and a deeper affection for the home of the nation.

The nation was prepared to accept Christianity as the national religion when the right man came to uphold the banner of the Cross—the man who always comes at the right time, who is the hope of your people and my people, under God; comes as Haig or Vartan, as Washington or Lincoln, but always with power and the might of faith and wisdom. So came Gregory, "the Illuminator," to Armenia. A prince of the ruling dynasty, he gave up the splendors of his position and became an humble preacher of the Gospel among his people. Cruel was the persecution that faced them, but, as martyrs of all ages, they met it undaunted. Prominent among those martyrs were thirty-six maidens, whose names are mentioned to this day in the services of the Church together with those of "our first Illuminators, Thaddeus and Bartholomew, and our Father Gregory, the Illuminator of the Land of Armenia." King Durtad, who led these persecutions, was smitten with disease. Released from the loathsome dungeon where he was thrown, St. Gregory healed the king, and thereupon both the court, and, by edict of the king, the entire nation, became Christian in the year 302, ten years before Constantine saw the illumined Cross; and thus the Armenian people became the first in the world to accept Christianity as a nation. The leaders of the infant Church at once undertook missionary labors among the surrounding Caucasian races, and had great influence, even among the Persians, of whom many became Christian.

I can only say a word about the immediate results of Christianity upon the nation. For one thing, it certainly presents a problem as to the power of this simple story of Bethlehem which the worldly philosopher of the nineteenth century will find it hard to explain. The land of war and conquest, of princes and generals, of peasants and artisans, suddenly became the land of Christian heroes, philosophers and valiant scholars. There arose a handful of men known as the Younger and the Elder Disciples. They went to Constantinople, Alexandria and Athens, and mastered the Greek language, in those days when there were none of the modern accessories of civilization, no universities, libraries or encyclopædias. They won fame in those cities as men of learning and power. They came back to Armenia and gave the Bible to the people in a translation of remarkable accuracy and beauty of diction, of which Prof. Brown, of the University of Edinburgh, told me that in the late revision of the Anglo-Saxon Bible, it was referred to and was regarded as a "queen translation." The nation found a fortress in that Bible. The nation's love of freedom, her inheritance of simple common sense and the devotion to an active, practical, natural life may have all concentrated themselves in producing that most important result in the life of the Church established in Armenia by Gregory the Illuminator, namely, that the Armenian Church laid hold of the cardinal truths of the Christian faith in the simple revelation of the Father, the Son and the Holy Ghost, and not only failed to understand anything more than that in that religion, but deliberately refused to enter into any theological discussion whatever.

The Armenian Church was represented at the Nicean Council by Arisdakes, the younger son of Gregory the Illuminator. When he came back and brought the creed, St. Gregory read it, and then he wrote under it: "But we, let us

AN ARMENIAN HIGH PRIEST.

glorify Him who was from before the eternities, worshiping the Holy Trinity and one God, Father, Son and Holy Ghost, now, ever and forever." That holy man seemed to see then with the wisdom that comes from above that the Byzantine mind had already begun its disastrous course of endless word-spinning. He seemed to say to them: "If you are going to talk of things incomprehensible to the human mind; if you are going to discourse of the eternal God, then I will tell you what we will do: We will worship Him who was from before the eternities." And so the Church has always repeated that affirmation with the creed for sixteen centuries, and it has been as a seal, forever shutting out all discussion of theological points, and has led the nation to find the expression of her faith in living intensely, in holiness and righteousness, and in worship with child-like devotion. It was for this cause principally, together with the political enmity of the Greek nation, that the Armenian Church took no part in the succeeding Church councils in the East.

Thus we have the phenomenon of a Christian Church living and holding the faith through sixteen centuries against fearful odds, and yet not having one single schism or heresy, nor one theological controversy of which there is any mention in all her history or in the magnificent Christian literature that was developed in the Golden Age of Armenian Christianity in the early centuries.

The liturgy of the Church was taken from that of St. James, of the Church of Jerusalem, and the form of church government has been one steady unchanging line of the episcopacy. But in that again we have this remarkable feature that in Armenia, of all lands the one where tyranny and high-handed hierarchical domineering should have developed because of the eternal example set to her people by her tyrant masters, the Armenian Church has had not a vestige of caste in her Church government or a tinge of the blight that has come upon the Church of the West in the form of ecclesiastical tyranny. Upon the same patriarchal throne of Etchmiadzin, near Erivan, in Russian Armenia, where in the year 302 sat Gregory the Illuminator, there sits today a man who rose from the ranks of the common peasantry of Armenia and became priest, bishop, patriarch, and now Catholicos, or chief Bishop of the Church; and yet, the venerable Catholicos Mugurditch Khrimian is called the "Beloved Father" of the nation, and is in reality nothing but a father and servant of his people and a brother in very deed to the clergy of the humblest rank. From the First Encyclical Letter of Blessing, which he sent out after his ordination, on December 15, 1893, I quote a few passages, to give you a glimpse of the spirit of the man that so worthily represents the spirit of the Church of Armenia:

"Mugurditch, Servant of Jesus Christ, and by the inscrutable will of God, Chief Bishop and Catholicos of all the Armenians: Supreme Patriarch of the national pre-eminent Throne of the Apostolic Mother Church of Ararat, in Holy Catholic Etchmiadzin:

"Salutations to thee, Apostolic Church of Armenia, born in Christ by the Gospel of Thaddeus and Bartholomew and Gregory, nurtured and developed in godly faith;

"Salutations to thee, Mother Mount Sion of God—Jerusalem; in thee appeared the Light of the World, the Incarnate Saviour, the Only-Begotten, who came down from the

Father, He who laid the foundations of the Church of Ararat, of Holy Etchmiadzin, built in Light;

"Salutations to you, Catholicoses and Patriarchs, who are brothers with me in equal yoke to conduct and to bear the services of the Church of Christ: Know ye how great is our responsibility in the presence of the great Chief Shepherd? For every one of us is to give an account for his fold;

"Salutations to you, Preachers of the Church, ye who teach and deliver the message of the Gospel! Comfort ye, comfort ye, my people, for great is their grief, and their sins are forgiven them, saith God;

"Salutations to you, Priests of the Most High God, who dispense the Holy Sacraments of the Church and are educators and guardians of the Holy Family. Know ye how great is your office?"

And after telling of his years, now past seventy, and how he is appalled at the sight of his flock scattered over the face of the earth, he calls upon the Armenian clergy to be eyes and hands to him, and to redouble their energy, and then adds:

"But what is the help of man? O, that the compassionate Samaritan might pass by you!

"Pray for me, my spiritual co-workers, for I know that most heavy is the cross that the Church of Armenia has laid upon my shoulders.

"And thou, Church and people of Armenia, who have chosen me to be your shepherd, I depend as a refuge upon your prayers, and I believe that the Lord will hear your supplications and keep me for the beloved Church. I shall live for you and you for Christ. Amen.

"Written this first Encyclical of Blessing on the fifteenth of December, 1893, and in the year of the nation 4383, on the Mother Throne of the Armenians, in Holy Etchmiadzin."

It cost Armenia torrents of blood and the lives of thousands upon thousands of her children, generation after generation, to keep the Armenian Church and thereby the nation itself alive, as a civilized people among the barbarous hordes which overran Armenia and laid it waste again and again. The Christ, indeed, brought a sword into Armenia from the day that her thirty-six maidens were slain as the first martyrs to the hour of the last awful massacre in the streets of Constantinople. Countless volumes could be filled with the story of Armenia's wars and battles in defence of the Christian Church; but the battle of the Armenian nation against Persia, in the fifth century, may well stand as an example of those holy wars. Armenia was then under Persia, and, as in all other ages, then, also, her people had found favor in the sight of her conquerors, and in the Persian army there was the valiant Armenian general, Vartan, with numbers of other high officers and 66,000 gallant warriors. The Persians worshiped fire. People call this or that faith a religion, and think that the name sanctifies faith, whereas the question is not how strong your faith is, but what you believe in. The fire worship of Persia carried with it awful corruption in morals, which went as a part of that religion. It was that which made the priests of Armenia call it darkness, and the faith of the Christ the Light of Heaven. The wicked king, Hazgerd, instigated by the more wicked priests of the fire-god, took it into his head to convert all races of men in his great empire to the "one true faith" of Zoroastrianism; and so the order went out, as it did in the days of Nebuchadnezzar. Then the Armenian priests and generals sat in council and indited an answer, giving the reasons of their faith and why they were compelled to refuse to comply with the order of the Shahinshah who had never known a refusal. They told of the

Christ who Himself was King of Kings and yet had been crucified, dead and buried, and how he rose the third day from the dead and ascended into heaven, there to be King of Kings and Lord of Lords forever. And this with many words that should have convinced anyone but that blind servant of the Evil Spirit. Well did they know what it meant to send up such an answer to the court of Persia, and they told the king that nothing could shake them from their faith, neither angels nor men, neither sword nor fire, nor water, nor all bitter stripes. "Of thee tortures, of us submission; thine is the sword, ours are the necks. We are not better than those that went before us who laid down upon this testimony their goods and their bodies. * * * Ask us no more, for the covenant of our faith is not with men that we should be deceived as children, but in bonds indissoluble with God, from whom there is no separation or departure, neither now, nor ever, nor forever, nor forever and ever." And out from the army of Persia came Vartan Mamigonian and his 66,000 braves, and there they stood in camp under the midnight skies; and with them were the priests and women of Armenia. And they set the altars and partook of the Holy Communion, and until the morning light told the story of men from the days of Joshua and Gideon until those of the martyrs of Armenia who had gone out to fight the battles in the name of Christ the King. There stood Vartan, the general-in-chief, and delivered an address to his soldiers which shall live much longer than the historic words of the great warrior of France. All this story, and of what followed in the battle of the following day, we have in a remarkable little book written by the priest Yeghishe, who was one of the Younger Disciples and an eye-witness of the battle. In the spring-time where the flowers covered the fields on the plains of Avarayr, by the river Dughmood, was fought a mighty battle by the 66,000 soldiers of Christ against the countless hosts of Persia, each 3000 men of whom, formed in the shape of a wedge, were led by an elephant. "It was not," says Yeghishe, "that one side or the other conquered, for brave men met brave men." Ten hundred and thirty-six Armenians fell together with Vartan Mamigonian to leave their names forever in the roll of the martyrs of Armenia. Thirty-five hundred and forty-four Persians fell, nine of whom were among the highest officials of the Persian army and personally favored by the Shah Hazgerd, so that they were afraid to tell the news of the battle in the court of Persia. But Armenia was conquered and devastated, her priests taken captive, tortured and murdered, and untold misery brought upon her people for years and years. Yet the battle of Vartan Mamigonian and his Christian warriors on the field of Avarayr became the Bunker Hill of Christianity in the East; for from that day to this, while the whole history of Armenia has been one of constant martyrdom, though unseen and unheard by the world, no potentate or conqueror has ventured to attempt to take Christianity away from the Armenians as a nation, surely knowing that the only alternative which the nation would accept would be extermination.

And now Persia was gone, and Rome fell under the weight of her own national crimes; the Spartan and the Athenian

AN ARMENIAN WOMAN.

philosopher found their resting-place in history, but the homes of Armenia, rising out of the overwhelming ruins of these empires—our beloved Church of Armenia swimming through pools of blood, creeping from under the crumbling battlements of ruined empires, stood once more upon the sacred soil of Mother Armenia; still the same home, where gentleness and purity made the atmosphere, and where patience and obedience were the law. The priest still held up the cross, broken and covered with the blood of martyrs, and the Church opened her gates that her people might still come in, and in spite of the disasters of the ages, still praise the God of Jacob, in whom they had learned to trust. But the cup was not full, and the greatest trial of the Church, and direst of all calamities for the nation, was yet to come at the hands of a countless host of stern and cruel warriors that moved onward to conquer and to destroy in the name of God and Mahomet.

THE MOHAMMEDAN DOMINATION.

When the Crusaders came from the West, with what gladness did the people of Armenia hail them, believing that the dawn of deliverance had come! They who had prayed, taught by their fathers, "for all holy bishops throughout the world," with what joy did they behold the vision of men who bore the image of the Cross and had come to deliver the tomb of the Saviour from the hands of the godless heathen! And the Armenians joined them for the Holy War. Back went the discomfited Crusaders, and the Armenians, who had helped them, had to stand and bear the whole brunt of the fury of fresh hordes of Arabs that came up from Egypt to wreak their vengeance upon them. Gladstone has said that history in future will show what the map of Europe would have been if that blighting hurricane of Mohammedan invasion in its onward march toward the gates of Vienna, where it finally lost its momentum, and, falling down, was driven back and back towards the sea, had not met its first resistance at the hands of the last remnant of Armenian warriors, who, in their fortresses of Cilicia, fought the desperate battle for home and liberty under the banner of the Cross.

CHAPTER VIII.

A TRIP THROUGH ARMENIA.

By Mrs. L. B. Bishop.

[This article was taken from Mrs. Bishop's book, "Travels in Persia." She is a woman widely known as an extensive traveler, and who has written a number of valuable books along this line. She is also a member of the Geographical Society of Scotland, and has attained a number of honors in other directions.—Ed.]

My room has an oven in the floor, neatly lined with clay, and as I write the women are making bread by a very simple process. The oven is well heated by the live embers of animal fuel. They work the flour and water dough, to which a piece of leaven from the last baking has been added, into a flat round cake, about eighteen inches in diameter and half an inch thick, place it quickly on a very dirty cushion, and clap it against the concave interior of the oven, withdrawing the cushion. In one minute it is baked and removed.

A sloping hole in the floor leads to the fowl-house. The skin of a newly-killed sheep hangs up. A pack-saddle and gear take up one corner, my bed another, and the owner's miscellaneous property fills up the rest of the blackened, cracked mud-hovel, thick with the sooty cobwebs and dust of generations. The door, which can only be shut by means of a wooden bolt outside, is six inches from the ground, so that the cats and fowls run in and out with impunity. Behind my bed there is a doorless entrance to a dark den, full of goats' hair, bones and other stores. In front, there is a round hole for letting in light, which I persistently fill up with a blanket, which is as persistently withdrawn. There is no privacy, for though the people are glad to let their rooms, they only partially vacate them, and are in and out all the time. Outside, there is mud a foot deep, then a steep slope, and a disgusting green pool, and the drinking water is nauseous and brackish.

* * * * * * * * * * * *

In this gloomy vault-like building prayers are said, as in all Nestorian churches, at sunrise and sunset by the priest in his ordinary clothing, the villagers being summoned by the beating of a mallet on a board.

Dr. Cutts, in his interesting volume, "Christians Under the Crescent in Asia," gives the following translation of one of the morning praises, which forms part of the daily prayer. The earlier portion is chanted antiphonally in semi-choirs:

"Semi-choir—1st. At the dawn of day we praise Thee, O Lord: Thou art the Redeemer of all creatures; give us Thy mercy a peaceful day, and give us remission of our sins.

"2d. Cut not off our hope, shut not Thy door against our races, and cease not Thy care over us. O God! according to our worthiness reward us not. Thou alone knowest our weakness.

"1st. Scatter, O Lord, in the world love, peace and unity. Raise up righteous kings, priests and judges. Give peace to the nations, heal the sick, keep the whole and forgive the sins of all men.

"2d. In the way that we are going may Thy grace keep us, O Lord, as it kept the child David from Saul. Give us Thy mercy as we are pressing on, that we may attain to peace according to Thy will. The grace which kept the prophet

Moses in the sea, and Daniel in the pit, and by which the companions of Ananias were kept in the fire, by that grace deliver us from evil.

"Whole choir—In the morning we all arise, we all worship the Father, we praise the Son, we acknowledge the Holy Spirit. The grace of the Father, the mercy of the Son, and the hovering of the Holy Spirit, the Third Person, be our help every day. Our help is in Thee. In Thee, our true Physician, is our hope. Put the medicine of Thy mercy on our wounds, and bind up our bruises that we be not lost. Without Thy help we are powerless to keep Thy commandments. O Christ, who helpest those who fulfil Thy will, keep Thy worshippers. We ask with sighing, we beseech Thy mercy, we ask forgiveness from that merciful One who opens His door to all who will turn unto Him. Every day I promise Thee that tomorrow I will repent; all my days are past and gone, my faults still remain. O Christ, have mercy upon me, have mercy upon me." * * *

Many a strange house I have seen, but never anything so striking as the dwellings of Qasha Ishai. Passing through the rude verandah, and through a lofty room nearly dark, with a rough stone dais, on which were some mattresses and berths one above another, I stumbled in total darkness into a room seventy feet by forty, and twenty feet or more high in its highest part. It has no particular shape, and wanders away from this lofty centre into low, irregular caverns and recesses excavated in the mountain side. Parts of the floor are of naked rock, parts of damp earth. In one rocky recess is a powerful spring of pure water. The roofs are supported on barked stems of trees, black, like the walls, wherever it was possible to see them, with the smoke of two centuries. Ancient oil-lamps on posts or in recesses rendered darkness visible. Goat-skins, with the legs sticking out, containing butter, hanging from the blackened crossbeams, and wheat, apples, potatoes and onions in heaps and sacks, piles of wool, spinning-wheels, great wooden cradles here and there, huge oil and water-jars, wooden stools, piles of bedding, plows, threshing instruments, long guns, swords, spears and gear encumbered the floor, while much more was stowed away in the dim caverns of the roof. I asked the number of families under the roof. "Seven ovens," was the reply. This meant seven families, and it is true that three generations, seventy-two persons, live, cook, sleep and pursue their avocations under that patriarchal roof.

The Gawar Christians are industrious and inoffensive, and have no higher aspirations than to be let alone; but they are the victims of a Kurdish rapacity which leaves them little more than necessary food. Their villages usually belong to Kurdish Aghas, who take from them double the lawful taxes and tithes. The Herkis sweep over the plain in their autumn migration "like a locust cloud," carrying off the possessions of the miserable people, spoiling their granaries and driving off their flocks. The Kurds of the neighboring slopes and mountains rob them by violence at night, and in the day by exactions made under threat of death. The latter mode of robbery is called "demand." The servants of a Kurdish Bey enter and ask for some jars of oil or roghan, a Kashmir shawl, women's ornaments, a jewelled dagger, or a good foal under certain threats, or they show the owner a bullet in the palm of the hand, intimating that a bullet through his head will be his fate if he refuses to give up his property or informs anyone of the demand.

In this way (among innumerable other instances) my host,

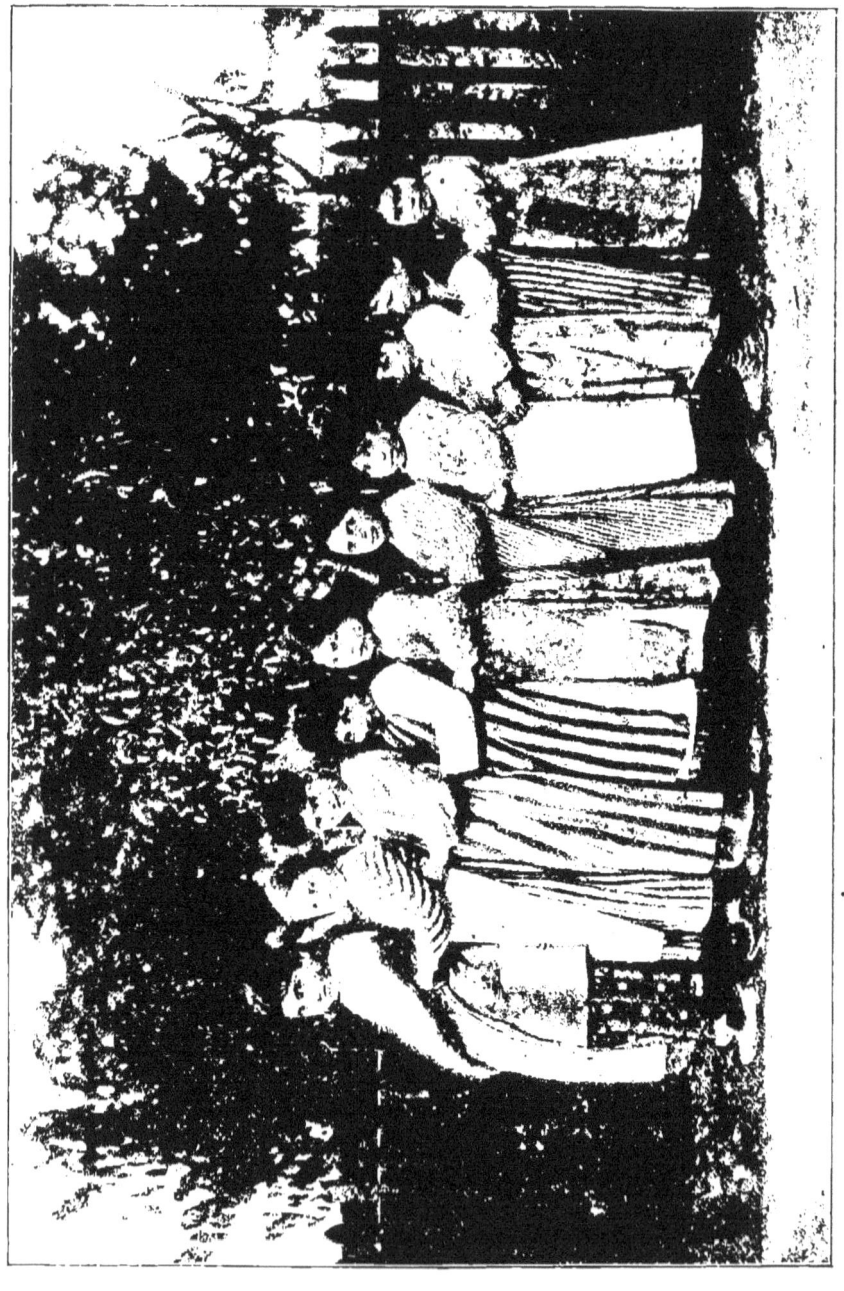

a much respected man, has been robbed of five valuable shawls, such as descend from mother to daughter, four handsome coats and 300 krans in silver. In the last two years ten and fifteen loads of wheat have been taken from him, and four four-foot jars filled with oil and roghan. Four hundred and fifty sheep have likewise been seized by violence, leaving him with only fifteen; and one night while I was at his house fifty-three of the remaining village sheep, some of which were his, were driven off in spite of the guards, who dare not fire. I was awakened by the disturbance, and as it was a light night, I saw that the Kurds who attacked the sheepfold were armed with modern guns. The reis of that village and this man's brother have both been shot by the Kurds.

The complaints to which I became a listener were made by maleks, bishops, priests, headmen and others. I cannot vouch for anything which did not come under my own observation. Those which I thought worthy of being noted down, some of which were published in the Contemporary Review in May and June in two papers, called the "Shadow of the Kurd," were either fortified by corroborative circumstances, or rest on the concurrent testimony as to the main facts of three independent narrators.

In some cases I was asked to lay the statements before the British consul at Erzeroum, with the names of the narrators as the authority on which they rested, but in the greater number I was implored not to give names or places, or any means of identification. "We are in fear of our lives if we tell the truth," they urged. Sometimes I asked them if they would abide by what they told me in the event of an investigation by the British vice-consul at Van. "No, no, no! we dare not!" was the usual reply. Under these circumstances, the only course open to me is to withhold the names of persons and places wherever I was pledged to do so, but as a guarantee of good faith I have placed the statements, confidentially, with the names, in the hands of Her Majesty's Principal Secretary of State for Foreign Affairs.

* * * * * * * * * * * * *

Mar—, Bishop of ——, mentioned previously as a fugitive from his diocese, is a fine, pleasant-looking middle-aged man, more like a sailor than an ecclesiastic. Late one night, in a whisper, with a trusty watch at the door, he told his story, through Qasha ——, in the following words:

"I fled, fearing for my life, because many times I had spoken against the oppressions. The Kurds have carried away most of the sheep and goats, besides taking all they wished to have, and they entered through the houses, plundering everything, and burning too. Their words are, "Give or die." I petitioned the government regarding the oppressions, and Mohammed Bey came, and by threat of death he got my seal, and wrote in my name a letter, saying it was all false, there were no oppressions, and he was a very good man, and he signed it with my seal, and it went to Stamboul. My seal has now been for one year in the hands of Mohammed Bey, who has killed about thirty Christians in Berwar. Three months ago I fled to save my life.

"Seventeen years the oppressions have begun; but it was ten years ago when we could easily keep ourselves and raise our bread; now we cannot. In ——, five years ago, all had plenty of dress and bread, and every family kept two cows and two hundred or more of sheep. But now, when I visited them, I would shame to look at the female persons, so naked were they, and so did they hide themselves for shame in the dark parts of their houses, for their dress was all in pieces, so that their flesh was seen. I was thirsty, and asked for milk, and they made reply, 'Oh, we have not a cow, or a sheep, or a goat; we forget the taste of milk.' And most of their fine fields were gone out of their hands by oppressions, for they could no longer find money wherewith to pay taxes, and they sold them for a vile price.

"K—— was the best village in Sopana, and more wealthy than any village of Kurds or Christians. There I went and asked for some milk. They said: 'Never a goat, or a sheep, or a cow have we.' I ask of all the families their conditions, and they make reply, with many tears, 'All that we have left has left our hands, and we fear for our lives now.' We were rich; now we have not bread to eat from day to day.

"Seventeen years ago the village of B—— had fifty families of wealthy villagers, but now I only find twelve, and those twelve could scarcely find bread. I had asked bread, but I could not find it. By day their things are taken by force out of their houses; at night their sheep and cattle were driven off. They could keep nothing. Our wheat, our sheep, our butter, is not our own. The chief, Mohammed Bey, and his servants ask of us, saying, "Give, or we will kill you."

This is a sample of innumerable tales to which I listen daily. Daily, from all quarters, men arrive with their complaints of robbery and violence, and ask the Patriarch to obtain redress for them; but he is powerless.

* * * * * * * * * * * * *

The wretched poverty of the people of this place made a very painful impression on me. They may have exaggerated when they told me how terribly they were oppressed by the Kurds, who, they say, last year robbed them of 900 sheep and this year 300, twenty-five and some cattle having been driven off a few days before; but it is a simple fact that the night of my visit, the twenty-four sheep for which there was no room in the stable were carried away by a party of well-armed Kurds in the bright moonlight, the helpless shepherds not daring to resist. It is of no use, they say, to petition the government; it will not interfere. The Kurds come into their houses, they say, and terrify and insult their women, and by demands, with violence, take away all they have. They say that the money for which they have sold their grain, and which they were keeping to pay their taxes with, was taken by the Kurds last week, and that they will be cruelly beaten by the zaptiehs because they cannot pay. Their words and air expressed abject terror.

* * * * * * * * * * * * *

I must ask my readers to believe that I crossed the Turkish frontier without any knowledge of or interest in the "Armenian Question;" that so far from having any special liking for the Armenians, I had rather a prejudice against them; that I was in ignorance of the "Erzeroum troubles" of June, 1890, and of yet more recent complications, and that the sole object of my journey by a route seldom traversed by Europeans from Urmi to Van was to visit the Patriarch of the Nestorians and the Kochanes station of the Archbishop of Canterbury's Assyrian Church Mission, and that afterwards I traveled to Erzeroum via Bitlis only to visit the American missionaries there. So far as I know, I entered Turkey as a perfectly neutral and impartial observer, and without any special interest in its Christian populations, and it is only the "inexorable logic of facts" which has convinced me of their wrongs and claims.

* * * * * * * * * * * * *

Their little church is poorer than poverty itself; a building of undressed stones without mortar, and its length of thirteen feet includes the rude mud dais occupied by the yet ruder altar. Its furniture consists of an iron censor, an iron saucer, containing oil and a wick, and an earthen flagon. There are no windows, and the rough walls are black with candle smoke. The young man who showed the church took a gospel from the said altar, kissing the cross upon it before handing it to me, and then, on seeing that I was interested, went home and brought a MS. of St. Matthew's Gospel, with several rudely-illuminated scenes from our Lord's life. "Christos," he said, with a smile, as he pointed to the central figure in the first illustration, and so on, as he showed me the others, for in each there was a figure of the Christ, not crowned and risen, but suffering and humiliated. Next morning, in the bitter cold of the hour before sunrise, the clang of the mallet on the sounding-board assembled the villagers for matins, and to the Christ crowned and risen, and "sitting on the right hand of power," they rendered honor as divine, though in the midst of the grossest superstition and darkness, and for Him whom they "ignorantly worship," they are at this moment suffering the loss of all things. Their empty sheepfold might have been full today if they had acknowledged Him as a prophet and no more. In another village, a young man, in speaking of their circumstances, said: "We don't know much, but we love the Lord Jesus well enough to die for Him."

* * * * * * * * * * * * *

Just as it was becoming dark, four mounted men, each armed with two guns, rode violently among the mules, which were in front of me, and attempted to drive them off.

In the melee the katirgi was knocked down. The zaptieh jumped off his horse, threw the bridle to me, and shouldered his rifle. When they saw the government uniform these Kurds drew back, let the mules go, and passed on. The whole affair took but a few seconds, but it was significant of the unwillingness of the Kurds to come into collision with the Turks, and of the power the government could exercise in the disturbed districts if it were once understood that the mauraders were not to be allowed a free hand.

* * * * * * * * * * * * *

VAN.

Van may be considered the capital of that part of Kurdistan which we know as Armenia, but it must be remembered that under the present government of Turkey Armenia is a prohibited name, and has ceased to be "a geographical expression." Cyclopedias containing articles on Armenia, and school-books with any allusions to Armenian history, or to the geography of any district referred to as Armenia, are not allowed to enter Asia Minor, and no foreign maps which contain the province of Armenia are allowed to be used in the foreign schools, or even to be retained in the country. Of the 4,000,000 of the Armenian race, 2,500,000 are subjects of the Sultan, and, with few exceptions, are distinguished for their loyalty and their devotion to peaceful pursuits.

Here as elsewhere I am much impressed with the excellence of the work done by the American missionaries, who

A STREET IN THE CITY OF VAN, ARMENIA.

are really the lights of these dark places, and by their exemplary and honorable lives furnish that moral model and standard of living which is more efficacious than preaching in lifting up the lives of a people sunk in the depths of a grossly corrupted Christianity. The boys and girls' schools in Van are on an excellent basis, and are not only turning out capable men and women, but are stimulating the Armenians to raise the teaching and tone of their own schools in the city, with one of which I was greatly pleased. The creation of churches, strict in their discipline, and protesting against the mass of superstitions which smother all spiritual life in the national Armenian Church, is undoubtedly having a very salutary effect far beyond the limited membership, and is tending to force reform upon an ancient church, which contains within herself the elements of resurrection.

I have already confessed to a prejudice against the Armenians, but it is not possible to deny that they are the most capable, energetic, enterprising and pushing race in Western Asia, physically superior, and intellectually acute, and, above all, they are a race which can be raised in all respects to our own level, neither religion, color, customs nor inferiority in intellect or force constituting any barrier between us. Their shrewdness and aptitude for business are remarkable, and whatever exists of commercial enterprise in Eastern Asia Minor is almost altogether in their hands. They have a singular elasticity, as their survival as a church and nation shows, and I cannot but think it likely that they may have some share in determining the course of events in the East, both politically and religiously. As Orientals, they understand Oriental character and modes of thought as we never can, and if a new Pentecostal afflatus were to fall upon the educated and intelligent young men who are being trained in the colleges which the Armenian churches have scattered liberally through Asia Minor, the effect upon Turkey would be marvelous. I think most decidedly that reform in Turkey must come through Christianity, and in this view the reform and enlightenment of the religion which has such a task before it are of momentous importance.

The town of Van is nearly a mile from the lake, and is built on an open level space, in the midst of which stands a most picturesque and extraordinary rock, which rises perpendicularly to a height of about 300 feet. It falls abruptly at both extremities, and its outline, which Colonel Severs Bell estimates at 1900 yards in length, is emphasized by battlemented walls, several towers and a solitary minaret, rising above the picturesque irregularity of the ancient fortifications.

The founding of Van is ascribed to Semiramis, who, according to Armenian history, names it Shemiramagerd, and was accustomed to resort to its gardens, which she had herself planted and watered, to escape from the fierce heat of the summer at Ninevah. The well of Semiramis and other works attributed to her bring her name frequently into conversation.

The town, which is walled, is not particularly attractive, but there is one very handsome mosque, and a very interesting Armenian church, eleven centuries old, dedicated to St. Peter and St. Paul. The houses are mean looking, but their otherwise shabby uniformity is broken up by lattice windows. The bazars are poorly built, but are clean, well supplied and busy, though the trade of Van is suffering from the general insecurity of the country and the impoverishment of the peasantry. In the Van bazars ladies can walk about freely, encountering neither the hoots of boys nor the petrifying Islamic scowl.

Fifty years ago Venetian beads were the only articles imported from Europe. Now, owing to the increasing enterprise of the Armenians, every European necessary of life can be obtained, as well as many luxuries. Peek and Frean's biscuits, Moir's and Crosse & Blackwell's tinned meats and jams, English patent medicines, Coats's sewing cotton, Belfast linens, Berlin wools, Jaeger's vests, and all sorts of materials, both cotton and woolen, abound. I did not see such a choice and abundance of European goods in any bazar in Persia, and in the city of Semiramis, and beneath the tablet of Xerxes, there is a bazar devoted to Armenian tailors, and, to the clatter of American sewing machines, stitching Yorkshire cloth. One of these tailors has made a heavy cloth ulster for me, which the American ladies pronounce perfect in fit and "style."

The Armenians, with their usual industry and thrift, are always enlarging their commerce and introducing new imports. Better than this, they are paying great attention to education, and several of their merchants seem to be actuated by a liberal and enlightened spirit. It is, however, to usury, not less than to trade, that they owe their prosperity. The presence of Europeans in Van, in the persons of the missionaries and vice-consuls, in addition to the admirable influence exerted by the former, has undoubtedly a growing tendency towards ameliorating the condition of the Christian population.

In the vilayet it is estimated by Colonel Severs Bell that the Christians outnumber the Moslems by 80,000, the entire population being estimated at 340,000. In the city of Van, with a population estimated by him at 32,000, the Christians are believed to be as 3 to 1.

Though the state of things among the Christians is not nearly so bad as in some of the Syrian valleys, the shadow of the Kurd is over this paradise. The Armenians complain of robbery, with violence, as being of constant occurrence, and that they have been plundered till they are unable to pay the taxes, and it is obvious that travelers, unless in large companies, are not safe without a government escort. In each village the common sheepfold is guarded from sunset to sunrise by a number of men, a heavy burden on villagers whose taxation should ensure them sufficient protection from marauders.

* * * * * * * * * * * * *

On the last two nights at Undzag and Ghazit I had my first experiences of the Turkish odah, or village guest-house or khan, of which, as similar abodes will be my lodgings throughout my journey to Erzeroum, I will try to give you an idea. Usually partially excavated in the hillside and partly embedded in the earth, the odah is a large rambling room, with an irregular roof, supported on rough tree-stems. In the centre, or some other convenient place, is a mud platform slightly raised; in the better class of odahs this has a fireplace in the wall at one end. Round this on three sides is a deep manger, and similar mangers run along the side walls, and into the irregular recesses, which are lost in the darkness. The platform is for human beings, and the rest of the building for horses, mules, oxen, asses and buffaloes, with a few sheep and goats probably in addition. The Katirgis and the humbler class of travelers sleep among the beasts; the remainder, without distinction of race, creed or sex, on the enclosed space. Light enters from the door and from a few small holes in the roof, which are carefully corked up at night, and then a few iron cups of oil with wicks, the primitive lamp in general use, hanging upon the posts, give forth a smoky light.

In such an odah there may be any number of human beings, cooking, eating and sleeping, and from twenty to a hundred animals or more, as well as the loads of the packhorses and the arms of the travelers. As the eye becomes accustomed to the smoke and dimness, it sees rows of sweet ox-faces, with mild eyes and moist nostrils, and wild horse-faces surrounding the enclosure, and any number more receding into the darkness. Ceaseless munching goes on, and a neigh or a squeal from some unexpected corner startles one, or there is a horse fight, which takes a number of men to quell it. Each animal is a "living stove," and the heat and closeness are so unsupportable that one awakes quite unrefreshed in the morning in a temperature of 80 degrees. The odah is one of the great features of traveling in Eastern

Asia Minor. I dined and spent the evenings in its warmth and cheeriness, enjoying its wild picturesqueness, but at Undzag I pitched my small tent at the stable door, and at Ghazit on the roof.

At sunset that evening 800 sheep were driven into the village sheepfold just below the roof on which my tent was pitched, and it was a very picturesque scene—men pushing their way through them to find their own sheep by ear-mark, women with difficulty milking ewes here and there, big dogs barking furiously from the roofs above, and all the sheep bleating at once. In winter they are all housed and hand-fed. The snow lies six feet deep, and Ghazit can communicate neither with Bitlis nor Van. It is the "milk of the flocks" which is prized. Cow's milk is thought but little of. I made my supper of one of the great articles of diet in Turkey—boiled cracked wheat, sugar and yo hoort, artificially soured milk, looking like whipped cream.

I was glad to escape to my tent from the heat and odors of the odah, even though I had to walk over sheeps' backs to get up to the roof. I had a guard of two men and eight more armed with useless matchlock guns watched the sheepfold. I was awakened by a tremendous noise, the barking of infuriated dogs close to me, the clashing of arms and the shouts of men, mixed up with the rapid firing of guns not far off on the mountain-side, so near, indeed, that I could see the flashes. It was a Kurdish alarm, but nothing came of it. A village which we passed a few hours later was robbed of 600 sheep, however.

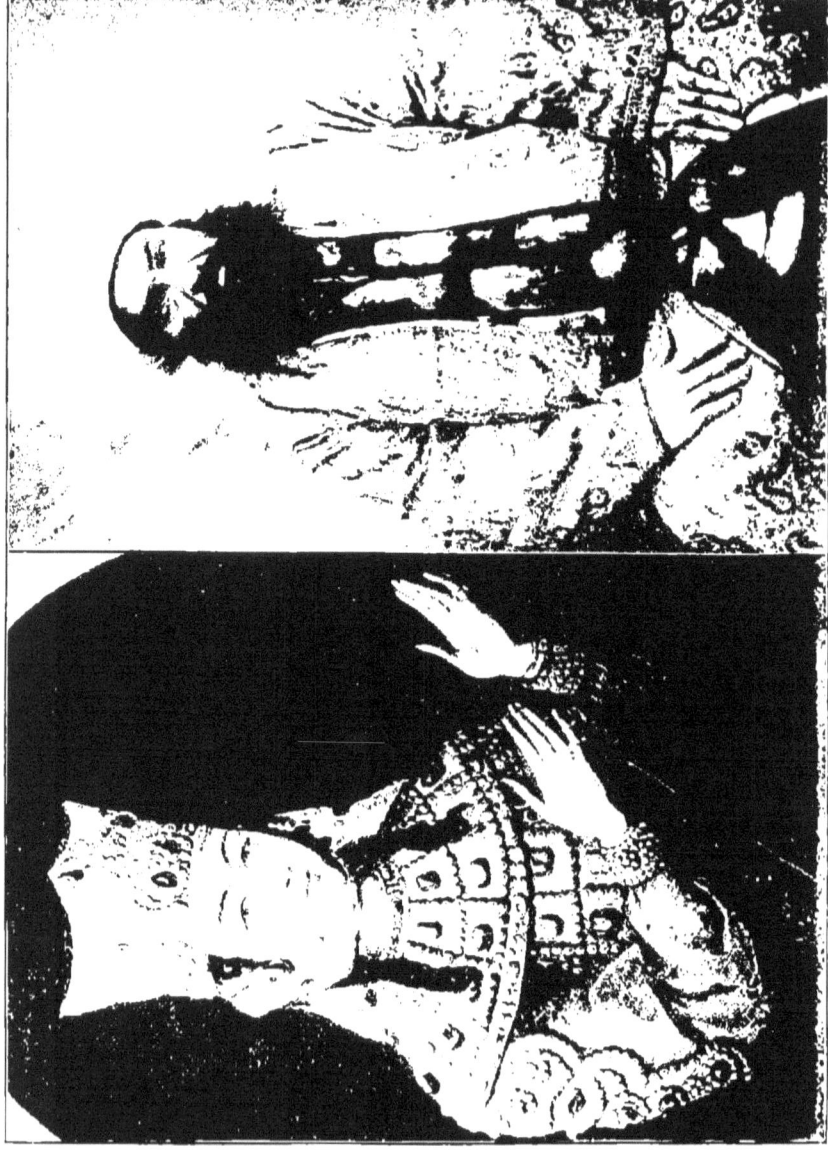

ARMENIAN PRINCESS   THE HIGH PRIEST

BITLIS.

This is the most romantically-situated city that I have seen in Western Asia. Five valleys appear to unite in Bitlis and to radiate from a lofty platform of rock supported on precipices, the irregular outlines of which are emphasized by walls and massive square and circular towers, the gigantic ruins of Bitlis Castle.

The massiveness of the houses is remarkable, and their courtyards and gardens are enclosed by strong walls. Every gate is strengthened and studded with iron, every window is heavily barred, all are at a considerable height, and every house looks as if it could stand a siege. There is no room to spare; the dwellings are piled tier above tier, and the flagged footways in front of them hang on the edges of precipices. Twenty picturesque stone bridges, each one of a single arch, span the Tigris and the torrents which unite with it. There are ancient ruins scattered through the town. It claims immense antiquity, and its inhabitants ascribe its castle and some of its bridges to Alexander the Great; but antiquarians attribute the former either to the Saracens or to the days when an ancient Armenian city, called Paghesh, occupied the site of the present Bitlis. It seems like the end of the world, though through the deep chasms below it, through which the Tigris descends with great rapidity to the plains, lies the highway to Diabekir. Suggestions of the ancient world abound. The lofty summits towering above the basin in which this extraordinary city lies are the termination of the Taurus chain, the Niphates of the ancients, on the highest peak of which Milton localized the descent of satan.

Remote as Bitlis seems, and is, its markets are among the busiest in Turkey, and its caravan traffic is enormous for seven or eight months of the year. Its altitude is only 4700 feet, and the mercury in winter rarely falls to zero; but the snowfall is tremendous, and on the Rahwan plain snow frequently lies up to the top of the telegraph poles, isolating the town and shutting up animals in their stables and human beings in their houses for weeks and occasionally months at a time.

Bitlis is one of the roughest and most fanatical and turbulent of Turkish cities, but the present governor, Raouf Pasha, is a man of energy, and has reduced the town and neighborhood to some degree of order. Considerable bodies of troops have been brought in, and the garrison consists of 2500 men. These soldiers are thoroughly well clothed and equipped, and look remarkably clean in dress and person. They are cheery, soldierly-looking men, and their presence gives a little confidence to the Christians.

The population of Bitlis is estimated at 30,000, of which number over 20,000 are Kurds. Both men and women are very handsome, and the striking Kurdish costume gives a great brilliancy and picturesqueness to this remarkable city. The short sleeveless jackets of sheepskin, with the black wool outside, which the men are now wearing over their striped satin vests, and the silver rings in the noses of the girls, give them something of a "barbarian" look, and, indeed, their habits appear to be much the same as those of their Karduchi ancestors in the days of Xenophon, except that in the interval they have become Moslems and teetotalers! Here they are Sunnis, and consequently do not clash with their neighbors the Turks, who abhor the Kurds of the mountains as Kizilbashes. The Kurdish physique is very fine. In fact, I have never seen so handsome a people, and their manly and highly picturesque costume heightens the favorable effect produced by their well-made, lithe, active figures.

The cast of their features is delicate and somewhat sharp; the mouth is small and well formed; the teeth are always fine and white; the face is oval; the eyebrows curved and heavy; the eyelashes long; the eyes deep-set, intelligent and roving; the nose either straight or decidedly aquiline, giving a hawk-like expression; the chin slightly receding; the brow broad and clear; the hands and feet remarkably small and slender.

The women, when young, are beautiful, but hard work and early maternity lead to a premature loss of form and to a withered angularity of feature which is far from pleasing, and which, as they do not veil, is always en evidence.

The poorer Kurds wear woolen socks of gay and elaborate patterns; cotton shoes like the gheva of the Persians; camlet trousers, wide at the bottom like those of sailors; woolen girdles of a Kashmir shawl pattern; short jackets and felt jerkins without sleeves. The turban usually worn is peculiar. Its foundation is a peaked felt cap, white or black, with a loosely-twisted rope of tightly-twisted silk, wool or cotton, wound round it. In the girdle the khanjar is always seen. Over it the cartridge belt is usually worn, or two cartridge belts are crossed over the chest and back. The girdle also carries the pipe and tobacco pouch, a long knife, a flint and steel, and in some cases a shot pouch and a highly-ornamented powder horn.

The richer Kurds dress like the Syrians. The undergarment, which shows considerably at the chest and at the long and hanging sleeves, is of striped satin, either crimson and white or in a combination of brilliant colors, over which is worn a short jacket of cloth or silk, also with long sleeves, the whole richly embroidered in gold. Trousers of striped silk or satin, wide at the bottom; loose mediaeval boots or carnation-red leather; a girdle fastened with knobbed clasps of silver as large as a breakfast cup, frequently incrusted with turquoises; red felt skull-caps, round which they wind large striped silk shawls, red, blue, orange, on a white or black ground, with long fringed ends hanging over the shoulders, and floating in the wind as they gallop; and in their girdles they carry richly-jeweled khanjars and pistols, decorated with silver knobs, besides a number of other glittering appointments. The accoutrements of the horses are in keeping, and at marriages and other festivities the head-stalls, bridles and breastplates are completely covered with pendent silver coins.

The dress of the women is a foil to that of their lords. It consists of a blue cotton shirt; very wide trousers, drawn in at the ankles; a silver saucer on the head, from which chains depend, with a coin at the end of each; a square mantle hanging down the back, clasped by two of its corners round the neck, and many strings of coins round the throat; a small handkerchief is knotted round the hair, and in presence of a strange man they hold one end of this over the mouth. The Turks in Bitlis are in a small minority, and the number of Armenian Christians is stated at from 2000 to 5000. The Old Church has a large monastery outside the town and several churches and schools. The Protestant Armenians have a substantial church edifice, with a congregation of about 400, and a large boarding-school for boys and girls.

The population is by far the wildest that I have ever seen in any Asiatic city, and is evidently only restrained from violence by the large garrison. It is not safe for the ladies of this mission to descend into the Moslem part of the city, and in a residence of more than twenty years they have never even passed through the bazars. The missionaries occupy a restricted and uncertain position, and the Armenian Christians are subject to great deprivations and restraints, and are distrusted by the government. Of late, they have been much harassed by the search for arms, and Christian gunsmiths have been arrested. Even their funeral ceremonies are not exempt from the presence of the police, who profess to believe that firearms are either carried in the place of a corpse or are concealed along with it. Placed in the midst of a preponderating and fully-armed Kurdish population, capable at any moment of being excited to frenzy against their faith, they live in expectation of a massacre should certain events take place which are regarded as probable within two or three years.

* * * * * * * * * * * * *

Yangaloo is a typical Armenian village; its ant-hill dwellings are half-sunk, and the earth which has been excavated is piled up over their roofs and sides. The interior of each dwelling covers a considerable area, and is full of compartments, with divisions formed by low clay walls or by the posts which support the roof, the compartments ramifying from a widening at the inner end of a long dark passage. In Yangaloo, as in other villages on the plains, the earth is so piled over the houses as to render them hardly distinguishable from the surrounding ground; but where a village burrows into a hillside only a small projection needs an artificial roof. The people live among their live-stock; one entrance serves for both, and in winter time the animals never leave the stables. The fireplace or tandur is in the floor, but is only required for cooking purposes, as the heat and steam of the beasts keep the human beings comfortably warm. From two to five families live in every house, and the people are fairly healthy. Xenophon, in his Anabasis, described the Armenian dwellings of his day thus: "Their houses were underground, the entrance like the mouth of a well, but spacious below; there were passages dug into them for the cattle, but the people descended by ladders. In the houses were goats, sheep, cows and fowls, with their young. All the cattle were kept in fodder within the walls." I have not seen the entrance by a well, but have understood that it still exists in certain exposed situations. Xenophon mentions buried wine, and it is not unlikely that the deep clay-lined holes in which grain is stored in some of the villages are ancient cellars, anterior to the date when the Karduchi became Moslems and teetotalers.

All the male members of a family bring their brides to live

under the parental roof, and one "burrow" may contain as many as three generations of married couples with their families. On becoming an inmate of her father-in-law's house, each Armenian bride, as in the country districts of Persia, has to learn the necessity of silence. Up to the day of the birth of the first child, she is the family drudge, and may not speak to anyone but her husband, and not to him in the presence of his parents. Maternity liberates her tongue, she may talk to her child, and then to the females of the household; but she may not speak freely till some years of this singular novitiate have passed by. She then takes a high place in the house, and eventually rules it if she is left a widow. The Armenian women are veiled out of doors, but only in deference to the Moslems, who regard an uncovered head as the sign of a bad women. The girls are handsome, but sheepish-looking; their complexions and eyes are magnificent.

Kurdistan is scarcely a "geographical expression," and, colloquially, the word is used to cover the country inhabited by the Kurds. They are a mysterious people, having maintained themselves in their original seats and in a condition of semi-independence through all the changes which have passed over Western Asia, though they do not exceed numerically 2,250,000 souls. Such as they were when they opposed the retreat of the Ten Thousand, they seem to be still War and robbery are the business of Kurdish life.

One great interest of this journey is that it lies through a country in which the Kurds, Turks and Armenians live alongside each other; the Kurds being of two classes, the tribal, which are chiefly nomads, owning no law but the right of the strongest; and the non-tribal or settled, who, having been conquered by Turkey, are fairly orderly, and are peaceable, except in their relations with the Christians. The strongholds of the tribal Kurds are in the wild mountains of Kurdistan, and especially in the Hakkiari country, which is sprinkled with their rude castles and forts. An uncurable love of plunder, a singular aptitude for religious fanaticism, a recklessness as to the spilling of blood, a universal rapacity and a cruel brutality when their passions are roused, are among their chief vices. The men are bold, sober and devoted to their kinsmen and tribe, and the women are chaste, industrious and maternal. Under a firm and equitable government, asserting vigorously and persistently the supremacy of law and the equal rights of race and creed, they would probably develop into excellent material.

The Christians, who, in this part of Kurdistan, are all Armenians by race, live chiefly on the plains and in the lower folds of the hills, and are engaged in pastoral and agricultural pursuits. My letters have given a faithful representation of them as dwelling with their animals in dark, semi-subterranean hovels. The men are industrious, thrifty, clannish, domestic and not given to vices, except that of intoxication, when they have the means and opportunity, and the women are hardworking and chaste. Both sexes are dirty, hardy, avaricious and superstitious, and ages of wrong have developed in them some of the usual faults of oppressed Oriental peoples. They cling desperately to their historic Church, which is represented among the peasants by priests scarcely less ignorant than themselves. Their bishops constitute their only aristocracy.

On the whole, the same condition of alarm prevails among the Armenians as I witnessed previously among the Syrian rayahs. It is more than alarm—it is abject terror, and not without good reason. In plain English, general lawlessness prevails over much of this region. Caravans are stopped and robbed, traveling is, for Armenians, absolutely unsafe, sheep and cattle are being driven off, and outrages, which it would be inexpedient to narrate, are being perpetrated. Nearly all the villages have been reduced to extreme poverty by the carrying off of their domestic animals, the pillage and, in some cases, the burning, of their crops, and the demands made upon them at the sword's point for every article of value which they possess, while, at the same time, they are squeezed for the taxes which the Kurds have left them without the means of paying.

In the village of ———, which has been swept bare by the Kurds, the people asserted that the zaptiehs had tied twenty defaulters together, and has driven them round and round barefooted over the thistles of the threshing-floor, flogging them with their heavy whips. My zaptiehs complain of the necessity they are under of beating the people. They say (and I think correctly) that they can never know whether a man has a hoard of buried money or not without beating him. They tell me also that they know that half of the peasants have nothing to pay their taxes with, but that unless they beat them to "get what they can out of them" they would be punished themselves for neglect of duty.

I have myself seen enough to convince me that, in the main, the statements of the people represent accurately enough the present reign of terror in Armenia, and that a state of matters nearly approaching anarchy is now existing in the vilayet of Erzeroum. There is no security at all for the lives and property of Christians, law is being violated daily, and almost with perfect impunity, and peaceable and industrious subjects of the Porte, taxed to an extent which should secure them complete protection, are plundered without redress Their feeble complaints are ignored, or are treated as evidence of "insurrectionary tendencies," and even their lives are at the mercy of the increased audacity and aroused fanaticism of the Kurds, and this not in nearly inaccessible and far-off mountain valleys, but on the broad plains of Armenia, with telegraph wires above and passable roads below, and with a Governor-General and the Fourth Army Corps, numbering 20,000 seasoned troops, within easy distance.

I have every reason to believe that in the long winter evenings which I have spent in these sociable odahs the peasants have talked to me freely and frankly. There are no reasons why it should be otherwise, for my zaptiehs are seldom present; Moussa is looking after his horses in distant recesses, quite out of hearing, and my servants are Christians. If the people speak frankly, I am compelled to believe that the Armenian peasant is as destitute of political aspirations as he is ignorant of political grievances; that if he were secured from the ravages of Moslem marauders he would be as contented as he is loyal and industrious; and this his one desire is "protection from the Kurds" and from the rapacity of minor officials, with security for his life and property. Not on a single occasion have I heard a wish expressed for political or administrative reform, or for autonomy. The Armenian peasants are "of the earth, earthy," and the unmolested enjoyment of material good is their idea of an earthly paradise.

With regard to the Kurds, they have been remorseless robbers for ages, and as their creed scarcely hesitates to give the appropriation of the goods of a Kaffir a place among the virtues, they prey upon the Syrian and Armenian peasants with clear consciences. To rob them by violence and "demand" month after month and year after year, till they have stripped them nearly bare, to cut their throats if they resist, to leave them for a while to retrieve their fortunes—"to let the sheeps' wool grow," as their phrase is—and then to rob them again, is the simple story of the relations between Kurd and Christian. They are well armed with modern rifles and revolvers. I have rarely seen a Kurd with an old-fashioned weapon, and I have never seen a Christian with a rifle, and their nearly useless long guns have lately been seized by the government The Kurds hate and despise the Turks, their nominal rulers; but the Islamic bond of brotherhood is stronger than the repulsion either of hatred or contempt, and the latent or undisguised sympathy of their co-religionists in official positions ensures them, for the most part, immunity for their crimes, for the new code, under which the evidence of a Christian has become nominally admissible in a court of law, being in direct opposition to the teaching of the Koran, to the practice of centuries, to Kurdish fanaticism, and to the strong religious feelings and prejudices of those who administer justice, is practically, so far as the Christians are concerned, a dead letter.

ARMENIAN WOMEN MAKING BREAD.

A GROUP OF KOORDS, ARMENIA.

CHAPTER IX.

GLADSTONE ON THE ARMENIAN QUESTION.

A meeting was held in the Town Hall, Chester, England, on the 6th of August, for the purpose of discussing the claims of the Armenians in Turkey. The assembly-room at the Town Hall was crowded to excess, and many thousands of persons had to be refused admission. The Duke of Westminster presided, and among those present were a great number of members of Parliament.

Mr. Gladstone, who was received with prolonged cheers, said: My Lord Duke, my Lords and Ladies and Gentlemen —My first observation shall be a repetition of what has already been said by the noble duke, who has assured you that this meeting is not a meeting called in the interests of any party, or having the smallest connection with those differences of opinion which naturally and warrantably in this free country will spring up in a complex state of affairs, dividing us on certain questions man from man. But, my lord duke, it is satisfactory to observe that freedom of opinion and even these divisions themselves upon certain questions give increased weight and augmented emphasis to the concurrence of the people to the cordial agreement of the whole nation in these matters where the broad principles of common humanity and common justice prevail.

A QUESTION OF HUMANITY.

It is perfectly true that the government whose deeds we have to impeach is a Mohammedan government, and it is perfectly true that the sufferers under those outrages, under those afflictions, are Christian sufferers. The Mohammedan subjects of Turkey suffer a great deal, but what they suffer is only in the way of the ordinary excesses and defects of an intolerably bad government—perhaps the worst on the face of the earth. That which we have now to do is, I am sorry to say, the opening up of an entirely new chapter. It is not a question of indifferent laws indifferently enforced. It is not a question of administrative violence and administrative abuse. It cuts further and goes to the root of all that concerns human life in its elementary conditions. But this I will say, that if, instead of dealing with the Turkish government and impeaching it for its misdeeds towards Christian subjects, we were dealing with a Christian government that was capable of similar misdeeds towards Mohammedan subjects, our indignation ought to be not less, but greater, than it is now.

THE ATROCITIES PROVED.

Now, it was my fate, I think some six or more months ago, to address a very limited number, not a public assembly, but a limited number of Armenian gentlemen, and gentlemen interested in Armenia, on this subject; and at that time I ventured to point out that one of our duties was to avoid premature judgments. There was no authoritative and impartial declaration before the world at that period on the subject of what is known as the Sassoun massacre; that massacre to which the noble duke has alluded and with respect to which, horrible as that massacre was, one of the most important witnesses in this case declares that it is thrown into the shade and has become pale and ineffective by the side of the unspeakable horrors which are being enacted from month to month, from week to week, and day to day in the different provinces of Armenia. It was a duty to avoid premature judgment, and I think it was avoided. There was a great reserve, but at last the engine of dispassionate inquiry was brought to bear, and then it was found that another duty, very important in general in these cases, really in this particular instance had no particular place at all, and though it is a duty to avoid exaggeration, a most sacred duty, it is a duty that has little or no place in the case before us, because it is too well known that the powers of language hardly suffice to describe what has been and is being done, and that exaggeration, if we were ever so much disposed to it, is in such a case really beyond our power. Those are dreadful words to speak. It is a painful office to perform, and nothing but a strong sense of duty could gather us together between these walls or could induce a man of my age and a man who is not wholly without other difficulties to contend with to resign for the moment that repose and quietude which is the last of many great earthly blessings remaining to him in order to invite you to enter into a consideration of this question—I will not say in order to invite you to allow yourselves to be flooded with the sickening details that it involves. I shall not attempt to lead you into that dreadful field, but I make this appeal to you. I do hope that everyone of you will for himself and herself endeavor in such a degree as your position may allow of you to endeavor to acquire some acquaintance with them, because I know that, when I say that a case of this kind puts exaggeration out of the question, I am making a very broad assertion, which would in most cases be violent, which would in all ordinary cases be unwarrantable. But those who will go through the process I have described, or even a limited portion of the process, will find that the words are not too strong for the occasion. What witnesses ought we to call before us? I should be disposed to say that it matters very little what witness you call. So far as the character of the testimony you will receive is concerned, the witnesses are all agreed. At the time that I have just spoken of, six or eight months ago, they were private witnesses. Since that time, although we have not seen the detailed documents of public authority, yet we know that all the broader statements which had been made up to that time and which have made the blood of this nation run cold, have been confirmed and verified. They have not been overstated, not withdrawn, not qualified, not reduced, but confirmed in all their breadth, in all their horrible substance, in all their sickening details.

The whole substance of the situation may be summed up in four awful words—plunder, murder, rape and torture. Every incident turns upon one or upon several of those awful words. Plunder and murder you would think are bad enough, but plunder and murder are almost venial by the side of the work of the ravisher and the work of the torturer, as it is described in these pages, and as it is now fully and authentically known to be going on. I will keep my word, and I will not be tempted by—what shall I say?—the dramatic interest attached to such exaggeration of human action as we find here to travel into the details of the facts. They are fitter for private perusal than they are for public discussion. I will not be tempted to travel into them; I will ask you for a moment, any of you who have not yourselves verified the particulars of the case, to credit me with speaking the truth, until I go on to consider who are the doers of these deeds. In all ordinary cases when we have before us instances of crime, perhaps of very horrible crime—for example, there is a sad story in the papers today of a massacre in a portion of China—we at once assume that in all countries, unfortunately, there are malefactors, there are plunderers whose deeds we are going to consider. Here, my lord duke, it is nothing of the kind; we have nothing to do here with what are called the dangerous classes of the community; it is not their proceedings which you are asked to consider; it is the proceedings of the government of Constantinople and its agents.

THE TURKISH GOVERNMENT RESPONSIBLE.

There is not one of these misdeeds for which the government at Constantinople is not morally responsible. Now, who are these agents? Let me tell you very briefly. They fall into three classes. The first have been mentioned by the noble duke—namely, the savage Kurds, who are, unhappily, the neighbors of the Armenians, the Armenians being the representatives of one of the oldest civilized Christian races, and being beyond all doubt one of the most pacific, one of the most industrious and one of the most intelligent races in the world. These Kurds are by them; they are wild, savage clans. There was but one word, my lord duke, in your address that I should have been disposed to literally criticize, and it was the expression that fell from you that the Sultan had "organized" these Kurds. They are, in my belief, in no sense organized—that is to say, there is no more organization among them than is to be found, say, in a band of robbers; they have no other organization, being nothing but a band of robbers. These the Sultan and the government at Constantinople have enrolled, though in a nominal fashion, not with any military discipline, into pretended cavalry regiments, and then set them loose with the authority of soldiers of the Sultan to harry and destroy the people of Armenia. Well, these Kurds are the first of the agents in this horrible business; the next are the Turkish soldiers, who are in no sense behind the Kurds in their performances; the third are the peace officers, the police and the tax-gatherers of the Turkish government; and there seems to be a deadly competition among all these classes which shall most prove itself an adept in the horrible and infernal work that is before them; but above them and more guilty than they are the higher officers of the Turkish government.

THREE PROPOSITIONS.

I think there are certain matters, such as those which have been discussed today and discussed in many other forms, on

which it is perfectly possible to make up our minds. And what I should say is, that the whole position may be summed up in three brief propositions I do not know to which of these propositions to assign the less or the greater importance. It appears to me that they are probably each and everyone of them absolutely indispensable. The first proposition is this: You ought to moderate your demands. You ought to ask for nothing but that which is strictly necessary, and that possibly according to all that we know of the proposals before us, the rule has been rigidly complied with. I do not hesitate to say, ladies and gentlemen, that the cleanest and clearest method of dealing with this subject, if we should have done it, would have been to tell the Turk to march out of Armenia. He has no right to remain there, and it would have been an excellent settlement of the question. But it is by no means certain that Europe, or even the three Powers, would have been unanimous in seeking after that end. Therefore, let us part with everything except what is known to be indispensable. Then I come to the other two rules, and of these the first is that you should accept no Turkish promises. They are absolutely and entirely worthless They are worse than worthless, because they may serve to elude a few persons who, without information or experience, naturally would suppose, when promises are given, that there is something like an intention of fulfilment. Recollect that no scheme is worth having unless it be supported by efficient guarantees entirely outside the promises of the Turkish government. There is another word which I must speak, and it is this: Don't be too much afraid if you hear introduced into this discussion a word that I admit, in ordinary cases, ought to be excluded from all diplomatic proceedings, namely, the word coercion. Coercion is a word perfectly well understood in Constantinople, and it is a word highly appreciated in Constantinople. It is a drastic dose, which never fails of its aim when it is administered in that quarter. Gentlemen, I would not use these words if I had not myself personally had large and close experience of the proceedings of the Turkish government. I say, first make your case good, and when your case is made good, determine that it shall prevail. Grammar has something to do with this case. Recollect that while the word "ought" sounded in Constantinople, passes in thin air, and has no force or solidity whatever attaching to it; on the contrary, the brother or sister monosyllable, the word "must," is perfectly understood; and it is a known fact, supported by positive experience, which can be verified upon the map of Europe, that a timely and judicious use of this word never fails for its effect. Gentlemen, I must point out to you that we have reached a very critical position indeed. How are three great governments in Europe, ruling a population of more than 200,000,000 souls, with perhaps eight or ten times the population of Turkey, with twenty times the wealth of Turkey, with fifty times the influence and power of Turkey, who have committed themselves in this matter before the world— I put it to you, that if they recede before an irrational resistance—and remember that I have in the first instance postulated that our demands should be reasonable—if they recede before the irrational resistance of the Sultan and the Ottoman government, they are disgraced in the face of the world. Every motive of duty coincides with every motive of self-respect, and, my lord duke, you, yourself, let drop a word which is a frightful word, unhappily not wholly out of place, the word

"EXTERMINATION."

There has gone abroad, I don't say that I feel myself competent to judge the matter, I don't think I do, but there has gone abroad and there is widely entertained a belief that the recent proceedings of the Turkish government in Armenia particularly, but not in Armenia exclusively, are founded upon deliberate determination to exterminate the Christians in that empire. I hope it is not true, but at the same time I must say that there are evidences tending to support it, and the grand evidence which tends to support it is this· the perfect infatuation of the Turkish government. Now, in my time there have been periods when Turkey was ruled by men of honesty and ability. I will say that until about thirty years ago you could trust the word of the Turkish government as well as any government in Europe; you might not approve of their proceedings, but you could trust their word. But a kind of judicial infatuation appears to have come down upon them. What has happened in Turkey? To hear of this vaunting on the part of its government, and this game of brag that is from time to time being played, that it cannot compromise its dignity, it cannot waive any of its rights. What would come of its rights in one-third part of its empire? Within my lifetime Turkey has been reduced by one-third part of her territory, and 16,000,000 or 18,000,000 people inhabiting some of the most beautiful and formerly most famous countries in the world, who were under the Ottoman rule, are now as free as we are The Ottoman government are as well aware of that as we, and yet we find it pursuing these insane courses. On the other hand, my lord duke most judiciously referred to the plan of government that was introduced in the Lebanon about 1861, whereby a reasonable share of stability to local institutions and popular control has been given in Turkey, and the results have been most satisfactory. There is also a part of the country, although not a very large part, where something like local self-government is permitted, and it has been very hopeful in its character. But when we see these things—on the one hand that these experiments in a sense of justice have all succeeded, and that when adapted to the Greeks and the Bulgarians and four or five other States have resulted in the loss of those States, then I say that the Turkish government is evidently in such a state of infatuation that it is fain to believe it may, under certain circumstances, be infatuated enough to scheme the extermination of the Christian population. Well, this is a sad and terrible story, and I have been a very long time in telling it, but a very small part of it; but I hope that, having heard the terms of the resolution that will be submitted to you, you will agree that a case is made out. I for one, for the sake of avoiding other complications, would rejoice if the Government of Turkey would come to its senses. If only men like Friad Pasha and Ali Pasha, who were in the government of Turkey after the Crimean war, could be raised from the dead, and could inspire the Turkish policy with their spirit and with their principles! That is, in my opinion, what we ought all to desire, and though it would be more agreeable to clear Turkey than to find her guilty of these terrible charges, yet if we have the smallest regard to humanity, if we are sensible at all of what is due to our own honor after the steps which have been taken within the last twelve or eighteen months, we must interfere. We must be careful to demand no more than what is just—but at least as much as is necessary—and we must be determined that, with the help of God, that which is necessary, and that which is just, shall be done, whether there will be a response or whether there be none.

CHAPTER X.

THE KURDS.

By Jesse Malek Yonan, of Oroomiah, Persia, at present in Rush Medical College, Chicago.

The recent reports concerning the massacre of the Armenians in Turkey and other places have been looked upon by many as incredible; not, however, to those acquainted with the character of the Kurds, who were the chief perpetrators. My intimate acquaintance with this people, and my knowledge of their hostility in my own Persian home, will help me to give a brief account of their history and present condition and also of the cruelties practiced by them on the unfortunate Christians of the Orient.

THEIR COUNTRY.

Kurdistan, which is a name very common in the East, is no more than a geographical appellation for the entire country inhabited by the Kurds. Its area is estimated to be more than 50,000 square miles. This region has no political boundaries, but includes both Persian and Turkish territory. It may be said to extend from Turkish Armenia on the north to the plains of the Middle Tigris and the Luristan mountains on the south. It contains many other people besides Kurds, among whom are Turks, Nestorians, Chaldeans, Persians and Armenians.

A "MOLLAH" NARRATING THE BATTLE OF KERBALA IN THE BAZAAR AT TABRIZ, PERSIA.

THEIR ORIGIN.

The origin and ancestry of the Kurds, like that of most Eastern nations, is still unsettled among ethnologists. They stand among the Asiatic races, like the Basques and Lapps in Europe, wrapt in obscurity. Whether they are of Iranian or Turanian origin, whether they are descendants of Medes or Parthians, or whether they are the Gardu, who at one time held the mountains north of Assyria, no one can say with certainty. It is safest to identify them with the Karduchie, with whom Xenophon and the ten thousand had so long a struggle. In regard to the Kurds, history is silent, except at certain epochs when they touched the more civilized world. It is said by some Eastern historians that the famous Saladin was a Kurd. Several governments of Western Asia have claimed them; but a people so rebellious has ever been a thorn in the side of every ruling power. In 1639 A. D. a treaty between one of the Sultans of Turkey and the Shah Sefavi, of Persia, established a frontier line between the two empires, which line, since that date, has served as a nominal division between the two. Their subsequent history is obscure They are a people without a literature and almost without a history. They number about 2,000,000, 700,000 of whom are under Persia, the rest being under Turkey. They are divided into many independent tribes. The tribal feeling is very strong, a very fortunate thing for Turkey and Persia, for could the Kurds be firmly united, these empires might often suffer much at their hands. At the present time, however, they are more subject to discipline than at any previous epoch in their history.

OCCUPATION AND CHARACTER.

Some of them are nomadic, not, however, wandering indefinitely, for they have well-defined circuits which they make annually. They spend the summer in the cool, bracing air of Northwestern Persia, and the winter in the milder plains of Assyria. It is interesting to watch them on the march during these migrations, moving with families, tents, flocks and herds, the hardy females bearing their little ones in cradles on their backs, the older children with only their heads emerging, being packed in large sacks, often with lambs to balance them, and thus slung over the backs of oxen or cows. Thus they move as the season advances, until midsummer finds them near the summits of the mountains or plateaus, in the neighborhood of perpetual snow, among cool rills, luxuriant pastures and blossoming flowers.

But some of them are agricultural people who live in villages, tilling ground on the plains and hillsides. It is amusing to notice them on their way to their work, dragging along their sluggish limbs as though they might drop asleep at any moment. They will waste two hours before they even start to work. After an hour of pretended labor, in which they have really accomplished nothing, they will have to sit down and smoke awhile. Up they are again, their long sticks in hand, to urge on the yokes of oxen which draw the wooden plows. Hardly have they begun afresh before they are again ready for a rest; out come the pipes, and down the hill the laborers go for a draught from a cool spring in the valley below. In this way they carry on all their work. Poor creatures, they are good for nothing. Others are shepherds. It is really inspiring to see how devoted they are to their sheep. See this one as he goes before his flocks. His staff is in his hand, and from his shoulder hangs a bag which contains his provisions for the day. Now he whistles, thus indicating to the sheep his desire that they travel rapidly. He has given them names, and often calls his favorite to him that he may pet her. Again we see him sitting on a rock, with his fond flock gathering around him, as he sings and plays his flute. How beautifully this illustrates the words of our Lord: "He calleth his own sheep by name and leadeth them out. He goeth before them and the sheep follow him, for they know his voice." This is a beautiful and peaceful picture of the Kurds. But let us look at him as he rides his Arabian steed, gun on shoulder, sword at side and spear in hand—a veritable fiend of death. His dark eyes and gloomy countenance are fearful to look upon. These warriors sleep most of the day, and at sunset start on their robbing expeditions. They descend to the numerous villages in the valleys and drive away the cattle and flocks, no one daring to oppose them, as their very name strikes terror to the hearts of the people. Robbing is their business, and they believe that God created them for this purpose only. I myself have conversed with many of them, and asked them why they steal. They answer that every man has some occupation. One is a judge, one a merchant, one a farmer, and "we are robbers." They make their living in this way. "Why don't you work?" I ask. "We do not know how to work." "Why do you kill people?" "When we meet a man that we wish to rob, if we find him stronger than ourselves, we have to kill him in order to rob him." "But you are liable to be killed some day." "We must die at some time," they answer. "What is the difference between dying now and a few days hence?"

They are always ready to defend their cause, and anyone who has not killed at least one or two men is not considered worthy to live. They are very cruel and as rugged as the region they occupy. Like Cain, their hand is against everybody, and everybody's hand against them. They are very brave and have no fear on the field of battle. In the late Russo-Turkish war they are said to have been Turkey's best soldiers. From the Persian Kurds several regiments are raised for the Persian army, which always prove themselves the bravest.

RELIGION AND LANGUAGE.

Their faith is that of the Sunni sect of Orthodox Mussulmans. They pretend to be very religious, and offer their prayers five times every day. Before leaving their homes for the purpose of robbery, they will offer a prayer, believing that God will hear them. They are very superstitious and bigoted. Their language is Koormanji (Kurdish). It is thought to be a branch of old Persian intermingled with alien words. It has never been reduced to writing The Kurds are profoundly ignorant and stupid, with neither books nor schools. Of the whole race, not one in ten thousand can read.

HOUSES AND WOMEN.

The most of the summer they live in tents in the cool places on the mountain slopes and valleys. Their winter houses are built underground, most of them having a single room, with one or two small holes on the top for light. This serves for a bedroom, parlor, kitchen and stable. In the daytime they are all away; towards sunset they come in one by one, at least a score of them, men, women and children, but already the hens have found their resting-place; sheep, oxen and horses each in their corner. After it is quite dark, coarse stale bread and sour milk are brought out for supper. Two spoons and one big dish are sufficient for all; each in his turn tries the spoon. Of course, this is always done in the dark, as they have no lights. Now it is bedtime, and one after another finds his place under the same quilt, without a pillow or bed, except some hay spread on the floor. In a few minutes all are fast asleep, and soon the heavy breathing and snoring of men and cattle is mingled, and the effect is anything but a sweet sound. The temperature of the room is sometimes as high as a hundred Fahr., and swarms of fleas (one of which would be enough to disturb the rest of an entire American family) attack the wild Kurds, but he stirs not until morning, the fleas being exhausted sooner than the men.

Their women wear an exceedingly picturesque costume. They have dark complexions, with eyes and hair intensely black. Their beauty is not of a refined type, but by a mass of paint is made sufficiently attractive for their easily-pleased husbands. Almost all the work, both in and out of doors, is done by them. Early in the morning, when they are through their home work, they hasten to the field to attend the flocks, or gather fuel for use in winter. In the evening they come in with large burdens on their backs, which appear to be quite enough for two donkeys to carry. So industrious are they that they frequently spin on their way to and from work, singing all the while, apparently as happy as if all the world were theirs. The difficulties and ailments of womanhood are nothing to them. A woman with child will go out among the rocks, climbing the mountain heights. Her time of labor is at hand, but she does not cease her usual toil. In the evening the woman may be seen coming singing down the mountain, a heavy burden of fuel on her back and in her arms the child to which she has given birth during the day. Even this the men do not appreciate or reward. They will not hesitate, when it is raining, to drag the women from the tent in order to make room for a favorite steed.

A WOMAN PHYSICIAN'S ACCOUNT OF A REMARKABLE OVERLAND JOURNEY THROUGH THE KURDS' LAND.

No civilized woman, says the San Francisco Chronicle, had ever made the journey from Oroomia, in Persia, through the mountains that separate it from Armenia and Kurdistan, and over the plains to ancient Nineveh, that were the theatre of the recent Turkish outrages against the Christian

IN A KURDISH CAMP.   A KURD CAPTURING AN ARMENIAN WOMAN.

Armenians, prior to the year 1874, in which year Dr. Catherine V. C. Scott, of this city, made the journey.

Mrs. Scott was at that time in charge of the College for Nestorians at Oroomia, Persia, and her journey was a self-imposed task, taken in the heroic endeavor to fulfil a duty which her father had annually performed unremittingly for twenty-four years. The mission of which the Rev. J. G. Cochran had charge embraced all the cities and villages west of the Tigris and north of the river Zab. Mrs. Scott, his daughter, was born at the village of Seiro, and remained as a pupil of the mission college until sixteen years of age, when she was sent to Philadelphia to be educated in the science of medicine at the Allopathic College. At the age of twenty she was recalled to Oroomia.

This she related to a gathering of friends at her house, 727 Geary street, as a preface to a most interesting account of her journey to Nineveh and return.

"On my return from Philadelphia my father met us at Constantinople. He had been compelled by the refusal of the Missionary Board to close the school earlier and to make a forced journey on horseback, traveling twenty-two hours out of twenty-four. On the return trip before Oroomia was reached my father was seized with typhoid fever and died shortly afterward. Being the only one at the mission who thoroughly understood the language of the Nestorians, the charge of my father devolved upon me, and I was forced to superintend the institution, as well as to practice medicine and treat the sick at the mission. I remained in this capacity for six years, until the close of the seminary."

Mrs. Scott spoke in a pleasant, conversational tone, and related the details of her life at the college and of the subsequent journey in a reminiscent vein, without previous preparation, just as her memory recalled the events. She began her narrative with the story of the famine, which resulted from a corner in grain, by which the people of Oroomia were compelled by the governor of the province in which Oroomia is situated to pay fabulous prices for their food, resulting in their being reduced to a state of beggary. During this famine Mrs. Scott says she prescribed for as many as 500 patients a day, and dispensed medicines and alms, herself superintending the distribution of $450,000 subscribed by American Jews and Protestants for the relief of the poor. "I have seen fully 10,000 starving, miserable people in front of the gates of the seminary, in rags and kneeling in the snow," said she, "begging, praying for relief; at nights sleeping under the hamams (baths), in the most miserable poverty and dying of dirt and disease."

She related how these miserable creatures would crowd about the horses of the missionaries, and falling upon their knees would clasp their arms about the legs of the horses. It having been a part of her father's duties to travel once a year to each of the villages within the district, she, together with the Rev. William Stocking and his wife and a numerous train of servants and attendants, undertook the journey.

In crossing the mountains from Persia into Armenia they encountered most dangerous passes and had many times narrowly escaped death. The roads were almost impassable and were purposely kept in such condition by the Armenians to prevent the incursions of bloodthirsty Kurds. She told of conditions of the most absolute poverty and degradation in which the mountaineers of Armenia dwelt. Her description of the city of Amadieh, a city of some 15,000 Kurds, likened the rock upon which the city stands to an immense bandbox, approach to which was made over a rough-hewn trail, guarded by iron gates. "It is the people of this city," said she, "who have taken so prominent a part in the recent massacres."

She told of several most perilous experiences of herself and party of crossing the river Zab on a narrow bridge of woven wickerwork, 240 feet in length, suspended at a great height above the foaming torrent beneath; of an encounter with Kurdish robbers; of a narrow escape of herself and her Arabian steed from death by falling over a cliff into a bottomless ravine; of sliding down the mountain-side upon burlaps; of the sunstroke and subsequent insanity of Mr. Stocking; the illness and death of Mrs. Stocking; of the massacre of a caravan of seventeen Europeans by Kurds, whose fate their own party narrowly escaped. After their arrival at Montserrat, Mrs. Stocking having succumbed to her illness, was buried, and the party proceeded home without further adventure. The tale of the horrors of that journey were sufficient to have shattered the mind and health of strong men, yet Mrs. Scott bore them with remarkable fortitude and courage, and spoke of some pleasant incidents of her life in that country with fervor and delight.

CHAPTER XI.

HOME-LIFE OF THE ARMENIANS.

The ceremonies at an Armenian birth are scarcely less superstitious than the Turkish rites. They are of a more vague and indefinite character. If possible, a mother and child should not be left alone the first few days; but the broom is replaced by the venerated image of the Holy Virgin or some saint, put on guard over the bed. Garlic is not resorted to as a safeguard against the evil eye, but holy water is nightly sprinkled over child and mother, who are also fumigated with the holy olive branch. The company received on these occasions is quiet, and only part of the Turkish show and pageantry is displayed in the adornment of the bed. The child has the same Bologna sausage appearance, modified by a European baby's cap.

About the ninth day the bath ceremony takes place; but instead of the mother's body providing food for her guests by the honeyed plaster of the Turkish woman, all sit down to a substantial luncheon, in which the Yahlan dolma and the lakana turshou (sauerkraut) play a prominent part, and which is brought into the bath on this occasion.

As the christening takes place within eight days, it cannot on that account be witnessed by the mother, who is unable to attend the church services before the fortieth day, when she goes to receive the benediction of purification. Part of the water used for the christening is presumably brought from the river Jordan, and the child is also rubbed with holy oil. The service concluded, the party walk home in procession, headed by the midwife carrying the baby. Refreshments are offered to the company, who soon afterwards retire. A gift of a gold cross or a fine gold coin is made to the child by the sponsors.

No system of diet is followed in the rearing of Armenian children, nor are their bodies refreshed by a daily bath. Few people in the East bathe their children, for a general idea prevails that it is an injurious custom and a fertile cause of sickness. Kept neither clean nor neat, they are allowed to struggle through infancy in a very irregular manner. Yet in spite of this they are strong and healthy.

ARMENIAN WEDDINGS.

The Armenian fiancailles, although contracted in a very simple fashion, are not easily annulled, and can only be set aside for very serious reasons.

A priest, commissioned by the friends of the aspirant, makes the proposals of marriage to the young lady's parents. Should the offer be accepted, he is again sent, accompanied by another priest, to present to the fiancee a small gold cross bought by her betrothed for the benefit of the church, and of a price proportioned to the means of the family.

Girls are given in marriage at a very early age; some when they are but twelve years old; but men seldom marry before they are twenty-one.

Like the Turkish wedding, it takes place on a Monday. A priest is sent by the bride's parents to inform those of the bridegroom that all is ready and the Duhun may begin. On the Friday, invitations are issued, and the bride is taken to the bath with great ceremony. On the Saturday, musicians are called in, and all the young maidens assemble to partake of a feast intended especially for them, and extended to the poor, who come in flocks to share in the good things.

Next day this festivity is repeated; the dinner is served at 3, and the young men are allowed to wait upon the girls—a rare privilege, equally pleasing to either sex, at other times excluded from each other's society, and, it is needless to say, that they now make the most of their opportunities.

As soon as this repast is over, the married people sit down to the wedding dinner in a patriarchal fashion, husband and wife side by side, while the young men are the last to partake of the bridal repast. In the evening, they are again admitted to the company of the ladies, on the plea of handing refreshments to them. About 10 o'clock the bride is taken into another room by her friends, who place upon her head a curious silver plate, over which a long piece of scarlet silk is thrown, falling to her feet, secured at the sides by ribbons, enveloping her in a complete bag, drawn tight at the top of her head, under the silver plate; two extraordinary-looking wings, called sorgooch, made of stiff cardboard, covered with feathers, are fastened on each side of the head. When this disguise is complete, the bride, blindfolded by her veil, is led forth from the apartment, and conducted by her father or nearest male relative to open a round dance, during the

MT. ARARAT.

performance of which money is showered over her. She is then led to a corner, where she sits awaiting the arrival of the bridegroom in the solitude of her crimson cage.

The bridegroom's toilet begins early in the afternoon. He is seated in the middle of the room, surrounded by a joyous company of friends; the gingahar, or best man, and a host of boys arrive, accompanied by the band of music sent in search of them.

The barber, an all-important functionary, must not be overlooked. Razor in hand, girded with his silk scarf, his towl over one shoulder, and a species of leather strap over the other, he commences operations, prolonged during an indefinite period, much enlivened by his gossip and bon mots, and turned to his advantage by the presents he receives from the assembled company, who, one by one, suspend their gifts on a cord, stretched by him for the purpose across the room. These gifts consist chiefly of towels, pieces of cloth, scarfs, etc. When the gossip considers the generosity of the company exhausted, he gives the signal for the production of the wedding garments, which, brought in state, together with the bridegroom's presents to his bride, must receive the benediction of the priest before they can be used.

After the evening meal has been partaken of, the gifts, accompanied by the musicians, are conveyed to the bride, the company following with the bridegroom, who walks between two torches, and is met at the door by another band of music.

On entering the presence of his future mother-in-law and

her nearest relatives, he receives a gift from her, and respectfully kisses her hand. Allowed a few moment's rest, he is seated on a chair between two flaring torches, after which he is led into the presence of his veiled bride, to whom he extends his hand, which she takes, extricating her own with difficulty from under her duvak, and is assisted to descend from her sofa corner, and stands facing her betrothed with her forehead reclining against his. A short prayer, called the "half-service," is read over the couple, their hands locked together, must not be loosened till they arrive at the street-door, when two bridesmaids, supporting the bride on each side, leads her at a slow pace to the church.

The procession is headed by the bridegroom and his men, followed by the bride and the ladies; no person is allowed to cross the road between the two parties. On entering the sacred edifice, the couple, making the sign of the cross three times, offer a prayer, believing that whatever they ask at this moment will be granted them; they then approach the altar-steps and stand side by side.

The first part of the service is read by the priest, standing on the altar-steps; the couples, placed in a row before him, with the best men and boys behind him. He asks each couple separately, first the bridegroom, and then the bride, the following question: "Chiorus topalus cabullus?" (Blind or lame, is he or she acceptable), to which the parties answer in the affirmative. Should either person object to the union, the objection is accepted, and the marriage cannot be proceeded with; but incidents of this kind are rare.

After the formalities of the acceptance have been gone

through, the couple stand facing each other, with their heads touching, and a small gold cross is tied with a red silken string on the forehead of each, and the symbol of the Holy Ghost pressed against them. The ceremony terminates by the partaking of wine, after which the married pair walk hand-in-hand to the door of the church; but from the church to her home the bride is once more supported by the bridesmaids. The moment they are about to cross the threshold, a sheep is sacrificed, over whose blood they step into the house.

When husband and wife are seated side by side, the guests come one by one, kiss the crosses on their foreheads, and drop coins into a tray for the benefit of the officiating priests.

The bride is now once more led to her solitary corner; the veil, which she has been wearing all the time of the ceremony, is momentarily lifted from her face, and she is refreshed with a cup of coffee, into which she drops money as she gives it back; a male child is then placed on her knees for a short time. This formality is followed by a regular scramble for her stockings by a flock of children, who make a great rush towards her feet, pull off her boots and stockings, which they shake, in order to find the money previously placed in them.

The bride and bridegroom soon after open a round dance, and during its performance money is again thrown over their heads.

The bride is again led back to her corner, where she remains a mute and veiled image; sleeping at night with that awful plate on her head, and guarded by her maiden friends, who do not desert her until Wednesday evening, when the bridegroom is finally allowed to dine tete-a-tete with the bride. The only guests admitted that day to the family dinner are the priest and his wife; the latter passes the night in the house, and is commissioned the next morning to carry the tidings to the bride's mother that her daughter has happily entered upon the duties of married life.

At noon a luncheon is given to the relatives and friends, who collect to offer their congratulations.

On Saturday, the ceremony of kissing the hands of her mother and father-in-law is again gone through; the bridal veil on this occasion is replaced by one of crimson crepe, which she wears until her father-in-law gives her a present, and allows her to remove it. Brides are not allowed to utter a word in the presence of a near relative of their husbands, until permitted to do so by his father. This permission, however, is sometimes not easily obtained, and years may elapse before it is given. Many a young wife has gone to her grave without having spoken to her father and mother-in-law.

Though the Armenians are sensual and despotic, they generally make good husbands, but the standard of morality is getting lax among the emancipated followers of the customs a la Granca, who, being entirely ignorant of the rules of true breeding, often abuse the freedom of European manners.

AN ORIENTAL BARBER.

In the warm climate of the Orient, a multitude of avocations which, with us, are followed indoors, are performed in the open air. In the great bazars of Palestine, Syria and Asia Minor, a majority of the merchants have their wares exposed outdoors, and they, with possibly one or more assistants (whenever the establishment is of sufficient consequence to require more than a single attendant) ensconce themselves in some shady nook or recess, or beneath some dingy awning, while the purchaser leisurely strolls along and examines their wares. Great stocks of valuable shawls, wrappings of silk and woven stuffs, cotton and linen, silverware and gold, antiques in brass, copper and other metals, swords and all kinds of weapons, are sold in the open air in many shops of Damascus, Aleppo, Beyrout, Smyrna, Jerusalem and even Constantinople. Workmen ply their trade on the sidewalk in little tents or booths, skilled artisans in precious metals as well as the humble maker of sandals.

Not the least picturesque of these alfresco Oriental workmen is the barber, who may be frequently seen plying his calling in a picturesque fashion. In all Eastern countries the barber is a much respected social functionary. Yet shaving is by no means the comfortable luxury in the East that it is among the Western people. Our later civilization has introduced many luxurious accompaniments to the art tonsorial that are totally unknown in the East, where the same appliances are still employed that have been used for many centuries. An Oriental barber shop or booth is usually found on some street aside from the main thoroughfare. Here the white-robed and turbaned attendant waits upon his patron, seating him upon a chair or stool, not unlike a "tabourette," or diminutive table, such as is used in

Syrian and Turkish homes. Tying a large towel about the neck of the sitter, the barber is ready to begin. Usually an attendant holds a platter or water-dish while the operation is in progress. The upright position is not calculated to add to the comfort of the patron, but this is atoned for, to some extent, by the skill and deftness with which the razor is handled by the barber himself.

Certain classes in the East shave the head or at least a portion of its surface, at regular intervals, and others the face alone, while still others approximate more closely to the European style of toilet. Shaving the head was customary among the Hebrews as an act of mourning, and was probably performed much in the same manner as is now usual in those latitudes, the operator rubbing the scalp gently and comfortably with his fingers moistened with water for a considerable time, and afterward applying the razor and shaving from the crown downward.

With few exceptions, the ancient nations attached a great value to the possession of a beard. In Egypt, however, it was the common practice to shave the hair of the face and head. Herodotus mentions it as a peculiarity that they permitted the hair and beard to grow as a sign of mourning. It is supposed that, during their captivity, the Israelites preserved their beards. Assyrians, Amalekites, Canaanites and Arabians were all more or less bearded in early times. One of the very oldest traditions is that Adam was created with a beard.

Modern Mohammedans no longer regard the beard as a sacred thing, as once did the followers of Islam. Sultan

A NEWSPAPER REPORTER BEING PURSUED BY TURKISH SOLDIERS.

Selim, in the sixteenth century, shattered all traditions by shaving off his beard, and since those days the Moslem has become more and more latitudinarian in this respect, so that one today cannot tell, by the mere presence or absence of a beard, whether a man be Moslem or Christian.

CHAPTER XII.

OPINIONS OF DISTINGUISHED WRITERS.

THE CRY OF ARMENIA.

A Sermon by Rev. T. De Witt Talmage, D. D. Text: II Kings 19: 37, "They escaped into the land of Armenia."

In Bible geography this is the first time that Armenia appears, called then by the same name as now. Armenia is chiefly a table-land, 7000 feet above the level of the sea, and on one of its peaks Noah's ark landed, with its human family and fauna that were to fill the earth. That region was the birthplace of the rivers which fertilized the Garden of Eden when Adam and Eve lived there, their only roof the crystal skies, and their carpet the emerald of rich grass. Its inhabitants, the ethnologists tell us, are a superior type of the Caucasian race. Their religion is founded on the Bible. Their Saviour is our Christ. Their crime is that they will not become followers of Mahomet, that Jupiter of sensuality. To drive them from the face of the earth is the ambition of all Mohammedans. To accomplish this, murder is no crime, and wholesale massacre is a matter of enthusiastic approbation and governmental reward. The prayer sanctioned by highest Mohammedan authority, and recited every day throughout Turkey and Egypt, while styling all those not Mohammedans as infidels, is as follows: "O Lord of all creatures! O Allah! Destroy the infidels and polytheists, Thine enemies, the enemies of the religion! O Allah! Make their children orphans and defile their bodies; cause their feet to slip; give them and their families, their households and their women, their children, and their relatives by marriage, their brothers and their friends, their possessions and the race, their wealth and their lands as booty to the Moslems, O Lord of all creatures!" The life of an Armenian in the presence of those who make that prayer is of no more value than the life of a summer insect. The Sultan of Turkey sits on a throne impersonating that brigandage and assassination. At this time all civilized nations are in horror at the attempts of that Mohammedan government to destroy all the Christians of Armenia. I hear somebody talking as though some new thing were happening, and that the Turkish government had taken a new role of tragedy on the stage of nations. No, no! She is at the same old business. Overlooking her diabolism of other centuries, we come down to our century to find that in 1822 the Turkish government slew 50,000 anti-Moslems, and in 1850 she slew 10,000, and in 1860 she slew 11,000, and in 1876 she slew 10,000. Anything short of the slaughter of thousands of human beings does not put enough red wine into her cup of abomination to make it worth quaffing. Nor is this the only time she has promised reform. In the presence of the warships at the mouth of the Dardanelles, she has promised the civilized nations of the earth that she would stop her butcheries, and the international and hemispheric farce has been enacted of believing what she says, when all the past ought to persuade us that she is only pausing in her atrocities to put nations off the track and then resume the work of death. In 1820 Turkey, in treaty with Russia, promised to alleviate the condition of Christians, but the promise was broken. In 1839 the then Sultan promised protection of life and property without reference to religion, and the promise was broken. In 1844, at the demand of an English minister plenipotentiary, the Sultan declared, after the public execution of an Armenian at Constantinople, that no such death penalty should again be inflicted, and the promise was broken. In 1850, at the demand of foreign nations, the Turkish government promised protection to Protestants, but to this day the Protestants at Stamboul are not allowed to build a church, although they have the funds ready, and the Greek Protestants, who have a church, are not permitted to worship in it. In 1856, after the Crimean war, Turkey promised that no one should be hindered in the exercise of the religion he professed, and that promise has been broken. In 1878, at the memorable treaty of Berlin, Turkey promised religious liberty to all her subjects in every part of the Ottoman Empire, and the promise was broken. Not once in all the centuries has the Turkish government kept her promise of mercy. So far from any improvement, the condition of the Armenians has become worse and worse year by year, and all the promises the Turkish government now makes are only a gaining of time by which she is making preparations for the complete extermination of Christianity from her borders.

Why, after all the national and continental and hemispheric lying on the part of the Turkish government, do not the warships of Europe ride up as close as possible to the palaces of Constantinople and blow that accursed government to atoms? In the name of the Eternal God, let the nuisance of the ages be wiped off the face of the earth! Down to the perdition from which it smoked up, sink Mohammedanism! Between these outbreaks of massacre the Armenians suffer in silence wrongs that are seldom, if ever, reported. They are taxed heavily for the mere privilege of living, and the tax is called "the humiliation tax." They are compelled to give three days' entertainment to any Mohammedan tramp who may be passing that way. They must pay blackmail to the assessor, lest he report the value of their property too highly. Their evidence in court is of no worth, and if fifty Armenians saw a wrong committed and one Mohammedan was present, the testimony of the one Mohammedan would be taken and the testimony of the fifty Armenians rejected; in other words, the solemn oath of a thousand Armenians would not be strong enough to overthrow the perjury of one Mohammedan. A professor was condemned to death for translating the English Book of Common Prayer into Turkish. Seventeen Armenians were sentenced to fifteen years' imprisonment for rescuing a Christian bride from the bandits. This is the way the Turkish government amuses itself in time of peace. These are the delights of Turkish civilization. But when the days of massacre come, then deeds are done which may not be unveiled in any refined assemblage, and if one speaks of the horrors, he must do so in well-poised and cautious vocabulary. Hundreds of villages destroyed! Young men put in piles of brushwood, which are then saturated with kerosene and set on fire! Mothers, in the most solemn hour that ever comes in a woman's life, hurled out and bayonetted! Eyes gouged out, and dead and dying hurled into the same pit! The slaughter of Lucknow and Cawnpore, India, in 1857, eclipsed in ghastliness! The worst scenes of the French revolution in Paris made more tolerable in contrast! In many regions of Armenia the only undertakers are the jackals and hyenas. Many of the chiefs of the massacre were sent straight from Constantinople to do their work, and having returned, were decorated by the Sultan. To four of the worst murderers the Sultan sent silk banners, in delicate appreciation of their services. Look at this picture. It is a copy of a private letter from Armenia: "Rev. Grigos Hachadoovian, a minister of the gospel, whom I knew personally, was the pastor of the Second Congregational Church of Kharpoot, my native city. When the Turkish soldiers commenced shooting all over the city, he took his wife and children and went to the church; soon about sixty of his congregation joined him. Naturally good and earnest Christians, as they were, they lifted their voices up to heaven for help. While in prayer, the Turks rushed in and demanded of the minister to become a Mohammedan then and there, with his congregation. He refused promptly. The Turks removed the pulpit, made a butchering platform, cut off the head of the minister and actually cut him to pieces before his congregation: mind you, on the platform from which he had preached Christ for twenty years! This horrible spectacle seems to have had no effect upon the devout Christian Armenians, as they all re-

ARMENIAN PEASANT WOMEN WEAVING TURKISH CARPETS.
KURDISH BANDITS.

fused to denounce Christ and pray to Mahomet, and all were killed in the church to the last man, woman and child." What do you think of that picture, Christian people of America? That is the Mohammedanism some people would like to have introduced into our country.

Five hundred Thousand Armenians put to death or dying of starvation! This moment, while I speak, all up and down Armenia sit many people, freezing in the ashes of their destroyed homes, bereft of most of their households, and awaiting the club of assassination to put them out of their misery. No wonder that the physicians of that region declared that among all the men and women that were down with wounds and sickness and under their care, not one wanted to get well. Remember that nearly all the reports that have come to us of the Turkish outrages have been manipulated and modified and softened by the Turks themselves. The story is not half told, or a hundredth part told, or a thousandth part told. None but God and our suffering brothers and sisters in that far-off land know the whole story, and it will not be known until, in the coronation of heaven, Christ will lift to a special throne of glory these heroes and heroines, saying, "These are they who came out of great tribulation and had their robes washed and made white in the blood of the Lamb!" My Lord and my God! Thou didst on the cross suffer for them, but Thou surely, O Christ! wilt not forget how much they have suffered for Thee! I dare not deal in imprecation, but I never so much enjoyed the imprecatory Psalms of David as since I have heard how those Turks are treating the Armenians. The fact is, Turkey has got to be divided up among other nations. Of course, the European nations must take the chief part, but Turkey ought to be compelled to pay America for the American mission-buildings and American school-houses she has destroyed, and to support the wives and children of the Americans ruined by this wholesale butchery. When the English lion and the Russian bear put their paws on that Turkey, the American eagle ought to put in its-bill.

Who are these American and English and Scotch missionaries who are being hounded among the mountains of Armenia by the Mohammedans? The noblest men and women this side of heaven. Some of them men who took the highest honors at Yale and Princeton and Harvard and Oxford and Edinburgh. Some of them women, gentlest and most Christ-like, who, to save people they never saw, turned their backs on luxurious homes to spend their days in self-expatriation, saying good-by to father and mother, and afterward good-by to their own children, as circumstances compel them to send the little ones to England, Scotland or America. I have seen these foreign missionaries in their homes all around the world, and I stamp with indignation upon the literary blackguardism of foreign correspondents who have depreciated these heroes and heroines who are willing to live and die for Christ's sake. They will have the highest thrones in heaven, while their defamers will not get near enough to the shining gates to see the faintest glint of any one of the twelve pearls which make up the twelve gates. This defamation of missionaries is augmented by the dissolute English, American and Scotch merchants who go to foreign cities, leaving their families behind them. Those dissolute merchants in foreign cities lead a life of such gross immorals that the pure households of the missionaries are a perpetual rebuke. Buzzards never did believe in doves, and if there is anything that nightshade hates it is the water lily. What the 550 American missionaries have suffered in the Ottoman Empire since 1820 I leave the archangel to announce on the day of judgment. You will see it reasonable that I put so much emphasis on Americanism in the Ottoman Empire when I tell you that America, notwithstanding all the disadvantages named, has now over 27,000 students in day-schools in that empire, and 35,000 children in her Sabbath-schools, and that America has expended in the Turkish Empire for its betterment over $10,000,000. Has not America a right to be heard? Aye! It will be heard! I am glad that great indignation meetings are being held all over this country. That poor, weak, cowardly Sultan, whom I saw a few years ago ride to his mosque for worship, guarded by 7000 armed men, many of them mounted on prancing chargers, will hear of these sympathetic meetings for the Armenians, if not through American reporters, then through some of his 360 wives. What to do with him? There ought to be some St. Helena to which he could be exiled, while the nations of Europe appoint a ruler of their own to clean out and take possession of the palaces of Constantinople. Tonight this august assemblage in the capital of the United States, in the name of the God of Nations, indicts the Turkish government for the wholesale assassination in Armenia, and invokes the interference of Almighty God and the protest of Eastern and Western hemispheres.

The Turkish government has in every possible way hindered Armenian relief. Now, where is that angel of mercy, Clara Barton, who appeared on the battlefields of Fredericksburg, Antietam, Falmouth, and Cedar Mountain, and under the blaze of French and German guns at Metz and Paris and in Johnstown floods, and Charleston earthquake, and Michigan fires, and Russian famine? It was comparatively of little importance that the German emperor decorated her with the Iron Cross, for God hath decorated her in the sight of all nations with a glory that neither time nor eternity can dim. Born in a Massachusetts village, she came in her girlhood to this city to serve our government in the Patent Office, but afterwards went forth from the doors of that Patent Office, with a divine patent signed and sealed by God Himself, to heal all the wounds she could touch, and make the horrors of the flood, and fire, and plague, and hospital fly her presence. God bless Clara Barton! Just as I expected, she lifts the banner of the Red Cross. Turkey and all nations are pledged to respect and defend that Red Cross, although that color of cross does not, in the opinion of many, stand for Christianity. In my opinion, it does stand for Christianity, for was not the cross under which most of us worship red with the blood of the Son of God, red with the best blood that was ever shed, red with the blood poured out for the ransom of the world? Then lead on, O Red Cross! And let Clara Barton carry it! The Turkish government is bound to protect her, and the chariots of God are twenty thousand, and their charioteers are angels of deliverance, and they would all ride down at once to roll over and trample under the hoofs of their white horses any of her assailants. May the $500,000 she seeks be laid at her feet! Then may the ships that carry her across Atlantic and Mediterranean seas be guided safely by him who trod into sapphire pavement bestormed Galilee! Upon soil incarnadined with martyrdom, let the Red Cross be planted, until every demolished village shall be rebuilded, and every pang of hunger be fed, and every wound of cruelty be healed, and Armenia stand with as much liberty to serve God in its own way as in this the best land of all the earth, we, the descendants of the Puritans and Hollanders, and Huguenots, are free to worship the Christ who came to set all nations free!

It has been said that if we go over there to interfere on another continent, that will imply the right for other nations to interfere with affairs on this continent, and so the Monroe doctrine be jeopardized. No, no! President Cleveland expressed the sentiment of every intelligent and patriotic American when he thundered from the White House a warning to all nations, that there is not one acre or one inch more of ground on this continent for any transatlantic government to occupy. And by that doctrine we stand now and shall forever stand. But there is a doctrine as much higher than the Monroe doctrine as the heavens are higher than the earth, and that is the doctrine of humanitarianism and sympathy and Christian helpfulness which one cold December midnight, with loud and multitudinous chant, awakened the shepherds. Wherever there is a wound it is our duty, whether as individuals or as nations, to balsam it. Wherever there is a knife of assassination lifted it is our duty to ward off the blade. Wherever men are persecuted for their religion it is our duty to break that arm of power, whether it be thrust forth from a Protestant church or a Catholic cathedral or a Jewish synagogue or a mosque of Islam. We all recognize the right on a small scale. If going down the road, we find a ruffian maltreating a child, or a human brute insulting a woman, we take a hand in the contest if we are not cowards, and though we be slight in personal presence, because of our indignation we come to weigh about twenty tons, and the harder we punish the villain the louder our conscience applauds us. In such case we do not keep our hands in our pockets, arguing that if we interfere with the brute the brute might think he would have a right to interfere with us, and so jeopardize the Monroe doctrine. The fact is, that that persecution of the Armenians by the Turks must be stopped, or God Almighty will curse all Christendom for its damnable indifference and apathy. But the trumpet of resurrection is about to sound for Armenia. Did I say in opening that on one of the peaks of Armenia, this very Armenia of which we speak, in Noah's time the ark landed, according to the myth, as some think, but according to God's "say-so," as I know, and that it was after a long storm of forty days and forty nights, called the Deluge, and that afterwards a dove went forth from that ark and returned with an olive leaf in her beak? Even so now, there is another ark being launched, but this one goes sailing, not over a deluge of water, but a deluge of blood—the ark of American

sympathy—and that ark, landing on Ararat, from its window shall fly the dove of kindness and peace, to find the olive leaf of returning prosperity, while all the mountains of Moslem prejudice, oppression and cruelty shall stand fifteen cubits under. Meanwhile we would like to gather all the dying groans of all the 500,000 victims of Mohammedan oppression, and intone them into one prayer that would move the earth and the heavens, hundreds of millions of Christian voices, American and European, crying out, "O God Most High! Spare Thy children. With mandate from the throne hurl back upon their haunches the horses of the Kurdish cavalry. Stop the rivers of blood. With the earthquake of Thy wrath shake the foundations of the palaces of the Sultan. Move all the nations of Europe to command cessation of cruelty; if need be, let the warships of civilized nations boom their indignation. Let the Crescent go down before the Cross, and the Mighty One who hath on His vesture and on His thigh a name written 'King of Kings and Lord of Lords,' go forth, conquering and to conquer. Thine, O Lord, is the kingdom! Hallelujah! Amen!"

THE BLOT ON THE CENTURY.

By Francis E. Clark, D. D., President of the United Society of Christian Endeavor.

The Armenian problem is by no means a new one, though it has reached its acute stages only within the last three years. Had there been no atrocities in Sivas and Harpoot, no massacres in Marash and Cesarea, there would still be abundant reason for the indignant remonstrance of the civilized world, and for the interference of the great Powers in behalf of long-suffering Armenia.

The rule of the Turk is hopelessly and remedilessly bad wherever that rule extends. The mildew and blight of his occupation are found wherever the Star and Crescent wave. Just as truly as in the olden days, destruction and desolation were left in the wake of the victorious "horse-tails" of the triumphant Sultans, so now desolation and destruction are left in the retreating wake of the decadent and conquered Sultan.

The history of six hundred years teaches us that it is of little use to talk about mending the reign of the Turk. There is nothing left but to end it. To mend it is out of the question; to end it is the only hope for Moslem and Christian alike who dwell within the Sultan's domains.

We hear less about the tribulations of the Syrians and the Arabs of Palestine and other parts of the Levant than of the dreadful fate of the Armenians; but their troubles are none the less real, even if they do not so much excite the horror of the civilized world.

Throughout a large section of the fairest part of the earth's surface, enterprise and intellectual progress, to say nothing of religious freedom, have long been dead. In the fair lands which border on the Mediterranean, lands which should be the garden spots of the earth, there is, and has been for many generations, poverty, wretchedness and squalor, which can hardly be credited in lands that are better governed.

Naturally the character of the people has deteriorated, and a hopeless fatalism or cunning mendacity, which seeks to win by deceit what it cannot gain by fairer methods, have become characteristic of the people. In fact, whether we consider the character of the people, the soil on which they live, the houses that cover them, or the institutions by which they are misgoverned, we find that the trail of the Turk is over them all.

The traveler through Palestine cannot but be impressed by these facts; still more he who takes the overland journey across Asia Minor, where the Turk has had more full and undisputed sway.

He will find himself in a land of great natural resources and large possibilities; a land with a fertile soil, and exhaustless mines of precious metals, a land of rushing rivers and bold and rugged mountain scenery. When the Turk is deposed and some decent government establishes its sway in Asia Minor, we shall read of Cook's Parties and Gaze's Tourists in the magnificent land of the Taurus. The Cilician gates will be open to the traveler, though for many years they have been practically closed by the inefficient shiftlessness of a government which taxes the people to death for roads which are never built, and bridges which are never constructed.

Then the mines which, with their hidden treasures, have been sealed to all enterprise, will pour their wealth into the world's coffers. But now the Turk reasons, with characteristic phlegm, that so long as the mines are undisturbed the wealth of the nation is intact, and he does not propose to allow outer barbarians to come in and open up mines and cart off his treasures of gold and silver. This is carrying the stocking-leg theory of finance to its absurdest limits. To be sure, the traveler finds one feeble, struggling little railway on the Mediterranean coast of Turkey from Mersin to Adana, a distance of about forty miles. It was built by foreign capital, however, and is managed by foreign enterprise, and has been hampered and taxed almost off the face of the earth by the ruling Turk.

There is also a passable wagon road for Turkey for a few miles from Tarsus toward the Cilician gates; but this passable road soon runs into an almost impassable cart-track, the cart-track degenerates into a camel-path, and though the camel-path does not exactly "run up a tree," it seems to lose itself when it gets to the most inaccessible portions of the Taurus mountains, or at least is fit only for the sure-footed "ships of the desert" that continually traverse it with their swaying loads and their tinkling bells. The only bridges in many parts of the country are those built by the Romans 1800 years ago, so substantially and so scientifically that the war of the elements and the neglect of the Turk for twenty centuries has not been able to destroy them.

It should be said that this road, which starts from Tarsus, comes to light here and there during the hundreds of miles which lie between the birthplace of St. Paul and the ancient city of Angora, in old Galatia; but it as often gets lost again or is obstructed and rendered impassable by falling trees and descending boulders, which no one has energy enough to move out of the way. And yet this road is the excuse for wringing tens of thousands of pounds every year out of the poverty-stricken inhabitants. To be sure, the money is not expended upon the road, and every year it is falling into a more utterly impassable condition; but, no matter, it furnishes an excuse for yearly taxes and for more misgovernment.

There are no hotels in our sense of the word, or inns, even, of the humblest character, along this highway, which is the only artery between Constantinople and the Mediterranean ports; but there are stone huts called khans, in which men and bullocks and camels and asses may rest their wearied bodies in delightful promiscuity, while all are impartially attacked by other occupants that are not recorded in the census, and are not registered upon the books even of a Turkish khan.

For much of the distance along this highway every tree and shrub and root has been plucked up to furnish a little scanty fuel for the shivering inhabitants. The broad stretches of table-land, naturally fertile, are so poorly tilled with the rude implements of the past, that only a scanty population can be maintained, and these at "a poor dying rate," where millions might thrive under a good government.

The villages in the interior are for the most part built of sun-dried mud, though sometimes of stone, and are filthy and squalid beyond all description—dead sheep and donkeys and camels lying in the streets. I have myself counted in one street of a little village more than a dozen dead animals, which the inhabitants were too unenterprising to bury or to haul away.

Very naturally, all enterprise and energy are killed out of such a people by hundreds of years of misrule and oppression. Why should a man strive to get on in the world, when he knows that he will only make himself by his enterprise the special prey of the oppressor? Why should he plant an orchard of superior fruit, when he knows that the tax-gatherer will get the best of it? Why should he try to improve his worldly condition in any way, when he knows that unless he can cover up his wealth and simulate poverty, he will but become the target for every corrupt and unscrupulous official?

The land of Turkey has been picked bare; even the pin feathers of enterprise, if we may be excused the expression, have been singed off by a rapacious officialism during many generations.

And now these centuries of atrocious misrule and almost inconceivable corruption are crowned by the murder and the pillage and the wholesale massacres, which have caused the blood of civilization to run cold, outrages that will mark the years of 1895-96 with such blots as no other years have known for many centuries. Yet the civilized world allows the great Powers, each disarmed against the Turk by their mutual jealousies, to look on supinely while the butchery in Armenia never ceases. Still the Queen's speech, read at the opening of Parliament in the year 1896, talks gingerly about the Sultan's promises to institute reforms, while very likely, at the very moment when her speech was read, the Sultan's hirelings were murdering Christians, pillaging their property and firing their villages!

What will our grandchildren think of the boasted civilization of the nineteenth century? How will the people of the happier age which is to come look back with shuddering horror, not only upon the deeds enacted in Turkey, but with scarcely less horror, upon the Christian nations, who by reason of their insane jealousy of one another, permitted those atrocities, which they might have prevented.

Alas, that this century should be known not only as the century of invention and discovery, of the railway and the steamship, and the telegraph and the telephone, the century of religious progress and missionary enterprise, the century of the Sunday-school, and the young people's movements, but also the century stained with the deepest dye of Christian blood and of which the great Christian Powers can never wash their hands!

God grant that before the record of the century is closed, before the Armenians are utterly exterminated, and no faithful Christians in Asia Minor are left to rescue, Europe and America may awake to their responsibilities and tardily save themselves from the reproachful scorn of future generations.

THE TYRANT TURK AND THE CRAVEN STATESMEN.

By Frances E. Willard, President of the Woman's Christian Temperance Union.

An ancient nation is being slowly slaughtered at the foot of Mt. Ararat, 50,000 victims stretched out under God's sky in the slow circle of a year; women, pure, devout and comely, suffering two deaths—a living and a dying death; little children poised on the bayonets of Moslem soldiers, villages burned and starvation the common lot.

On the other hand, Christian Europe, with 7,000,000 soldiers, who take their rations and their sacrament regularly; statesmen, who kneel on velvet cushions in beautiful cathedrals, and pray, "We beseech Thee to hear us, good Lord;" diplomatists who can "shape the whisper of a throne" and shade the meaning of an ultimatum; but neither statesman, diplomat nor soldier has wit, wisdom or will to save a single life, shelter a single tortured babe, or supply a single loaf of bread to the starving Christians on the Armenian hillsides; "vested interests" are against it, "the balance of power" does not permit it, the will of the Sultan is the only will in the Empire of Turkey, and all the wills of all the Christian nations cannot move it one hair.

The Turk is a savage, while the statesmen are—over-civilized; he is a tyrant, while they are—craven cowards.

Meanwhile a star moves towards the East; it caught its light from the Star of Bethlehem. One woman, well nigh seventy years of age, takes her life in her hands and goes forward to the rescue; she goes to bind up wounds, to give out bread, to light the fires on blackened hearthstones, to put hope into broken hearts. She is a greater power today for God and brotherhood than all the statesmen, diplomatists and soldiers. The world's eyes follow her with love; they cannot see her plainly for tears.

Did our Heavenly Father overrule the wickedness of leaders to put before humanity an object lesson, on the broadest scale, of the futility of force and the omnipotence of love?

WHAT I WOULD DO.

By Senator Frye, of Maine.

At the last session of the last Congress two missionaries appeared here from Armenia, both of whom I knew personally, one of whom was formerly a resident of my own city, and stated the grievances, the troubles, the massacres, their fears. They were asked what was the remedy, and they said to the committee that, in their judgment, if a consulate could be established at Erzeroum and another at Harpoot and consuls appointed, then there would be no trouble in that great interior, because the eye of America would then be upon it. In less than a week after that the Committee on Foreign Relations reported a bill establishing two consulates, one at Erzeroum and the other at Harpoot, and it became a law. The President of the United States appointed the consuls.

Surely, the committee and Congress did everything then as expeditiously as anybody could ask, and did exactly what these missionaries desired should be done. Turkey refused exequaturs to those two consuls. I do not know what the executive department has done as to that refusal. I do not know what the executive department can do as to it; but it seems to me that some pressure ought to be brought somehow, that when there can be no objection to the persons of the consuls appointed exequaturs shall be granted.

Now, consider this incident. If that consul had been received by Turkey, had gone to Harpoot, a consulate building had been provided for, and an American flag raised, more than 20,000 lives would have been saved. One of the most terrible massacres perpetrated in Turkey anywhere took place at that point.

The good people of the United States have planted in Turkey over $6,000,000 for a single purpose, to improve and better the condition of the people of that country. They have erected as fine colleges as there are in the world. They have been maintained by American money. They have educated thousands of Turks, or Armenians, who are subject to Turkey. It has been a work of wonderful beneficence, a work which has had marvelous success, and yet it is stopped absolutely today. That American capital now is held up; it cannot do an ounce of work. At Harpoot the American colleges were burned down, and the Americans themselves were compelled to flee for their lives.

I do not know how far the United States of America can interfere in Turkey. I am in favor of these resolutions as an expression of our opinion upon the awful tragedies there; but if I had had my way, after the powers of Europe have waited now a solid year looking each other in the face with suspicious eyes and neither one daring to make a move lest the other shall receive a benefit—I say if I had had my way, I would have Congress memorialize Russia and say to her: "Take Armenia into your possession. Protect the lives of these Christians there. And the United States of America will stand behind you with all of its power." That is the memorial and resolution I would have passed.

American citizens are suffering there. I care not what our Minister reports to the State Department. I know from better opportunity to learn it than Minister Terrell has or can have; that is, from the headquarters of the foreign missions of the United States of America, where information is received by every mail, and where the information is absolutely accurate, but where the informants dare not have their names known because their lives would immediately pay the penalty.

Now, so far as American citizens are concerned, I would protect them there at any cost. We never agreed that the Dardanelles should be closed to us. There cannot be found a line in the policy of the United States of America which ever permitted any great navigable water to be closed to our ships; not one. On the contrary, we have been ready to go to war at any time to keep navigable waters open to our ships. We have given no assent to the agreement of the concerting nations over there that the Dardanelles shall be closed. If it was necessary to protect our American citizens and their property, I would order United States ships of war, in spite of foreign agreements, to sail up the Dardanelles and plant themselves before Constantinople, and then demand that American citizens should have the protection they are entitled to.

I think one of the grandest things in the history of Great Britain, and one thing for which I admire her, is that she does protect her citizens everywhere and anywhere, under all circumstances. Her mighty power is put forth for their relief and protection, and it is admirable. I do not wonder that a British citizen loves his country. Why, that little incident which all of you are familiar with is a marvelous illustration of that. The King of Abyssinia took a British citizen of the name of Campbell, about twenty years ago, carried him up into the fortress of Magdala, on the heights of a lofty mountain, and put him into a dungeon without cause. It took six months for Great Britain to find that out, and then she demanded his immediate release. King Theodore refused to release him. In less than ten days after the refusal was received 3000 British soldiers and 5000 sepoys were on board ships of war sailing for the coast. When they arrived, they were disembarked, were marched 700 miles over swamp and morass under a burning sun, then up the mountain to the very heights, in front of the frowning dungeon, and then they gave battle. They battered down the iron gates, the stone walls. King Theodore had killed himself with his own pistol. Then they reached down into the dungeon, with that English hand, lifted out from it that one British citizen, and carried him down the mountain heights, across the same swamps and morass, landed him on the white-winged ships, and sped him away to his home in safety. That cost Great Britain $25,000,000 and made General Napier Lord Napier of Magdala.

That was a great thing for a great country to do. A country that has an eye that can see away across an ocean, away across the many miles of land up into the mountain heights, down into the darksome dungeon one, just one, of her 38,-

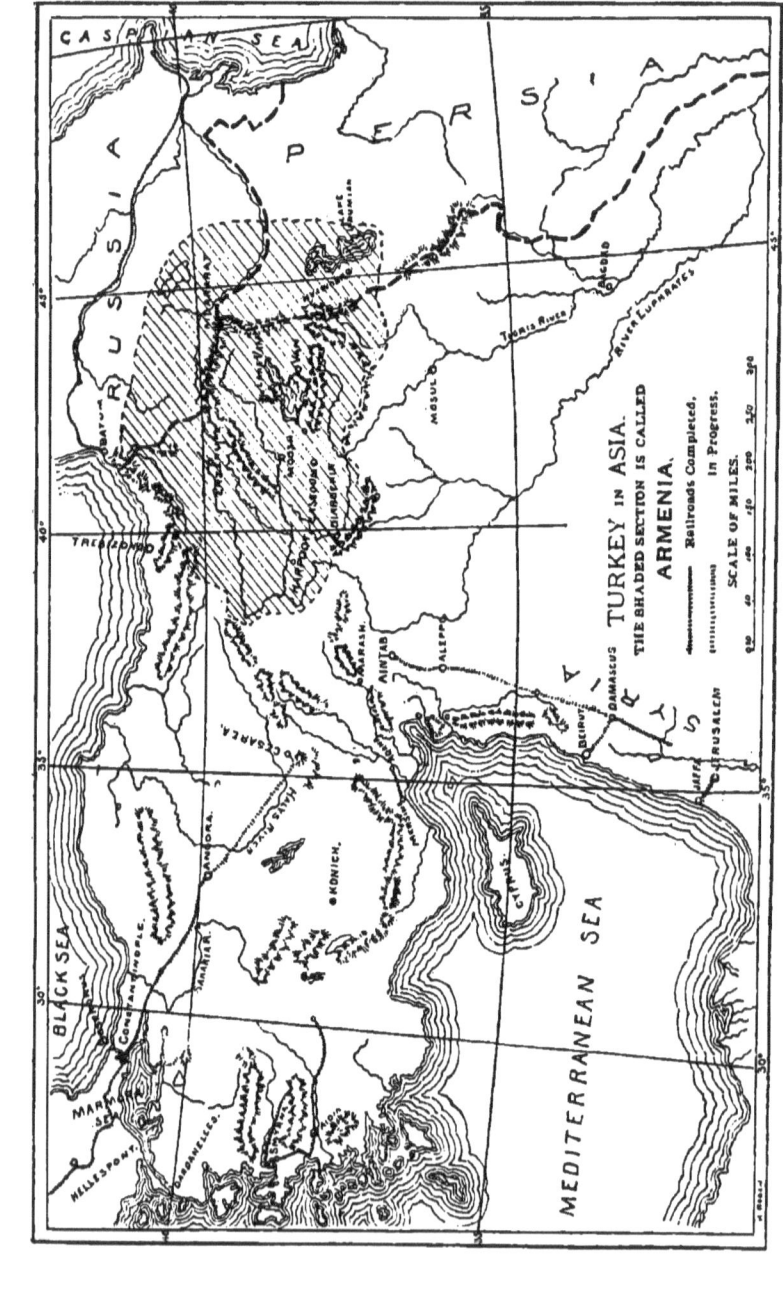

000,000 people, and then has an arm strong enough and long enough to reach across the same ocean, across the same swamps and marshes, up the same mountain heights, down into the same dungeon, and pluck him out and carry him home to his own country a free man—in God's name, who will not die for a country that will do that?

Our country will do it, and our country ought to do it. All that I ask of this grand republic of ours is that it shall model itself after Great Britain, if it pleases, in this one thing, that the life of an American citizen shall be protected wherever he may be, whether in Great Britain or in Turkey, and in no other thing whatsoever.

CHAPTER XIII.

THE ARMENIAN OUTRAGES.

By United States Senator Shelby M. Cullom, of Illinois.

Mr. Collum reported on January 24, 1896, the following resolutions to the Senate, and also made a speech in favor of their adoption. This speech, with some changes, which he has kindly sent, is as follows:

Whereas the supplementary treaty of Berlin, July 13, 1878, between the Ottoman Empire and Great Britain, Germany, Austria, France, Italy and Russia, contains the following provisions:

"LXI. The Sublime Porte undertakes to carry out without further delay the ameliorations and reforms demanded by local requirements in the provinces inhabited by the Armenians, and to guarantee their security against the Circassians and Kurds.

"It will periodically make known these steps taken to this effect to the powers, and will superintend their application.

"LXII. The Sublime Porte, having expressed the wish to maintain the principle of religious liberty, to give it the widest scope, the contracting parties take note of this spontaneous declaration.

"In no part of the Ottoman Empire shall difference of religion be alleged against an individual as a ground for exclusion or incapacity as regards the discharge of civil and political rights, admission to the public service, functions, and honors, and the exercise of the different professions and industries.

"All persons shall be admitted, without distinction of religion, to give evidence before the tribunals.

"Liberty and the outward exercise of all forms of worship are assured to all, and no hindrance shall be offered either to the hierarchial organization of the various communions or to their relations with their spiritual chiefs.

"The right of official protection by the diplomatic and consular agents of the powers in Turkey is recognized both as regards the above-mentioned persons and their religious, charitable, and other establishments in the holy places;" and

Whereas the extent and object of the above-cited provisions of said treaty are to place the Christian subjects of the Porte under the protection of the other signatories thereto, and to secure to such Christian subjects full liberty of religious worship and belief, the equal benefit of the laws, and all the privileges and immunities belonging to any subjects of the Turkish Empire; and

Whereas by said treaty the Christian powers parties thereto having established, under the consent of Turkey, their right to accomplish and secure the above-recited objects; and

Whereas the American people, in common with all Christian people everywhere, have beheld with horror the recent appalling outrages and massacres of which the Christian population of Turkey have been made the victims:

Resolved by the Senate of the United States (the House of Representatives concurring), That it is an imperative duty, in the interest of humanity, to express the earnest hope that the European concert brought about by the treaty referred to may speedily be given its just effect in such decisive measures as shall stay the hand of fanaticism and lawless violence, and as shall secure to the unoffending Christians of the Turkish Empire all the rights belonging to them both as men and Christians and as beneficiaries of the explicit provisions of the treaty above recited.

Resolved, That the President be requested to communicate these resolutions to the governments of Great Britain, Germany, Austria, France, Italy and Russia.

Resolved further, That the Senate of the United States, the House of Representatives concurring, will support the

President in the most vigorous action he may take for the protection and security of American citizens in Turkey, and to obtain redress for injuries committed upon the persons or property of such citizens.

I am astounded and appalled at the brief accounts which I have had of the awful carnival of havoc, destruction and blood which has prevailed for a time in a country with which the United States maintains amicable relations. The concurrent and accumulated testimony of hundreds and thousands of intelligent, humane, honest and courageous Christians and Jews alike, Catholics and Protestants, Europeans and Americans, makes it absolutely certain as a dreadful truth that a massacre of innocence unparalleled for ages has been perpetrated in the Armenian provinces of Turkey. How can we believe that in 1894 and 1895, along the very borders of the land where scriptural history was made, and where the patriarchs of old fed their flocks, almost in sight of Hermon and Lebanon, and only a short journey from Bethlehem, the most gigantic and brutal enormities have been committed upon a wholly unoffending people?

We believe, without questioning, those words which have long been part of our religion, that "of one blood God made all the nations of the earth," but I confess that my faith is somewhat shattered in the accepted belief when I see the soldiers of an organized and recognized government, where there is no war and no enemy, killing, bayoneting and outraging an unarmed and unoffending people—a Turkish army, under the pay of the Turkish government, composed of Circassians, Kurds and other barbarian soldiers, led through the rural and pastoral districts to devastate and destroy every living thing, to rob, to murder and flay alive, old and young, male and female. Destruction and rapine have been and now are the orders obeyed in the beautiful valleys and on the rugged hills of Armenia. There has been no war, no conflict between two contending powers, but a merciless, pitiless tornado of bloody ruin. Over many square miles of territory, fire and the sword have swept the last vestige of Armenian human life. Through hundreds of Eastern villages, towns blessed with schools and colleges, with churches and missionaries, the demon of damnable and fanatical hate has spread ruin, desolation and death.

Has it come to this, that in the last days of the nineteenth century humanity itself is placed on trial? There is responsibility somewhere. There is to be retribution some time. Who is responsible? Not alone the poor, weak, slavish Sultan who sits at Constantinople, and has been forced to let Austria manage one province and to permit other nations to manage and govern other provinces. But there are what we know as the great powers of Europe, who have practically determined that they will not allow Turkey to abdicate her autonomy until they can agree among themselves as to how her territory shall be apportioned between themselves. In my judgment, if Great Britain had consented that Russia should look after Armenia, as Austria has been permitted to control Bosnia for some years, this era of blood would not have stained the history of Europe. But the fear that Russia might obtain some greater share of the "sick man's" estate than herself caused England to prevent the establishment of decent government in Armenia.

But without going into the detail of the disputes between the countries of the European alliance, it is not wrong to say that upon those great powers rests the responsibility. They have for years practically "held up" the Turkish government and allowed her to say nothing and do nothing which they did not direct. They could have in six days put a perfect and absolute stop to the reign of death. They are responsible for the policy which has allowed this. The Turk is the puppet in their hands, and his soldiers and people are but the toys of their will and pleasure.

I favor the adoption of the resolutions reported from the Committee on Foreign Relations in reference to the condition of affairs in the Turkish Empire. It is a matter of some embarrassment to this nation that it cannot, consistent with its declarations in the past, consent to send a fleet and an army to that country with orders to use whatever power may be necessary to put a stop at once to the indiscriminate murder and slaughter of all classes of Armenians who have so far offered practically no resistance.

As I have shown, a condition of affairs has for some time past existed in the Armenian portion of Turkey so appalling to the human heart that it is scarcely fit to be told. The Committee on Foreign Relations are not disposed to sit idly by and take no notice of such condition. They have, therefore, reported certain resolutions, reciting in connection with them certain provisions of the treaty made between the Ottoman Empire, Great Britain, Germany, Austria, France,

ARMENIAN VILLAGERS PURSUED BY KURDS.

Italy and Russia, which would seem almost sufficient to excuse any other nation from having anything to say with reference to the conditions existing in Turkey.

The treaty of 1878, made between the powers as above indicated, substantially obligates those powers to see to it that the Ottoman Empire shall in no way interfere with any class of its subjects on the ground of difference of religion. In that treaty the Ottoman Empire bound itself to make no distinctions for any reason whatever between one class of its subjects and another, and the combined powers in effect obligated themselves to give protection to the Armenian portion of that country, guaranteeing the same against any imposition by the Porte or any other authority in the Turkish Empire.

The people of the United States are intensely excited over the condition of affairs reported to exist in that country. It cannot be questioned that such condition is well known to the Allied Powers, and yet, so far as we are informed, nothing has been done, except by diplomatic correspondence, to stop the further slaughter of innocent people or to care for the hundreds of thousands of Armenians who have been left homeless, helpless and starving. The purpose of the resolutions reported and under consideration is to plead with great earnestness to those Allied Powers who have undertaken to care for those people to put a stop to such brutality as is practiced upon them by the Circassians and Kurds; and not entirely without the help or connivance of the Turkish soldiers themselves.

The sixty-first article of the treaty referred to recites that the Sublime Porte undertakes to carry out the ameliorations and reforms demanded by the local requirements in the provinces inhabited by the Armenians, and to guarantee their security against the Circassians and Kurds.

The Sultan appears to have done nothing to protect the Armenians from those savage robbers and murderers, but it is believed, and I think correctly, by the Christian world, that the Sultan is knowingly allowing such slaughter to go on, the object being, it is said, to so reduce the Armenian population that they will no longer be of sufficient consequence to give him any concern.

It is unnecessary for me to say that it is amazing to the people of this country, at least, to witness such a terrible slaughter of those innocent people, and at the same time witness the apparent indifference manifested by the powers who agreed to see that they were protected.

Before the treaty of Berlin was entered into by the great powers in 1878, Great Britain announced its own treaty of defense with the Porte, which, it is said, caused a great sensation among the Allied Powers. This treaty between Turkey and England provides that England was to join His Imperial Majesty the Sultan in defending certain portions of his territory against any future attempt on the part of Russia to take possession of the same, and the Sultan promised England to introduce the necessary reforms, to be agreed upon between the two powers, in his government, and for the protection of the Christian and other subjects of the Sultan. As a guarantee of good faith, the Sultan consented to the occupation by England of the island of Cyprus. That compact was secretly signed at Constantinople on the 4th day of June, 1878, only a few days before the congress convened at Berlin to make the treaty of 1878.

So that the English government, making greater pretensions to the observance of the rights of the people than perhaps any other government in Europe, has an additional obligation resting upon it to protect the Armenians in Turkey, and yet nothing has been done by it, notwithstanding this double obligation resting upon it, nor by any of the other powers looking to the enforcement of their treaty obligations beyond a mere diplomatic correspondence between them and the Sultan.

So it seemed to the Committee on Foreign Relations that we could not do less, that we could not say less, by way of a recital of the obligations of the Allied Powers to protect those people, and an appeal to them to carry out their pledges, than we have done by the resolution which is now under consideration.

It may be proper for me to say that yesterday dispatches came from that country, saying that Turkey and Russia had made a treaty, by which Russia was to dominate Turkey and hold it as a vassal. I see, however, what I anticipated might be true, that the former dispatches have been substantially denied this morning. So the condition prevails that these several allied powers, having taken upon themselves practically the special right, if such a right could be conferred, to protect the Armenians by name, consisting of over 2,000,000 in European Turkey and more than 1,500,000 in Asiatic Turkey, have, notwithstanding that obligation, permitted the indiscriminate slaughter which has been going on there for the last year, to say nothing of what occurred before that time, almost distancing any description of slaughter in the history of the world. I do not myself believe that there can be found in all the history of the world such a condition as has existed in that country for the last year and a half.

The heart of all Christendom is stirred to its very depths as it witnesses the piteous pleas of the suffering Armenians beseeching the Christian world to give them protection.

I said that nothing had been done by the combined powers looking to putting a stop to the murder of the Armenians since the treaty of 1878, aside from mere diplomatic protests. I ought to say that some eight months ago a scheme of reform for the Armenian provinces was presented to the Sultan by the English, French and Russian governments, which was sanctioned October 17, 1895, by imperial irade for the provinces of Bitlis, Diarbekir, Seevas, Erzeroum, Van and Harpoot. These provinces cover the region where the majority of the Armenians reside. Since the sanction by the Sultan of this proposed reform, wholesale slaughter and plunder have been perhaps more frequent than before.

It is unnecessary for me to detail the history of what has been going on at any greater length; but it would seem, from all the information that can be obtained, that there has been a determination on the part of the Sultan of Turkey to allow the Armenian population to be almost exterminated. It appears to be an assault upon the Armenians because of their religion. The religious leaders of those engaged in the indiscriminate slaughter which has been carried on incite the people to action by crying from the housetops: "Woe to the Mussulman who does not kill at least one Christian and carry away some of their belongings, in the name of Mahomet and His Imperial Majesty the Sultan."

This country of ours may be said to be a neutral government, so far as interference with the internal affairs of any government in Europe is concerned. It has no disposition to interfere in the affairs of European governments, except in the cause of humanity itself. And we now appeal most earnestly, in the name of humanity, to the governments which have contracted to protect those people, that they shall carry out their obligations. As to the right of this government to protect American citizens everywhere we ask no odds from any nation upon earth.

In earlier days, the crusaders from Western Europe swarmed over this very country in their misguided efforts to establish religion through the agency of the sword. Of late it has seemed almost necessary to inaugurate another crusade in the interest of peace and humanity, that possibly a few people might be saved from a nation numbering about 4,000,000 in all. They are greater in number than were the people of the American colonies in the days of the American Revolution. Is it necessary, in the economy of the civilized governments of Europe, that the blood of 4,000,000 people shall be spilled, that it shall water the soil of that vast area of country?

The sympathy of America has always gone out to the oppressed and misgoverned peoples of other countries. We extended our hands and gave of our means to Greece when

Turkey, years ago, strove to crush her to the earth. We sympathized with Hungary and did what we could to relieve the people there when they were held in bonds and difficulties.

I cannot refrain from giving here the thrilling words of our great Webster, in an address referring to the affairs of Hungary. He said:

"I see that the Emperor of Russia demands of Turkey that the noble Kossuth and his companions shall be given up to be dealt with at his pleasure, and I see that this demand is made in derision of the established laws of nations.

"Gentlemen, there is something on earth greater than arbitrary or despotic power. The lightning has its power, the whirlwind has its power, and the earthquake has its power; but there is something among men more capable of shaking despotic power than the lightning, the whirlwind or the earthquake, and that is the excited and aroused indignation of the whole civilized world."

I know of no condition which has existed in this world for centuries which has called upon civilized nations and peoples for interference equaling the necessity for stopping the indiscriminate slaughter which has been going on in Turkish Armenia.

ARMENIANS BEING SENT AWAY TO EXILE.

CHAPTER XIV.

THE CONDITION OF ARMENIA.

By E. J. Dillon.

[The "Condition of Armenia" was originally prepared by Mr. Dillon and published in the Contemporary Review, and no one is more competent to speak with authority on this subject. He was sent as special commissioner by the Daily Telegraph, London, to write articles for this paper on the condition of Armenia. He has a wide reputation as a careful and graphic writer, and his letters to the Telegraph, and this article in the Contemporary Review, were accepted as authority by such men as Mr. Gladstone, Canon MacColl, Bishop of Chester, Bishop of Hereford and many other eminent men of England.

The article attracted widespread attention, and possibly we would be unable to give a better and more graphic account of the condition of Armenia than pictured by Mr. Dillon; and that he has not overdrawn the condition of affairs has been completely confirmed and established by the inquiries of the delegates appointed by the three Powers, England, France and Russia. The article has been abridged.—Ed.]

Turkey's real sway in Armenia dates from the year 1847, when Osman Pasha gave the final coup de grace to the secular power of the Kurdish Derebeks in the five southeastern provinces (Van, Bitlis, Moush, Bayazed and Diarbekir). During that long spell of nearly fifty years, we can clearly distinguish two periods: one of shameful misgovernment (1847-1891), and the other (1892-1894) of frank extermination. This plain policy of extermination has been faithfully carried out and considerably extended from that day to this, and unless speedily arrested will undoubtedly lead to a final solution of the Armenian problem. But a solution which will disgrace Christianity and laugh civilization to scorn. The enlisted Kurds were left in their native places, exempted from service, supplied with arms, invested with the inviolability of ambassadors, and paid with the regularity characteristic of the Sublime Porte.

The massacre of Sassoun itself is now proved to have been the deliberate deed of the representatives of the Sublime Porte, carefully planned and unflinchingly executed in spite of the squeamishness of Kurdish brigands and the fitful gleams of human nature that occasionally made themselves felt in the hearts even of Turkish soldiers.

An eminent foreign statesman, who is commonly credited with Turcophile sentiments of uncompromising thoroughness, lately remarked to me in private conversation that Turkish rule in Armenia might be aptly described as organized brigandage, legalized murder and meritorious immorality.

The first step in carrying out the plan of extermination was the systematic impoverishment of the people. This is natural in a country whose officials are kept waiting eight or ten months for their salaries, and must then content themselves with but a fraction of what is due. "I have not received a para* for the past twenty weeks, and I cannot buy even clothes," exclaimed the official who was told off to "shadow" me day and night in Erzeroum. "Do they pay you your salary regularly?" I inquired of the head of the telegraph office at Kutek. "No, Effendi, not regularly," he replied; "I have not had anything now for fully eight months. Oh yes, I have; a month's salary was given to me at Bairam." "How

*A Turkish coin. Forty paras are equivalent to twopence.

do you manage to live, then?" "Poorly." "But you must have some money to go on with, or else you could not keep body and soul together?" "I have a little, of course, but not enough. Allah is good. You have now given me some money yourself." "Yes, but that is not for you; it is for telegrams, and belongs to the State." "Well, my shadow will have grown considerably less before the State beholds the gleam of it. I keep for myself all money paid in by the public. I take it as instalments of my salary. It does not amount to very much. But whatever it happens to be, I pocket it." These men are, of course, petty officials, but their case is not essentially different from that of the majority of their betters, and judges, officers, deputy-governors and valis, etc., are to the full as impecunious and incomparably more greedy.

Tahsin Pasha, the late Governor-General of Bitlis, is a fair specimen of the high Turkish dignitary of the epoch of extermination. An avaricious skinflint, he was as cruel as Ugolino's enemy, Ruggieri, and as cold as Captain Maleger in Spenser's "Fairy Queen." He cultivated a habit of imprisoning scores of wealthy Armenians, without any imputed charge or show of pretext. Liberty was then offered them in return for exorbitant sums representing the greater part of their substance. Refusal to pay was followed by treatment compared with which the torture of the Jews in mediaeval England, or the agonies of the eunuchs of the princesses of Oude in modern India, were mild and salutary chastisements. Some men were kept standing up all day and night, forbidden to eat, drink or move. If they lost strength and consciousness cold water or hot irons soon brought them round, and the work of coercion continued. Time and perseverance being on the side of the Turks, the Armenians generally ended by sacrificing everything that made life valuable for the sake of exemption from maddening pain. It was a case of sacrificing or being sacrificed, and that which seemed the lesser of the two evils was invariably chosen.

In the Vilayet of Bitlis several hundred Armenians who possessed money, cattle or crops were arbitrarily imprisoned and set free on the payment of large bribes. Some of them, unable to produce the money at once, were kept in the noisome dungeons until they raised the sum demanded, or were released by death. About 100 Armenian prisoners died in the prison of Bitlis alone. The following petition, signed and sent to me—and if I mistake not, also to the foreign delegates at Moush—from a well-known man, whose name and address I publish, will help to convey some idea of how the Vali of Bitlis governed his province and prospered the while: "We, who have served the Turkish government with absolute loyalty, are maltreated and oppressed, more particularly of late years, now by the government itself, now by Kurdish brigands. Thus last year (1894) I was suddenly arrested at my own house by Turkish police and gendarmes, who escorted me to the prison of Bitlis, where I was insulted and subjected to the most horrible tortures. Having been kept four months there, I was released on condition of paying £450, by way of ransom. No reason, no pretext, has been given for this treatment. On my return home, I found my house in disorder, my affairs ruined, my means gone. My first thought was to appeal to the Turkish government for redress, but I shrank from doing so, lest I should be condemned again. Hearing that you have come to Armenia for the purpose of investigating the condition of the people, I venture to request you, in God's name, to take notice of the facts in my case. Signed, Boghos Darmanian, of the village of Iknakhodja of the Kaza of Manazkerd."

In 1890, the village elder of Odandjor in Boolanyk, Abdal by name, was a wealthy man, as wealth goes in that part of the world. He possessed 50 buffaloes, 80 oxen, 600 sheep, besides horses, etc. The women of his family wore golden ornaments in their hair and on their breast, and he paid £50 a year in taxes to the treasury. In 1894 he was a poverty-stricken peasant, familiar with misery and apprehensive of death from hunger. His village and those of the entire district had been plundered, and the inhabitants stripped, so to say, naked, the Turkish authorities smiling approval the while.

In July, 1892, a captain of His Majesty's Hamidieh cavalry, Idris by name, an ornament of the Hassnanlee tribe, came with his brother to demand a contribution of fodder from the inhabitants of Hamsisheikh. They accosted two of the Armenian notables, Alo and Hatchadoor, and ordered them to provide the hay required. "We do not possess such a quantity in the whole village," they replied. "Produce the hay without more ado, or I'll shoot you dead," exclaimed Idris. "But it does not exist, and we cannot create it." "Then die," said the gallant captain, and shot them dead on the spot. A formal complaint was lodged against Idris, and the Kaimakam, to his credit, arrested him and kept him in prison for four weeks, when the valiant Kurd, having paid the usual bribe, was set at liberty. About thirty similar murders were committed in the same district of Boolanyk during that season, with the same publicity and the same impunity.

At first the Armenians were wont to complain when their relatives or friends were killed, in the hope that in some cases the arm of the law might be raised to punish the murderers and thus produce a deterrent effect upon others who might feel disposed to go and do likewise. But they were very soon weaned of this habit by methods the nature of which may be gathered from the following incident: In July, 1892, a Kurd named Ahmed Ogloo Batal rode over to Govandook (district of Khnouss) and drove off four oxen belonging to an Armenian named Mookho. In 1892 the law forbidding Christians to carry arms was not yet strictly observed, and Mookho, possessing a revolver, and seeing that the Kurd was about to use his, fired. Both weapons went off at once and both men fell dead on the spot. What then happened was this: Nineteen Armenians of the village, none of whom had any knowledge of what had occurred, were arrested and put in jail and told that they would be released on payment of a heavy bribe. Ten paid it and were set free at once. The remainder, refusing, were kept in prison for a long time afterwards. None of the Kurds were molested. "Why should Mohammedans be punished for killing Armenians?" asked a Kurdish brigand who was also a Hamidieh officer, of me. "It is unheard of."

In August, 1893, the Djibranlee Kurds attacked the village

A GROUP OF VILLAGERS, ARMENIA.

A HARVEST SCENE.

of Kaghkik, plundered it, and wounded a merchant named Oannes, who was engaged in business in his shop. Next day Oannes went to the deputy-governor (Kaimakam) in Khnoussaberd, and lodged a complaint, whereupon the Kaimakam put him in prison for "lying." The sufferings inflicted upon him in that hotbed of typhoid fever exceed belief—but that is another story. After eight days his neighbors brought a Kurd before the Kaimakam who bore out their evidence that Oannes had been really wounded in the manner described, and that he was not lying. Then, and then only, the authorities allowed the people to pay a bribe of £10 for the release of the wounded man.

There is no redress whatever for a Christian who has suffered in property, limb, or life at the hands of Mohammedans; not because the law officers are careless or lethargic, but because they are specially retained on the other side. And the proof of this, if any proof were needed, is that the complainants themselves are speedily punished for lodging an information against their persecutors. But whenever a Kurd or a Turk is the victim of a "crime," or even an accident, the energy of the government officials knows no bounds. In the spring of last year, when the snows were thawing and the waters rose high in the rivers and streams, some needy Kurds were moving along the bank of the river, hard by Hussnakar. They were wretched beggars, asking alms, and battling with fate. In an attempt to ford the river they were carried away and drowned. Forthwith the villagers were accused of having murdered them, and four Armenian notables were arrested and imprisoned in Hassankaleh on this trumpery charge, the real object of which was not disguised. After the lapse of seven or eight months the villagers were told that on payment of a bribe of £75 the prisoners would be discharged. The money had to be scraped together and paid to the authorities, whereupon the men were released. I saw two of them, Atam and Dono, myself.

To give a fair instance of the different rates of taxation for Christians and Mohammedans in towns, it will suffice to point out that in Erzeroum, where there are 8000 Mohammedan houses, the Moslems pay only 395,000 piastres, whereas the Christians, whose houses number but 2000, pay 430,000 piastres.

In the country districts everything without exception is highly taxed by the government, and the heaviest burden of this legal exaction is light when compared with the extortion practiced by its agents, the Zaptiehs. A family, for instance, is supposed to contribute, say, £5, and fulfils its obligation. The Zaptiehs, however, ask for £3 or £4 more for themselves, and are met with a rash refusal. Negotiations, interlarded with violent and abusive language, ensue, and £1 is accepted. But the Zaptieh's blood is up. In a week they return and demand the same taxes over again. The Armenians wax angry, protest, and present their receipt; whereat the Zaptiehs laughingly explain that the document in question is no receipt but a few verses from a Turkish book. The villagers plead poverty and implore mercy. Greed, not compassion, moves the Zaptiehs to compromise the matter for £3 more, but the money is not forthcoming. Then they demand the surrender of the young women and girls of the family to glut their brutal appetites, and refusal is punished with a series of tortures over which decency and humanity throw a veil of silence. Rape, and every kind of brutal outrage conceivable to the diseased mind of Oriental profligates, and incredible to the average European intelligence, varied perhaps with murder or arson, wind up the incident.

I have seen and spoken with victims of these representaives of the Sublime Porte; I have inspected their wounds, questioned their families, interrogated their priests, their persecutors and their gaolers (some of them being incarcerated for complaining), and I unhesitatingly affirm not merely that these horrors are real facts, but that they are frequent occurrences. The following is the translation of an authentic document in my possession, signed and sealed by the inhabitants of Melikan (Kaza of Keghi), addressed as recently as March 26 of the present year to his Beatitude, the learned and saintly Metropolitan Archbishop of Erzeroum, a dignitary who enjoys the respect and esteem of friends and foes:

For a long time past the four or five Zaptiehs charged with the collection of the imperial taxes have chosen our village for their headquarters, and compel the inhabitants of the outlying country to come hither and pay their contributions. They eat, drink, and feed their horses at our expense, undisguisedly showing that they are resolved to reduce us to beggary.

Lately seven other Zaptiehs, who had not even the pretext of collecting the taxes, entered our village, insulted the Christian religion, and dishonored our wives and daughters, after which they seized three men who protested—Boghos, Mardig and Krikor—bound them with a twofold chain and hung them up by the feet from the rafters. They left them in this position until the blood began to flow from their nostrils. These poor men fell ill in consequence. The Zaptiehs, however, declared publicly that they had treated the people thus merely in obedience to the special orders of the chief of the police.

We therefore appeal to imperial justice to rescue us from this unbearable position. The inhabitants of the village of Melikan, Kaza of Keghi.

        (Signed) KATSHERE.
26th March, 1895.

The Armenians are naturally peaceful in all places: passionately devoted to agriculture in the country, and wholly absorbed by mercantile pursuits in the towns. Lest their inborn aversion to bloodshed, however, should be overcome by the impulse of duty, the instinct of self-defense, or deep-rooted affection for those near and dear to them, they are forbidden to possess arms, and the tortures that are inflicted on the few who disregard this law would bring a blush to the cheek of a countryman of Confucius. They must rely for protection exclusively upon the Turkish soldiers and the Turkish law.

Kevork Vartanian, of the village of Mankassar (Sanjak of Alashkerd), testified, among other things, as follows:

In 1892, a Kurd, Andon by name, son of Kerevash (of the tribe of Tshalal), came with his comrades to my house and took £5 in gold belonging to me, which I had saved up to buy seed corn with. I lodged a complaint against him, but the authorities dismissed me with contempt. Andon, hearing of my attempt to have him punished, came one night with twelve men, stood on our roof and looking down through the aperture, fired. My daughter-in-law, Yezeko, struck by a bullet, fell dead. Her two boys and my child Missak (two years old) likewise lost their lives then and there. Then the

Kurds entered the apartments and took my furniture, clothing, four oxen and four cows.* I hastened to the village of Karakilisse and complained to Rahim Pasha. Having heard my story, he said: "The Hamidieh Kurds are the Sultan's warriors. To do thus is their right. You Armenians are liars." And we were imprisoned. We did not obtain our release until we had paid £2 in gold.

The following winter 200 soldiers entered our village under the leadership of Rahim Pasha himself. He at once told us that it was illegal to complain of the doings of the Kurds. Then he quartered himself and his troops upon us and demanded daily eight sheep, ten measures of barley, besides eggs, poultry and butter. Forty days running our village supplied these articles of food gratis, receiving curses and blows for our pains. Rahim Pasha, angry with his host, Pare, for grumbling, had a copper vessel hung over the fire, and, when heated, ordered it to be placed on Pare's head. Then he had him stripped naked and little bits of flesh nipped out of his quivering arms with pincers.

These ruffians had scarcely quitted our village when Aipe Pasha, with sixty horsemen, took their places. Seeing that there were no more sheep to be had in the village, they slaughtered and ate our cows and oxen, and having inflicted much suffering upon us during six days, they too left. To whom could we address our complaints, seeing that the legally constituted authorities themselves perpetrated these

---

*Cows, horses, etc., are frequently lodged in the apartment in which the inmates live and sleep. I have passed many a restless night in a spacious room along with horses, buffaloes, oxen, sheep and goats

things? Nothing was left for us but to quit the country, which we did.

Take another case, in which the victim was the wife of a Protestant Armenian missionary, Madame Sookyassian, of the village of Todoveran (district of Bassen). I am personally acquainted with that family, and possess the portraits of all the members of it, including the lady, who was afterwards murdered. "On September 12, 1894," deposed Armenag Sookyassian, the son of the missionary's wife, "we were seated at table in my father's house, when a boy came and told us that the Turks and Kurds had come to attack us Christians. My brother crossed over to the other side of the street, where our shop was, to fetch a revolver. Sixteen Kurdish horsemen meanwhile entered the street, ascended the roofs, and opened fire. We barricaded the door, but they broke it in. A bullet struck my mother on the shoulder, but without inflicting a serious wound. She defended herself (being on the roof) by throwing stones. Meanwhile one of the Mohammedans leveled his gun, and, taking aim, fired. The bullet struck her on the cheek and passed out under the ear, carrying away the whole side of her face. She dropped, was carried in, and asked for water, which could only be given by raising her upper jaw. Next morning she was dead. We complained, but no one was punished."

One more typical instance, and I shall be done with this branch of the subject. The case which I am now about to narrate is taken not merely from the depositions of the parties interested, but from the official records, signed and sealed by government employes, which I myself have seen. It

ARMENIAN REFUGEES.

throws a more powerful light upon Turkish justice, and teaches a more useful lesson to those who still honestly believe in Turkish promises than the most eloquent diatribe.

In the month of June, 1890, the village of Alidjikrek was the scene of a double crime. The Armenian shepherds who were tending the flocks of the villagers rushed in excitedly, asking for help. "The Kurds of Ibil Ogloo Ibrahim came up with their sheep and drove us out of the village pastures." Four young men set out to reason with the Moslems and assert the rights of property; but scarcely had they reached the ground when the Kurds opened fire and killed one of the youths, named Hossep, on the spot. Another fell mortally wounded; his name, Haroothioon. Their comrades fled in horror to the village; the people, dismayed, abandoned their work; the parish priest and several of the principal inhabitants ran to the scene of the murder, others rode off to inform the gendarmes.

The Zaptiehs (gendarmes), accompanied by an official, were soon on the spot. They found Hossep dead, and the parish priest, Der Ohannes, administering the last consolations of religion to the dying Haroothioon. They ordered the prayers to cease, and menacing asked, "Where are the Kurdish murderers?" "They have fled," was the reply. "Indeed; probably you, dogs, have killed them, and buried them out of sight. You are all my prisoners." (Turning to the priest)—"You, too, come!" And they were all taken to Hassankaleh and thrown into the loathsome dungeon there.

The parish priest, Der Ohannes, was a well-to-do man. The process of systematic impoverishment was then only beginning. His brother, Garabed, and their ten comrades in misfortune, were likewise men of substance, and it seemed desirable to the officials that their property should change hands. They were left, therefore, to soak in the feted vapors of a reeking Eastern prison-house. The time dragged slowly on, day by day, week by week, and month by month, till they seemed to have been completely forgotten. Their families were in an endless agony of fear, their affairs were utterly neglected, their health was wholly undermined. In this pandemonium they passed a year—the most horrible period of their lives.

Then they humbly besought their persecutors to help them to their liberty and to name the price. The terms were agreed to and they were advised to send Kurds to hunt up traces of the Kurdish murderers whom they were accused of having murdered in turn. "If they be found you will be set free." The cost of this advice and of the ways and means of carrying it out amounted to about £400, which the prisoners were compelled to borrow at 40 per cent. interest.

The search was, of course, successful, Kurdish and Turkish assassins, when their victims are Christians, having no need to hide their persons, no motive to hang their heads. What they do is well done. These particular heroes were found enrolled in a battalion of His Majesty's favorite cavalry —the Hamidieh of Alashkerd. They confessed and did not deny; a cloud of witnesses—Turks and Kurds of course, Christians being disqualified—testified in court in favor of the twelve Armenian prisoners, who were then set at liberty, with ruined fortunes and broken health. The sentence of the court set forth that the Armenians, charged with the crime of having killed certain Kurds who had assassinated two Armenian villagers, had proved their innocence, the Kurds in question having been discovered living and well, serving the Commander of the Faithful in the Hamidieh Corps.

The Kurdish murderers, about whose precious lives so much fuss was made, were left in peace, and they still continue to serve His Majesty the Sultan with the same zeal and contempt of consequences as before.

The stories told of these Kurdish Hamidieh officers in general, and one of them, named Mostigo, in particular, seemed so wildly improbable that I was at great pains to verify them. Learning that this particular Fra Diavolo had been arrested and was carefully guarded as a dangerous criminal in the prison of Erzeroum, where he would probably be hanged, I determined to obtain, if possible, an interview with him and learn the truth from his own lips. My first attempt ended in failure; Mostigo, being a desperate murderer, who had once before escaped from jail, was subjected to special restrictions, and if I had carried out my original plan of visiting him in disguise, the probability is I should not have returned alive. After about three weeks' tedious and roundabout negotiations, I succeeded in gaining the gaoler's ear, having first replenished his purse. I next won over the brigand himself, and the upshot of my endeavors was an arrangement that Mostigo was to be allowed to leave the prison secretly, and at night, to spend six hours in my room, and then to be reconducted to his dungeon.

When the appointed day arrived, the gaoler repudiated his

part of the contract, on the ground that Mostigo, aware that his life was forfeited, would probably give the prison a wide berth if allowed to leave its precincts. After some further negotiations, I agreed to give two hostages for his return, one of them a brother Kurd, whose life the brigand's notions of honor would not allow him to sacrifice for the chance of saving his own. At last, he came to me one evening, walking over the roofs, lest the police, permanently stationed at my door, should espy him. I kept him all night, showed him to two of the most respectable Europeans in Erzeroum, and, lest any doubt should be thrown on the story, had myself photographed with him next morning.

The tale unfolded by that Kurdish noble constitutes a most admirable commentary upon Turkish regime in Armenia. This is not the place to give it in full. One or two short extracts must suffice.

Q. Now, Mostigo, I desire to hear from your own lips and to write down some of your wonderful deeds. I want to make them known to the "hat-wearers"*

A. Even so. Announce them to the Twelve Powers.†

There were evidently no misgivings about moral consequences; no fears of judicial punishment. And yet retribution was at hand; Mostigo was said to be doomed to death. Desirous of clearing up this point, I went on:

I am sorry to find that you are living in prison. Have you been long there?

A. I, too, am sorry. Five months, but it seems an age.

Q. These Armenians are to blame, I suppose?

---

*The Kurds call all Europeans hat-wearers, and generally regard them with respect and awe.

†I. e., to the whole universe.

A. Yes.

Q. You wiped out too many of them, carried off their women, burned their villages, and made it generally hot for them, I am told.

A. (Scornfully)—That has nothing to do with my imprisonment. I shall not be punished for plundering Armenians. We all do that. I seldom killed, except when they resisted. But the Armenians betrayed me and I was caught. That's what I mean. But if I be hanged it will be for attacking and robbing the Turkish post and violating the wife of a Turkish colonel, who is now here in Erzeroum. But not for Armenians! Who are they that I should suffer for them?

After he had narrated several adventures of his, in the course of which he dishonored Christian women, killed Armenian villagers, robbed the post and escaped from prison, he went on to say:

We did great deeds after that: deeds that would astonish the Twelve Powers to hear told. We attacked villages, killed people who would have killed us, gutted houses, taking money, carpets, sheep and women, and robbed travelers. * * * Daring and great were our deeds, and the mouths of men were full of them.

Having heard the story of many of these "great deeds," in some of which fifty persons met their death, I asked:

Q. Do the Armenians ever offer you resistance when you take their cattle and their women?

A. Not often. They cannot. They have no arms, and they know that even if they could kill a few of us it would do them no good, for other Kurds would come and take vengeance; but when we kill them, no one's eyes grow large with rage. The Turks hate them, and we do not. We only want money and spoil, and some Kurds also want their lands, but the Turks want their lives. A few months ago I attacked the Armenian village of Kara Kipriu and drove off all the sheep in the place. I did not leave one behind. The villagers, in despair, did follow us that time and fire some shots at us, but it was nothing to speak of. We drove the sheep towards Erzeroum to sell them there. But on the way we had a fight near the Armenian village of Sheme. The peasants knew we had lifted the sheep from their own people, and they attacked us. We were only five Kurds and they were many—the whole village was up against us. Two of my men—rayahs* only—were killed. We killed fifteen Armenians. They succeeded in capturing forty of the sheep. The remainder we held and sold in Erzeroum.

Q. Did you kill many Armenians generally?

A. Yes. We did not wish to do so. We only want booty, not lives. Lives are of no use to us. But we had to drive bullets through people at times to keep them quiet; that is, if they resisted.

Q. Did you often use your daggers?

A. No; generally our rifles. We must live. In autumn we manage to get as much corn as we need for the winter and money besides. We have cattle, but we take no care of them. We give them to the Armenians to look after and feed.

Q. But if they refuse?

A. Well, we burn their hay, their corn, their houses, and we drive off their sheep, so they do not refuse. We take back our cattle in spring, and the Armenians must return the same number that they received.

Q. But if cattle disease should carry them off?

A. That is the Armenians' affair. They must return us what we gave them, or an equal number. And they know it. We cannot bear the loss. Why should not they? Nearly all our sheep come from them.

After having listened to scores of stories of his expeditions, murders, rapes, etc., I again asked: "Can you tell me some more of your daring deeds, Mostigo, for the ears of the Twelve Powers?" to which I received this characteristic reply:

---

*The Kurds are divided into Torens or nobles, who lead in war time, and possess and enjoy in peace; and Rayahs, who sacrifice their lives for their lords in all raids and feuds, and are wholly dependent on them at all times. A rayah's life may be taken by a toren with almost the same impunity as a Christian's.

A SCENE IN ARMENIA.

Once the wolf was asked: "Tell us something about the sheep you devoured?" and he said: "I ate thousands of sheep; which of them are you talking about?" Even so it is with my deeds. If I spoke and you wrote for two days, much would still remain untold.

This brigand is a Kurd, and the name of the Kurds is legion. And yet the Kurds have shown themselves to be the most humane of all the persecutors of the Armenians. Needing money, this man robbed; desirous of pleasure, he dishonored women and girls; defending his booty, he killed men and women, and during it all he felt absolutely certain of impunity, so long as his victims were Armenians.

The following case has been inquired into and verified by the foreign representatives in Turkey: In the spring of 1893 Hassib Pasha, the Governor of Moush, feeling the need of some proofs of the disaffection of the Armenians of Avzoot and the neighboring villages, dispatched Police Captain Reshid Effendi thither to seach for arms. Reshid set out, made careful inquiries and diligently searched in the houses, on the roofs, under the ground, but in vain. There were no firearms anywhere. He returned and reported that the villagers had strictly observed the law forbidding them to possess weapons of any kind. But Hassib Pasha waxed wroth. "How dare you assert what I know to be untrue?" he asked. "Go back this minute and find the arms. Don't dare return without them!" The Police Captain again rode off to Avzoot and searched every nook and corner with lamps, so to say, turning the houses inside out. But he found nothing. Then he summoned the village elder, and said: "I have been sent to discover the hidden arms here. Tell me where they are." "But there are none." "There must be some." "I assure you, you are mistaken." "Well, now, listen. I have to find arms here, whether there are any or none, and I cannot return without them. Unless you deliver me some, I shall quarter myself and my men upon your village." This meant certainly plunder and probably rape. The elder was dismayed. "What are we to do?" he asked. "We have no arms." "Go and get some, then; steal them, buy them, but get them." Two or three persons were accordingly sent to the nearest Kurdish village, where they purchased three cartloads of old daggers, flintlock guns and rusty swords, which were duly handed over to Reshid. With these he returned to the Governor of Moush exulting. Hassib Pasha, seeing the collection, rejoiced exceedingly, and said: "You see now, I was right. I told you there were arms hidden away there. You did not seek for them properly at first. Be more diligent in future."

Verto Popakhian, an inhabitant of the village of Khalil Tshaush (Khnouss), narrated the following, the story of his troubles, which throws a curious sidelight on Turkish justice and Armenian peasant-life generally:

A Kurd, named Djundee, endeavored to carry off my niece, Nazo, but we took her to Erzeroum, and gave her in marriage to an Armenian. We often have to give our young girls in marriage when they are mere children, eleven to twelve years old, or else dress them up in boys' clothes, to preserve them undefiled. Nazo's husband was the son of the parish priest of Hertev. The Kurds vowed vengeance upon me for saving the girl thus. Djundee beat my brother so seriously that he was ill in bed for nearly six months, and he and his men drove off my cattle, burned our grain, threshing-floor and hay and ruined us completely. When the girl came home on a visit, Djundee and his Kurds attacked the house and carried her off. We complained to all the authorities in the place and in Erzeroum too. By the time they agreed to examine the girl publicly, she had borne a child to the Kurd, and shame prevented her return. She remained a Mohammedan. We then bought a gun for our protection, the law forbidding firearms not existing yet. In 1893 we sold the gun to a Kurd named Hadji Daho, but in 1894 the police came and demanded it. We said we had sold it, and the Kurd bore out our assertion. He even showed it to them. But they arrested my brother and myself, and compelled us to give our two buffaloes in exchange for two guns, which they took away as incriminating proof of our guilt; and then sent us to Erzeroum prison. We were kept here, suffering great hardships, for a long time. When eight months had passed away, my brother died of ill-treatment. Then they promised me my liberty in consideration of large bribes, which reduced me to absolute beggary. I had no choice. I gave them all they asked, leaving myself and family of nineteen persons completely destitute. And then they condemned me to five years' imprisonment.

Justice in all its aspects is rigorously denied to the Armenians. The mere fact that he dares to invoke it as plaintiff or prosecutor against a Kurd or a Turk is always sufficient to metamorphose him into a defendant or a criminal, generally into both, whereupon he is invariably thrown into prison. What the prison really is cannot be made sufficiently clear in words. If the old English Star Chamber, the Spanish Inquisition, a Chinese opium den, the ward of a yellow-fever hospital, and a nook in the lowest depths of Dante's Hell be conceived as blended and merged into one, the resulting picture will somewhat resemble a bad Turkish prison. Filth, stench, disease, deformity, pain in forms and degrees inconceivable in Europe, constitute the physical characteristics: the psychological include the blank despair that is final, fiendish, fierce malignity, hellish delight in human suffering, stoic self-sacrifice in the cultivation of loathsome vices, stark madness raging in the moral nature only—the whole incarnated in grotesque beings whose resemblance to man is a living blasphemy against the deity. In these noisome dungeons, cries of exquisite suffering and shouts of unnatural delight continually commingle; ribald songs are sung to the accompaniment of heartrending groans; meanwhile the breath is passing away from bodies which had long before been soulless, and are unwept save by the clammy walls whereon the vapor of unimagined agonies and foul disease condenses into big drops and runs down in driblets to the reeking ground. Truly, it is a horrid nightmare quickened into life.

I despatched a friend of mine to visit the political prisoners in the Bitlis penitentiary, and to ask them to give me a succint account of their condition. Four of them replied in a joint letter, which is certainly the most gruesome piece of reading I have beheld ever since I first perused a description of the Black Hole. Only the least sensational passages can be stripped of the decent disguise of a foreign language and exposed to the light of day. It is dated "Bitlis Prison, Hell, March 28 (April 9), 1895," and begins thus:

In Bitlis prison there are seven cells, each one capable of containing from ten to twelve persons. The number they actually contain is from twenty to thirty. There are no sanitary arrangements whatever. Offal, vermin and the filth that should find a special place elsewhere are heaped together in the same cell. * * * The water is undrinkable. Frequently, the Armenian prisoners are forced to drink "Khwlitsh" water—i. e., water from the tank in which the Mohammedans perform their ablutions. * * *

Then follows a brief but suggestive account of the treatment endured by the writers' comrades, many of whom died from the effects. For example, "Malkhass Aghadjanian and Serop Malkhassian of Avzoot (Moush) were beaten till they lost consciousness. The former was branded in eight places, the latter in twelve places, with a hot iron." The further outrage which was committed upon Serop must be nameless. "Hagop Seropian, of the village of Avzoot, was stripped and beaten till he lost consciousness; then a girdle was thrown around his neck, and having been dragged into the Zaptieh's room, he was branded in sixteen parts of his body with red-hot ramrods." Having described other sufferings to which he was subjected, such as the plucking out of his hair, standing motionless in one place without food or drink till nature could hold out no longer, the writer goes on to mention outrages for which the English tongue has no name, and civilized people no ears. Then he continues:

Sirko Minassian, Garabed Malkhassian and Isro Ardvadzadoorian, of the same village, having been violently beaten, were forced to remain in a standing position for a long time, and then had the contents of certain vessels poured upon their heads. Korki Mardoyan, of the village of Semol, was violently beaten; his hair was plucked out by the roots, and he was forced to stand motionless for twenty-four hours. Then Moolazim Hadji Ali and the gaoler, Abdoolkadir, forced him to perform the so-called Sheitantopy,* which resulted in his death. He was forty-five years of age. Mekhitar Saforian and Khatsho Baloyan of Kakarloo (Boolanyk) were sub-

---

*Literally "Devil's ring." The hands are tightly bound together, and the feet, tied together by the great toes, are forced up over the hands. The remainder of the Sheitantopy consists of a severe torture and a beastly crime.

jected to the same treatment. Mekhitar was but fifteen and Khatsho only thirteen years old. Sogho Sharoyan, of Alvarındj (Moush), was conveyed from Moush to Bitlis prison handcuffed. Here he was cruelly beaten, and forced to maintain a standing position without food. Whenever he fainted they revived him with douches of cold water and stripes. They also plucked out his hair, and burned his body with red-hot irons. Then * * * (they subjected him to treatment which cannot be described). * * * Hambartzoon Boyadjian, after his arrest, was exposed to the scorching heat of the sun for three days. Then he was taken to Semal, where he and his companions were beaten and shut up in a church. They were not only not allowed to leave the church to relieve the wants of nature, but were forced to defile the baptismal fonts and the church altar. * * * Where are you, Christian Europe and America?

The four signatures at the foot of this letter include that of a highly respected and God-fearing ecclesiastic.

I am personally acquainted with scores of people who have passed through these prison mills. The stories they narrate of their experiences there are gruesome, and would be hard to believe were they not amply confirmed by the still more eerie tales told by their broken spirits, their wasted bodies and the deep scars and monstrous deformities that will abide with them till the grave or the vultures devour them. But let us take one of the usual and by no means most revolting cases of arrest and imprisonment as an illustration.

A young man from the village of Avzood (Moush district) went to Russia in search of work, and found it. He also married, and lived there for several years. Towards the close of 1892 he came back to his native village, and the police, informed that "an Armenian who has lived in Russia is returned," despatched four of their number under the orders of

AN ARMENIAN FAMILY.

Isaag Tshaush to Avzood. They arrived two hours after sundown, and while three of them guarded the house where the young man was staying, the leader entered. Shots were heard immediately after, and the young Armenian and Isaag lay dead. The authorities in Bitlis then sent a Colonel of the Zaptiehs to Avzood to see "justice" done. And it was done very speedily. The colonel summoned the men of the village —none of whom were mixed up in the matter—and put them in prison. Then the officials deflowered all the girls, and dishonored all the young women in Avzood, after which they liberated the men, except about twenty, whom they conveyed to the gaol of Bitlis. A few of these died there, and ten others were soon afterwards dismissed. Finally they decided to charge a young teacher, Markar, of the village of Vartenis, with the murder of Isaag Tshaush, and as there was no evidence against him, the other prisoners were ordered to testify.

When the trial came on, and the incriminating document was read, the signatories stripped themselves in court, exhibited the ugly marks left by the red-hot irons, and called God to witness that that evidence of theirs, wrung from them by maddening torture, was a lie. Markar, on the other hand, declared that he was not in Avzood village at all on the night in question. But these statements were unavailing; he was hanged last year, and the "witnesses" condemned to various terms in fortified towns. Some of the women dishonored by the Zaptiehs died from the effects of the treatment to which they were subjected.

All accounts of the prisons in Armenia, Turkish, Kurdish

and Christian, agree in essential characteristics. I lately called on a very respectable Armenian—a man of good education and once a person of property—who has passed through several prisons, the object of his incarceration being the desire to deprive him of all he possessed. Him I questioned about the treatment of the prisoners, and what he said was this:

Armenian prisoners are very often tortured; but a good deal depends upon the place. Some prisons are very bad, being noted for the abominable things that go on inside their walls; others are not so horrible. The prison of Erzeroum, for example, is not nearly so bad as that of Bitlis, though there, too, torture is occasionally employed in a fiendish way. The reason is, I conjecture, that the foreign consuls in Erzeroum can always get information about what goes on in the prison there, and the authorities are restrained by the knowledge of this.

Q. Then there is no torture in Erzeroum?

A. There is sometimes, but not nearly so often as elsewhere. I have seen the "Standing Box" there, and I know it was used some time ago, but I fancy it would not be often employed—certainly not nearly so often as in Bitlis.

Q. What is the Standing Box?

A. It is a small cupboard, just large enough for one man to stand in, something like a sentry-box in shape. The prisoner put there could not sit, lean or move.

Q. Surely he could lean, at least, against the wall?

A. No; because it bristles all over with sharp iron points, and on the ground there is barely room enough for his two feet to stand. He is kept here for twenty-four, thirty-six, forty-eight hours, as the case may be; sometimes longer still. Two or more Zaptiehs always stand guard, and see that the thing is properly carried out. He receives nothing to eat or to drink, and is not allowed to leave even to attend to the wants of nature. This is a horrible torture. It was applied to Markar, the teacher, and to numbers of my friends and acquaintances. Damadian's servant, Sogho Sharoyan, was subjected to it; so were Hagop Seropian, of Avzood, Sirko Minassian, Garabed Molkhassian, Korki Mardoyan, Saghatiel Mirzoyan of Khosgheldi (Boolanyk), and scores of others. But this is by no means the worse. The torture of Sheitantopy, which is also an outrage that—

Yes, I know all about that.

The gaolers grow rich on the money they wring from the inmates of the cells. The prison-keeper of Bitlis prison, Abdoolkader, a wretch who, God having presumably made him, may be called a man, earns enormous sums in this way. He lately spent £500 on his house, and two or three Turkish merchants are said to be doing business on his capital, although his salary is only about 50s. a month. These sums are received as bribes, not for any positive return made to the prisoners, but for mere relief from torture, employed solely for this purpose. The following case may give some idea of the nature of the relief thus highly paid for. Some five months ago three men of the village of Krtabaz were arrested and imprisoned. The fact that they were released without trial ten weeks later is evidence enough of their innocence of crime. They were taken to the prison of Hassan-kaleh. The room in which they were confined was overcrowded. The term overcrowding does not connote the same thing in Armenia as in European prisons. They had no room to lie down at all. Some Kurdish prisoners confined in the same dismal den, who enjoyed special privileges, had but two and one-half feet space to sleep in. In one corner of the dungeon a hole in the wall represented the prison-equivalent of sanitation, and these three Armenians were told that they must stand up by this hole, and might lean against the wall to sleep. This they did for fifteen consecutive nights. The stench, the filth, the vermin exceed all conception. After the lapse of fifteen days, by dint of starving themselves, they were enabled to give part of their food to some of the Kurds, one of whom allowed the Armenians to take his place in turn during the day. This was not much, for the Kurds themselves had only sitting space, about two and one-half feet long; still it did afford relief. But the Kurd was severely punished for this benevolence or enterprise. His rations of bread were cut off, and he was put in irons for several days. The men he thus befriended, who now aver they owe their lives to him, were notables of their village, and innocent persons, to boot, who were released some weeks later because "they had done no wrong."

"The Armenians could help themselves if they really wished," I lately heard an Englishman say, with a serious and convinced air; "they have only to turn Mohammedans. Surely God would not punish them for that." It is certainly true that the moment they embraced Islam their troubles would cease, and that now, though martyrs by suffering, deprived of the palm, they are but contemptible "criminals" in name.

The following story is calculated to bring out in strong relief the temptation which the Armenians have to give up their faith. The narrative will be found interesting on other grounds besides.

Melik Agha was a notable and noble Armenian of the village of Abri (Boolanyk district), blessed with sons and grandsons, cattle, sheep, land, corn and hay in abundance—

a sort of Armenian Job on a small scale. A noble Mohammedan of the same village, Kiamil Sheikh, by name, envying his riches, desired to draw them to himself, and failing that, to destroy them and their owner. Last autumn for this purpose he had Melik's hay, corn, etc., burned to ashes. Then the Sheikh's men came and took away five of his horses and killed 150 of his sheep, leaving their carcasses to rot where they fell. This was wanton waste in a country where people are continually poor and frequently hungry. Melik, therefore, went to Kop where the Kaimakam resides and invoked the strong arm of the law. While he was in Kop complaining, and his sons were away on business, the Sheikh's people, ever on the watch, dropped into his house, murdered the two children of Melik's eldest son and abducted their mother, who was very far gone with child. Melik Agha, hearing of this calamity, set out for Erzeroum to lay the matter before the chief authorities of the Vilayet. The upshot of his application was that Selim Pasha was deputed to inquire into the business and to get the woman back—the children, of course, could not be resuscitated, nor could their murderer be punished. The captor refused to deliver up the young woman, saying, "She will publicly declare that she embraces Islam." Then the Pasha, turning to Melik, asked, "What will you say or do if your daughter-in-law does publicly affirm that she becomes a Mohammedan?"

"I shall say that we too will become Mohammedans rather than allow our wives and daughters to pass into other hands." Then the woman was fetched, but seeing her surrounded by Sheikhs, and afraid of speaking the truth, Melik said to the

Pasha: "She is ill. In a few days she will become a mother. Give her peace until then, and meanwhile send her to any Turkish house you like in Erzeroum. In a fortnight we shall hear what she has to say." To this all agreed, and the Pasha departed. Three days later the woman's husband (Melik's eldest son) was killed by Kiamil's people in broad daylight. Even the Turkish family in which the woman lived were horrified, and requested the Sheikhs to come and take her away, as they refused to have anything more to do with the business.

Soon after this, Melik's second son, Mgirdeetch, shot two of the Sheikhs in the field. It was a very wrong and un-Christian thing to do, and cases of the kind give correct people in Europe a pretext for complaining of the vindictiveness of the Armenians. What he should have done, we know, was to entertain the Sheikhs at dinner, or at least to let them pass on in peace; though there are certain highly civilized Europeans—nay, ministers of Christian churches, known to me, who virtually say:

"God be praised for every instinct which rebels against a lot,
Where the brute survives the human and man's upright form is not."

However this may be, Mgirdeetch and his younger brother, feeling that they and their relatives were doomed, ran into the house of Mussah Bey and proclaimed themselves Mohammedans. Then they sent a messenger to their father informing him of what they had done and exhorting him to go and do likewise. And he did. A Mullah was appointed to teach the newly-converted family the doctrines and wor-

ship of Islam, and, as fate would have it, the Mullah in question was a man who had been Melik's faithful servant for many long years, and was far more disposed to become a Christian than his former master was to recognize the teachings of the Koran. Melik having discussed his plans with this friendly Mullah, sent his widowed daughter with a grown-up girl and three boys to Russia. When they drew near to the frontier, at Gara-Ghedook, the Kurds attacked them and strove to obtain possession of the girl. But she held her mother's hand and refused to be delivered up to the lusts of these savages. Then the Kurds shot her dead. Her mother took the body on her back and carried it to the village Ghairavank, about three miles from Kaghziman, where it was buried by Father Raphael. After some time Melik himself and the other members of his family escaped to Russia, leaving behind his house, lands, hay, corn, cattle, etc., and taking only a little money, of which the Kurds robbed him on the road. He was thankful to God for having allowed him to get across the frontiers with his life.

The difficulty of emigrating from Turkey, with money, clothing, or women, will be best understood in the light of a few concrete examples. Not that the Turks object to their leaving. On the contrary—and this is the most conclusive proof of the existence of the plan of extermination—they actually drive them over the frontier, and then persistently refuse to allow them to return.

Sahag Garoyan, questioned as to the reasons why he and his family of ten persons emigrated from his village of Kheter (Sanjak of Bayazid), deposed as follows:

We could not remain because we were treated as beasts of burden by Rezekam Bey, son of Djaffar Agha, and his men, who belong to His Majesty's Hamidieh corps, and can therefore neither be punished nor complained of. I emigrated towards the end of last year. Rezekam had come with his followers, as if it were war time, and taken possession of the houses of the Armenians, driving the occupants away. Only seven families were allowed to stay on. The others, having no place to go to, took refuge in the church. We had to feed the Kurds for three months, giving them our corn, sheep, etc., and keeping their cattle in fodder. We had to serve some of them as beasts of burden. Rezekam himself paid a weekly visit to the village of Karakilisse, and levied a contribution of £10 Turkish on the inhabitants, besides hay, barley, etc., for his men. At last, unable to bear this burden any longer, we addressed a complaint to the authorities. They told us to be gone. Then a Kurd, named Ghazaz Teamer, ordered us to sign a document setting forth that we were prosperous and happy. This was to be sent to Constantinople, as he wished to be appointed Yoozbashi of the Hamidiehs. No one signed the paper, whereat Teamer grew angry, and killed Avaki and his brother. Five months later he killed Minass, son of Kre, of the village of Mankassar. When the winter came on last year, Rezekam Bey imprisoned our neighbor Sarkiss, son of Sahag, had his head plunged in cold water and dried; after that it was steeped in petroleum and his hair burned off. Then he endeavored to violate Sara, Sarkiss's sister, but she was smuggled away in time. Rezekam's servant, Kheto, dishonored Moorad's wife, and a few days later entered the house of Abraham, an inhabitant of the same village, commanding him to go and work for Rezekam Bey. Abraham's wife, who was about to become a mother, begged that he might be allowed to stay at home, but Kheto kicked her in the stomach, and she was delivered of a dead child an hour or so after. Oh, we could not live there—not if we were beasts, instead of Christians.

Mgirdeetch Mekhoyan, aged thirty-five, of the village of Koopegheran (Sandjak of Bayazid), deposed: "I emigrated in 1894, because Aipa Pasha came with forty Kurdish families, demolished our church, and took everything we had." The same story, with variations, comes from every Sanjak, almost from every village, of the five Armenian provinces. Bedross Kozdyan, aged fifty-five, of the village of Arog (Sandjak of Van), testified:

I left my village and my country with my family in August last year (1894), because we were driven away by the Kurds under Tri, son of Tshalo, who was abetted by the Turkish authorities. He first came and violated three girls and three young married women, whom he took away in spite of their cries and prayers. Three Armenians tried to protect the wetched women, who implored them not to let them go. But the Kurds killed the three on the spot. Their names were Sarkiss, Khatsho and Keveark. Next day he and his men drove off the sheep of the villagers. We complained to the Governor of Van, but he said he could not move in the matter. Ten days later the Kurds came again, and carried away our wheat, barley and live stock, and burned the hay which they could not transport. Then they knocked down the altar of our church, hoping to find gold and silver hidden away there. We again besought the authorities to protect us, but they replied, "We'll slaughter you like sheep if you dare to come again with your complaints against good Mohammedans." Then we took what we could with us and set out for Russia. When we reached Sinak six armed Kurds attacked us, robbed us of everything we had, and sent us over the frontier with nothing but our clothes.

Ove Oviants, of the village of Leez, Sandjak of Boolanyk, deposed:

I emigrated with my family of eight persons, because we were driven off by the Kurds under Terpoi Neato, with the connivance of the Imperial authorities. He came to our village and took three yoke of oxen, seventy sheep and two mules. A month later they drove off seventy more sheep and two mules, the latter and seventeen of the sheep my own property. We were 250 Armenian families, but against a handful of Kurds we could do nothing, having no firearms. One night they broke open my door and took away the clothing and ornaments of the women of our family and two cows. Modego Tilo, seeing that one of our neighbors had a handsome daughter, carried her off and forced her to become a Moslem. The girl's father appealed to the Vali of Bitlis, who ordered the Kaimakam of Kop to flog him soundly and then imprison him for seven days. This was done. He was warned on being released that if he complained again he would be tortured to death. My family and four others then left for Russia. At Apazin the Kurds attacked us and took everything we possessed.

Khatsho Garabedian, of the village of Kiavoormi (Sandjak of Khnouss), declared:

I am forty-five years of age. The reason I left with my family was because the Turkish authorities allowed the Kurds under Heasso to strip me of nearly everything I possessed, and then the Turkish Zaptiehs came and demanded the taxes, which I had no means of paying. The chief of these Zaptiehs then said: "You have no money, but you have a pretty wife. Lend her to me, and I will give you a receipt for the taxes." I contrived to have my wife taken to another house, and when the Turkish official saw that he could not dishonor her, he punished me. First, cold water was poured over me, then dung and other filth was rubbed into my face, and a strap thrown around my neck. In this way I was dragged through the village. On my return, they took my ox, the only possession that was still left me, and had it not been for that ox they would have taken my life. I then fled with my family, and we had only two Turkish pounds in money among us. The soldiers, however, stopped us and made us deliver up that, and we entered Russia as poor as the day we were born.

The plan of extermination is obviously working smoothly and well. The Christian population is decimated, villages are changing hands almost as quickly as the scenes shift in a comic opera, and the exodus to Russia and the processions to the churchyard are increasing.

Three hundred and six of the principal inhabitants of the District of Khnouss gave me a signed petition when I was leaving Armenia, and requested me to lay it before "the humane and noble people of England." In this document they truly say:

We now solemnly assure you that the butchery of Sassoun is but a drop in the ocean of Armenian blood shed gradually and silently all over the empire since the late Turko-Russian war. Year by year, month by month, day by day, innocent men, women and children have been shot down, stabbed or clubbed to death in their houses and their fields, tortured in strange fiendish ways in fetid prison cells, or left to rot in exile under the scorching sun of Arabia. During the progress of that long and horrible tragedy no voice was raised for mercy, no hand extended to help us. That process is still going on, but it has already entered upon its final phases, and the Armenian people are at the last gasp. Is European sympathy destined to take the form of a cross upon our graves?

English people have not even a remote notion of the extent to which young married women and girls are outraged all over Armenia by Turkish soldiers, imperial Zaptiehs, Kurdish officers and brigands—and outraged with such accompaniments of nameless brutality that their agonies often culminate in a horrible death. Girls of eleven and twelve—nay, of nine—are torn from their families and outraged in this way by a band of "men" whose names are known, and whose deeds are approved by the representatives of law and order.

In 1893 six Kurds came to the village of Tshekhi, entered the house of Garabed Ghiragossian, and compelled the host to provide them with an abundant meal and their horses with fodder. Having eaten their fill, they went out into the garden and partook of green fruit and cucumbers till they sickened. Then they accused Garabed of having poisoned them, and set about punishing him condignly. They tied him tightly to a pillar in the apartment, then seized his wife, and each of them dishonored her in turn. After this they told the wretched man that they would set him free if he paid them a certain sum for his liberty.

On November 7 last, a Turk of the city of Bayazid asked Avedis Krmoyan to pay a little debt. The Armenian, not having the money at the time, besought his creditor to wait a few weeks. The Turk refused, and insisted on taking Krmoyan's wife as a pledge that the money would be paid. Entreaties and tears were unavailing; the woman was carried off, and then forced to become a Moslem. She can never return to her husband again.

In the village of Khosso Veran (Bassen) a girl named Selvy was seized by a Turk as security for a debt contracted by her father. The creditor kept her three months and dishonored her; nor would he consent to set her free until Giragoss Ohannissean went bail for her. As the debt, however, is unpaid, the Turk has a mortgage on her still. This sort of thing cannot be said to be uncommon, for although I knew but three cases of it from personal knowledge I heard of more than a score in different parts of Armenia.

The following case is one in which I took a very lively interest, because I am well acquainted with the victim and her family. Her name is Lucine Mussegh, her native village Khnoossaberd. Born in 1878, Lucine was sent at an early age to the Armenian Missionary School at Erzeroum,

OMDURMAN BAZAAR, OR THE SUQ OF BAYT AL MAL

where she was taught the doctrines of evangelical Christianity, her father, Aghadjan Kemalian, having always manifested a strong sympathy for Protestantism. Armenian girls are in chronic danger of being raped by Turks and Kurds, and Armenian parents are continually scheming for the purpose of shielding them from this calamity, which, as we have seen, occasionally results in death. The means usually employed are very early marriages or attempts to pass off the girls as boys. I have known children to be taken from school, married, allowed to live a few months with their husbands or wives, and then sent back to school again. This is what happened to Lucine, who, taken from school at the age of fourteen, was wedded to a boy of her own age, Milikean by name, and having lived some time with him under his father's roof, was sent to the Protestant school once more. One night, during her husband's absence from home, she was seized by some men, dragged by the hair, gagged, and taken to the house of Hussni Bey. This man is the son of the Deputy-Governor of the place. He dishonored the young woman and sent her home the next day; but her husband refused to receive her any more, and she is now friendless and alone in the world.

Lucine's father presented a complaint to the colonel of the Hamidiehs, and a petition to the parish priest. The Metropolitan Archbishop of Erzeroum likewise took the matter in hand, and appealed to the Governor-General of the Vilayet and to the court of Khnouss. But all to no purpose. Lucine is now a pariah. In her Appeal to the Women of England, which is too long and too naive to find a place here, Lucine says:

We suffered in patience when our corn, butter and honey were seized, and we were left poor and hungry; we bowed our heads in sorrowful resignation when our kith and kin were cut down by the Kurds and the Turks. Are we also to be silent and submissive now that our race is being poisoned at its source? Now that child-mothers and baby-daughters are being defiled and brutalized by savages? Say, Christian sisters, is there in truth no remedy? * * * We ask for no revenge, for no privileges; we ask only that * * * but need I be more explicit to English matrons, wives and sisters? * * * Although we are Armenians, we are Christians; I was brought up in a Protestant school, as you were; I drew my moral sustenance from the Bible, as you did; I was taught to feel and think, as you were. * * * For the love of the God, then, whom we worship in common, help us, Christian sisters, before it is too late, and take the thanks of the mothers, wives, sisters and daughters of my people, and with them the gratitude of one for whom, in spite of her youth, death would come as a happy release.

(Signed) LUCINE MUSSEIGH.

I have also received a piteous appeal to the women of England from some hundreds of Armenian women of the District of Khnouss, begging as an inestimable favor to be shielded from the brutal treatment to which they are all subjected. It is needless to publish it here. Written appeals are seldom very forcible. If the reader had seen the wretched women themselves, as I saw them, and heard them tell their gruesome tales in the simplest of words, punctuated by sobs and groans, emphasized by misery and squalor, they would be in a condition to form some idea of the state of things in Armenia, which in the good old times of theocracy would have brought down consuming fire from heaven. In the village of Begli Akhmed, for example, I met a woman of about twenty-eight, clothed in ragged pieces of dirty carpets, with a pale, emaciated boy of twelve, suffering from a terrible cough, who looked like a typhus patient aged only six or seven. I asked her to tell her story, and this is what she said:

My name is Atlass Manookian; I come from the village of Khrt (Khnouss district). We were very well off, but the Kurds took away everything we had. Everything, Effendi; still my poor husband worked for me and the child here, though they told us to go. One day when I was bringing bread to my husband in the field, they struck me on the head and dishonored me. That was in the daytime.

"It was at noon, mother, when father used to eat his bread, that they did that to you," broke in the ghost of a child. I never in my life witnessed anything more horrible than the sight of those two friendless, hopeless wretches, as they stood there trembling in the cold, the dying child, thus simply bearing witness that his mother was dishonored in the fields by a number of neighboring Kurds. She then went on: "I complained to the head officer, Sheikh Moorad, but the Bimbashi beat me cruelly about the head and back, and knocked me down. Then, last spring, when my husband was sowing corn, Ali Mahmed came up and killed him." "With an axe, mother," said the boy. "We are now alone in the world, wandering and begging, and nobody knows us," said the woman. Having given her some coins, I hurried away, vainly striving to shake off the horrible impression which clung to me like a hideous ghost for weeks afterwards.

Mr. Dillon very clearly sets forth the condition of the Armenians in his article, but we have three more letters which have been sent for publication. One of these was written to the students of one of the leading theological seminaries in this country by a former graduate; one by the Rev. Dr. Whittle, and the other by Dr. Grace N. Kimball.

FROM A MISSIONARY TO HIS FORMER FELLOW-STUDENTS.

November 30, 1895.

My Dear Friends: The role of a "Prophet of Ills" is not a pleasant one to play. Many hundred letters have been written within a year predicting great calamity, and no one seems to have heeded the warnings. Four months ago I sent an article in which I enlarged on the statement that if the Powers acted there was no danger, but if they failed to act and were delayed, the consequence would be awful. Now the storm has broken, and it is more horrible than anyone conceived of. After Sassoun, after the Commission of Inquiry, after all the pressure that has been applied in Constantinople, under the very eyes of the Powers, in this month of November the Kurds and the soldiery have slaughtered over 20,000 Christians and committed awful atrocities on the human race. They have sacked every city and town in the provinces covered by the Reform Scheme, and the carnival of blood is extending in ever-widening circles to all parts of the empire. The calling out of the reserves, the sending of warships, the conference in Vienna, have all come too late. There are said to be 250,000 destitute tonight in the empire.

And now the Turks have waked up to the value of a certain modern invention, e. g., the telegraph, and they will fill the earth with their "official" lies. Hitherto no newspaper in the Armenian language or the Arabic language has been allowed to mention Armenia. Now they are teeming with the most atrocious misrepresentations and fabrications. Nothing is straight that can be made crooked. And the copying of these lies will throw dust in the eyes of half the world, while the "weaknesses," not the "Powers," are talking great things about the Armenian question, the Turks have decided to dispose of it by wiping the Armenians from the face of the earth. Give them a few months more, and the Armenian question will be settled forever, as far as all human affairs are concerned. The fact is, that never for a moment have they paused in their awful purpose. Perhaps this last grand carnage is their kindest act. Death is easier and sweeter than the life they are living. And perhaps this last scene in the tragedy will open the eyes of those who must act to the real character of the rulers in this empire.

For many reasons, which I need not mention, I have kept my name and pen from these matters, but I can see no good reason for silence now. . . . . .

I wonder if anyone in all America realizes fully the awful enormity of the calamities being heaped upon Christians here? One murder in any town is a pall to the whole people; ten murders would create a panic. Multiply that by fifty; think of corpses heaped by hundreds into holes and rivers! In Diarbekir more than 5000 were slaughtered within three days. Those who died are but a fraction of those on whom have been heaped outrage, indignities, fear, fever, hunger, and cold will add another 5000, and tens of thousands will never know another pleasant home, a peaceful night while life lasts. Think of men, women and children being hunted and beaten to death as people hunt and kill a dog! A refugee came into our house a few days ago whose aunt was treated to outrage and death in ways that cannot be described. His brother lived in Constantinople, and when fourteen corpses were rolled out from under a bridge, that brother was among them, with his face almost cut off. In the government centre, one-half an hour away from our house, are Kurds who have helped at such barbarities, and their conversation the whole day long is of the things they did and saw enacted. No wonder our people here are in great consternation. No wonder that all fear for the people of Damascus! Could they look forward to death alone, that would be easy; but there are many things more horrible which loom up as possibilities. A dog will not eat a dog, one of his own kind; but the outrages, indignities, barbaric and fiendish, which these human devils heap on defenseless women and children are horrible beyond all conception. It makes one shudder to see the battalions of Kurds and Arnaruts being poured into Syria, massed in Damascus and quartered in every section of the outlying districts. May God hasten and make no tarrying.

* * * * * * * * * * * *

Our duty at the present time is to be at our posts. I am sure I could cause a semi-panic tomorrow by sending my family over the mountain to Beyrout. But not being con-

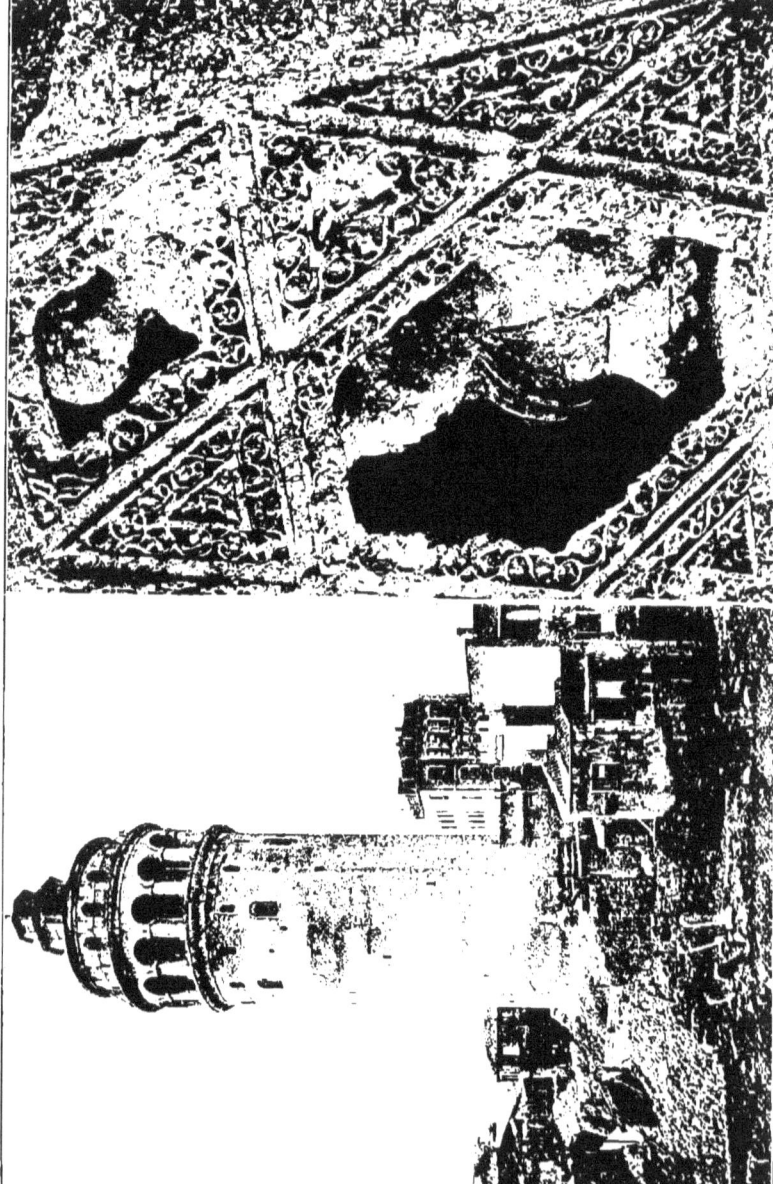

scious of any immediate danger, we go right on in our daily duties, and our presence does help many troubling souls to keep still. The whole town is buying arms, making powder and casting bullets. We can hardly view these preparations with favor, seeing that even before the danger is past they may quarrel and use these on each other. A week ago after midnight some drunken rowdies went out of their haunts and tried their guns on the midnight air. So many shots were fired that the whole town was aroused. A woman in a house near our own went crazy from fear, and did not recover her reason for days. Many of the older people remember the massacre of 1860, and their horror at the possibility of another such experience is pitiable to behold.

December 6.—Our latest news here is that cholera has appeared among the half-famished soldiers in Damascus. This is another woe added to the woes of the empire. What these soldiers will do when driven to desperation no one can foretell. They are strangers in language and customs. The Turkish government never allows a man to serve in his own country. Soldiers living in Syria are sent either to Yemen or Crete or Constantinople, and Damascus is filled with troops who live in the north of the empire. There is a prime wisdom in this. When they are ordered to fire on a mob, they do not hesitate, for they are sure they are not firing on any of their own families or friends.

* * * * * * * * * * * * *

If I would tell you one in a thousand of the wild rumors afloat, I would need to keep writing all night. They range from the most incredible to the actual, and often take on the nature of prophecy—of coming events which cast their shadows before. Where they rise no one knows. They are one of the sad fruits of a muzzled press. Not a newspaper in the Turkish Empire dares refer to passing events, and hence the poor people prevented from knowing the truth, torture themselves with the most lonesome stories and apprehensions.

FROM REV. W. A. WHITTLE, D. D.

Having just returned from a second and somewhat extended tour through Asia Minor and other countries bordering on Armenia, I feel that I owe it to the Christian people of America, and our fellow-religionists in the far East, to relate some of my recent observations and experiences.

Some fifteen years ago, the Sultan of Turkey, together with his high officials, determined as a stroke of political policy to create a revival of Mohammedanism. Since this decision was arrived at, Turkey has been more of a religious than a political government. Hundreds of mosques throughout the Turkish Empire were immediately turned into schools, so-called colleges and universities. Into these schools multitudes of boys and young men were gathered, and there they were compelled to spend from two to six years in studying the Koran. Philosophy, mathematics, history, natural history, algebra, geometry and astronomy, so assiduously cultivated by the ancient Arabs, are unknown in these schools; indeed, the scientific studies of the Western world are by these self-complacent people utterly despised. I have made personal visits to a number of these theological seminaries—a strange name you will say for institutions from which issue such direful influences.

The largest one of these schools that I have visited, indeed I believe it is the largest in the world, is in Cairo, Egypt, where there are said to be 10,000 students. Their ages ranged from five years upwards; many of them were blind. The pupils were barefoot and half-clothed; each of them had a pigeon-hole less than three feet square assigned to him, in which he kept his books, clothes and food. On entering a large open court, with marble pavement, I saw hundreds of students sitting flat on the floor, grouped around their several teachers. Many of the teachers and students were stretched out full length on the pavement, with bread and dates in one hand and the Koran in the other. Many, if not all of them, were studying aloud; the buzz and confusion arising from such a concourse the reader can well imagine.

The schools are hotbeds of Mohammedanism; both the instructors and the pupils are wildly fanatical; many of them know the Koran well-nigh by heart, but they are wholly incapable of comprehending the meaning of its simplest sentences; intolerant of those who refuse the Koran, they are ready to use the sword. Only one thing more is left for the graduates of these institutions to do to prepare them for their bloody work, namely, to visit Mecca, which every good Mohammedan is expected to do once in a lifetime.

In approaching the sacred city, the devotee strips himself literally stark naked; this done, he goes out into a dark valley, and there, for an hour, "throws stones at the devil." He then returns to the sacred city to listen to a sermon against

Christians, which is well calculated to inflame his passions and arouse his fanaticism to the highest point. The green turban wound around his head is ever afterwards a sign that he has obtained the Prophet's favor by visiting the heavenly city. He now puts on the war paint; unsheathes his sword and flings away the scabbard; perhaps nothing would now more delight him than to shed the innocent blood of "Christian dogs." In many instances pupils from such schools as I have described have armed themselves with sharp knives and clubs, and roamed the streets in search of Christians, and as often as they were found they were left bruised, mangled and generally in a dying condition. So much for the cause of these unspeakable troubles.

What shall I say as to the extent of these atrocities? The massacres are by no means confined to Armenians. Only a few weeks ago in Macedonia I saw a burning village, whose Christian inhabitants had just been massacred; indeed, nothing but the timely arrival of the British fleet at Salonica prevented this slaughter from attaining fearful proportions. Having a personal letter from the Secretary of the American Navy, I obtained an interview with Lord Seymour, Admiral of the English Mediterranean Fleet, who was full of grave apprehensions at these massacres, fearing that they would soon become general throughout the Turkish Empire.

In Northern Syria, a number of Christian men came to my tent and detailed to me some of their recent experiences. Only a week before, several members of their families and friends had been butchered. They said that if they had a cow, a horse, or any other personal property that a Mohammedan wanted, he, without ceremony, possessed himself of it. They appealed to me for help to get away from Turkey and come to America or any other country where they could live in peace and safety. They are willing to sell themselves into perpetual slavery if they could only thereby purchase these inestimable blessings.

At Alexandretta, whither the Marblehead and the California have been sent, several members of my party had a narrow escape. Turkish soldiers from the interior were brought to this port awaiting ships to transport them to some field of action unknown to them. But these soldiers were unprovided for; they were receiving no pay from the government and had no means of sustenance; they slept on the ground under the broad sky; so pinched were they by hunger that they broke into the stores and shops and helped themselves. This caused a great strife between the citizens on the one hand and the soldiers on the other, and soon a mob many hundreds strong was seen struggling in the streets and devastating property. It was a scene of wild confusion. Before I knew it, several members of my party were surrounded by the mob; some of them were arrested, but after great anxiety and considerable delay, they were extricated.

A sight enough to move a heart of adamant was to see twenty Armenian prisoners brought into Alexandretta, each with a huge chain about his neck, and all chained together. They were immediately thrust into prison, where no one, not even foreign officials, was allowed to see them. No doubt some of these poor, unfortunate prisoners were murdered in their chains.

No one who studies the subject with an unbiased mind can, with the facts before him, come to any other conclusion than that the Armenians are a down-trodden, oppressed and long-suffering people.

What are the emergencies of the case? The Armenian people are in deep need of our sympathy, our moral support and our financial aid. These people are full of self-respect, and are heroically struggling for freedom; though outnumbered many times by their foes, they are contending for their religious liberty, and are bravely defending the sanctity of their homes and the honor of their wives and daughters with their lives.

Every civilized nation, especially Christian nations, should in this hour of despair extend to them a protecting hand. Some told me they did not know whence relief would come, but they said they believed that God in His own good time would provide some means of sustenance. Have they exercised this faith in vain? I think not. But the question will have to be answered largely by the Christian people of America.

FROM DR. GRACE N. KIMBALL, VAN.

Ah, my dear friend, what shall I say of the condition of things here! I am heartsick with it all. As I write, and not only now, but all the day and every day, from morning to night, the clamor of wretched men, women and children comes up from below in the street, as they crowd upon us for help. They come by scores and hundreds, the most wretched, forlorn-looking people you ever saw—you never saw!

WALL AND GATE OF LIBASGUN.

Their story is simply that after a hard fight with every disadvantage of Turkish oppression, they had managed to make more or less adequate provision for living in their miserable villages through the winter, when they were descended upon by armed bands of Kurds, robbed of everything, many killed and the rest driven forth, after being stripped even of the clothing on their backs, to wander in snow and mud, and cold, hungry and naked, often entirely barefooted, to find refuge and safety in the city. Many traveled for four, five and six days in this way. I have no idea of how many little babies I have seen, their hands and feet frostbitten, not to speak of the feet of the grown people. Many come in with terrible wounds from rifle or sword or club, and for all there is no hope and no adequate help. During the past ten days we have registered people from over sixty pillaged villages, and daily the number grows. Moreover, there are large districts terribly ravaged, whose inhabitants, through fear of the Kurds or by reason of the deep snow, cannot get here.

Meanwhile, it has been five weeks that the entire business of the city has been stopped, through fear of massacre; hence a large part of the city people are on the verge of starvation and utterly desperate. People in civilized countries have no conception of the utter poverty and misery of these people.

It is nonsense to talk about the Armenians being in revolt against the Turkish government: as well talk of the sheep being in revolt against the wolves. A more submissive, obedient, subject people never existed. What they have suffered and are suffering will never be known—their desolate homes, their murdered fathers, and brothers, and priests, their dishonored women, their children dead and thrown away in their flight, priests cut up in pieces and burned. One faithful old man, abbot of a monastery, was killed with horrible tortures, skinned, and his skin stuffed with straw and placed standing at the door of his monastery. Young women have been stripped naked, outraged, and then turned loose on the mountain-side in the cold and snow. A man today told us of his flight from his village, where he was robbed of sixteen oxen, six cows, thirty sheep, all his winter wheat and supplies and household goods, even the very clothes from the backs of his women and children. They fled to the lake shore, and there in the cold and wet, without shelter or even protection for decency, his son's wife gave birth to a child, and they had not even a rag to wrap it in. These are the things that have become commonplace to our ears, so constantly do we hear them.

CHAPTER XV.

STORY OF THE MASSACRES—HOW CAUSED.

Conversions to Islam—Armenians Terrorized into Abandoning Christianity—Disgrace of European Diplomacy—The Powers Look Calmly on the Turk's Savage Slaughter—Turkish Government Methods.

In newspaper discussion and in press dispatches in this country the responsibility for Armenian massacre has been laid primarily on the Sultan, the Turkish government and the fanatical Moslems of Turkey, and, secondarily, on the different European powers who signed the Berlin Treaty. Under this view, which is the one generally accepted by those best able to judge, the successive massacres were begun under secret orders from the Sultan and continued with the connivance of his officers, the European powers being prevented by their divisions from preventing these appalling outrages or punishing them.

Professor Edwin A. Grosvenor, of Amherst College, in a recent speech at a meeting of the Amherst Alumni in Boston, has precipitated an active and virulent discussion in the press of New England by declaring that the early massacres were deliberately fomented by Armenian revolutionary committees, agitating from a safe distance in Europe and America. Their intrigues, he asserts, precipitated bloody reprisals, natural, and indeed inevitable, under an Oriental despotism. While, therefore, in Professor Grosvenor's opinion "the direct responsibility lies upon the Ottoman government and its Mussulman subjects," the massacres never would have taken place but for the deliberate intention and plan of sundry Armenian revolutionary committees to precipitate disturbances which would lead to European intervention.

This view of the occurrences in Turkey and of the causes of the terrible misery and bloodshed which overspread a region far larger than this State, has the august sanction of the German Emperor, who spoke of the Sultan in his speech at the opening of the Reichstag as he might have spoken of any sovereign suppressing rebellious subjects. It is held and urged by a number of French papers, including the Temps, a well-informed and most able journal. It has evidently colored and influenced Lord Salisbury's policy, and he in his last speech denied that the Sultan had ordered any of the horrible cruelty which has destroyed all revenue over fully a sixth of his empire, and that one of its most fertile divisions.

But this support and corroboration of the view of Professor Grosvenor, for many years a resident in Constantinople and an erudite student of Turkish history, cannot carry conviction to anyone familiar with all the facts. "Till a few months ago," says Professor Grosvenor, "the Armenians were in a state of contemptuous tranquility. The vast majority were even contented with their lot, for they had known no better." This is not true. It would have been true twenty, perhaps even ten, years ago. Up to twenty years ago Turkish despotism, great as were its evils, had come as a relief from the worse, because more irregular, oppression and plunder of local Kurdish feudal lords. Within the last twenty years—it might be more accurate to say since the Berlin Treaty singled out the Armenians as subjects for reform in Turkish administration—the provinces in which they live have been the scene of steadily increasing cruelty, rapine and oppression. The Kurds, hereditary enemies and oppressors, were armed and let loose on the neighboring Armenian villages. The Turkish postoffice and police have begun a systematic espionage. Any letters which admitted of a compromising interpretation were liable to be followed by the arrest or domiciliary search of those to whom they were addressed, if Ottoman subjects. A copy of Armenian national verses, though legendary in character, a national motto among a man's papers, a patriotic schoolboy composition—all these things have been enough in the past ten years to doom men to a lingering death in Turkish prisons or to banishment and slow torture in the distant oases of Fezzan.

For ten years past the condition of all the vilayets which contain Armenians have seen the old, dull, merciless indifference of Oriental despotism edged and armed with the espionage, the arrests, the executions and the banishment of skilled European oppression. This Turkish policy has led to revolutionary committees among expatriated Armenians. With folly unspeakable, with rash temerity, in reckless disregard of all the terrible consequences, these committees began two and three years ago to endeavor to precipitate massacre by futile rising on the deliberate conviction that European interference would follow. The massacres have come. Europe has not interfered.

But the massacres would never have come if the experience and experiments of ten years had not persuaded the Turkish government that it could add to the individual cruelties of the past decade wholesale massacre, the familiar and awful instrument of Oriental rule in all time. These massacres once begun, and there can be no reasonable doubt that the orders for some of them came from Abdul Hamid, the flame of Moslem fanaticism and of Kurdish rapine, so long fostered by the Turkish government, broke forth. Horror unspeakable succeeded. In 2500 villages, men, women and children have been slaughtered, and the miserable survivors, numbering at least 250,000, have been left starving and naked in a winter as severe as our own. In thirteen cities wholesale plunder has followed official massacre, and, while one-third to one-half of the adult Armenian breadwinners have been slaughtered in their shops and homes, the rest of the Armenian population is left destitute and starving, without even doors to their dwellings, every Armenian house being often stripped of every article of value in or on the walls in most cities.

This colossal crime and this appalling misery, like all such terrible catastrophes, have a mingled origin, but the ultimate and exclusive responsibility rests with Turkish misgovernment. Into its reform Armenia cannot enter; but it is possible to begin widespread, general and generous relief, whose distribution has already begun in the massacre district, and which only needs free support and contribution in order to become immediately effective.

Government officials are now forcing the people still left

ARMENIANS SLAIN IN THE STREETS OF BAIBURT.

alive to sign documents that they have no cause of complaint and no needs which are not supplied by the most benign of rulers. Signatures to these documents are obtained by imprisonment, threats of massacre and actual bodily torture. In spite of all these denials, there is reason to believe that over 40,000 may prove to be the number killed. Two hundred and fifty thousand of the survivors are in danger of perishing unless foreign aid reaches them, and as many more have been entirely impoverished. An unknown number of women and children have been carried off by the Turks and Kurds.

Of the devastated region, the province of Harpoot has suffered the most. Sivas, Bitlis and Van come next, and then Erzeroum and Diarbekir. In the provinces of Trebizond, Angora, Aleppo and Adana the devastation was not systematic, as in the other six provinces to which the reform scheme applied. A Turk just in from the province of Sivas has told us of villages through which he passed where none of the people had any clothing, but were huddled in empty houses, without fuel or bedding, sitting on heaps of half-burned straw, with pieces of sacking tied about the waist. This was a region 4000 feet above sea level, where winter is comparable to New York. The rule observed throughout was to strip every house that was plundered, and destroy all that could not be carried away. All the cattle and sheep were carried off, shops were ruined and artisans' tools taken away or broken up. The need of aiding those who live through the winter to make a new start is a pressing one.

The relief thus far has been only in the large cities and to the refugees who have flocked in from the villages. The food supply in the country is sufficient, if funds were in hand to buy it, and two cents a day will keep a man alive. There is no need of bringing food to Turkey from outside. In many places the people are dying from exposure quite as much as from actual starvation. The plunderers are willing to sell off the stolen goods at reduced rates, so that at present all that is needed can be had on the ground.

It is no easy task to save some of the Armenians from death, but the people of America are able and willing to give help, and there are facilities for its prompt and faithful distribution. There cannot be a more worthy cause.

APPEAL BY THE BISHOPS.

Bishops of the Protestant Episcopal Church in the United States who sent a petition to President Cleveland, asking that the government interfere in saving the Christian Armenians from continued massacre at the hands of the Turks, forwarded to the powers of Europe and to the Archbishop of Canterbury a memorial, praying that immediate measures be adopted to compel the Turks to cease from slaughter and persecution.

At the time the petition was sent to President Cleveland, the State Department was consulted as to the best procedure to be followed in order that the petition should reach the eye of the various European potentates to whom it was to be addressed. On the advice of the State Department, the several memorials were forwarded addressed to the Ministers of

Foreign Affairs of France, Germany, Austria and Russia. At the same time in which the letter was dispatched to President Cleveland, a letter was sent to the Archbishop of Canterbury, as head of the English Church. Notice of the reception of the letter to the Archbishop of Canterbury has already been received.

SLAUGHTER OF ARMENIANS BY THE TURKS SHOULD BE STOPPED.

This action thus taken by the Bishops of the Episcopal Church in behalf of Armenia is the result of a letter sent to each of the Bishops by the Right Rev. John Williams, D. D., Bishop of Connecticut, and presiding Bishop, inclosing a circular showing the condition of affairs in Turkey. The circular reads:

As is now generally known, during the months of October and November, the Mussulman population of Eastern Turkey, in many places actively aided by Ottoman troops, put to death from 30,000 to 40,000 Gregorian and Protestant Armenians. The killed were chiefly males, and included a considerable portion of the educated and influential classes in the six provinces named in the reform scheme, namely, the provinces of Erzeroum, Bitlis, Van, Diarbekir, Harpoot and Sivas. A part of the whole number massacred were killed in the cities of Trebizond, Aintab, Marash, Ourfa and Caesarea, which are outside the provinces named above. The massacres were accompanied by pillage on such a scale that nearly the whole Armenian agricultural population in the villages and the greater part of the Armenian traders and artisans in the cities and towns of the provinces and districts named above have been plundered of money, goods, food supplies, clothing, implements, cattle and sheep, their houses being destroyed and themselves reduced to abject want.

The purpose of this paper is to invite the attention of the

Christian world to a progressive aggravation of this awful crime which has been brought to light since the middle of November.

In a territory some 60,000 miles in area an effort has been and is now being made to extinguish Christianity among the Armenian race, by destroying church edifices, killing the clergy, and forcing the surviving members of their flocks in all places where foreign consuls are not present to report the facts to become Mohammedans. It now seems probable that a large part of those who have been killed in the country districts are martyrs, who have refused life at the price of denying their Lord. Multitudes are now being singly approached and put under pressure of the most awful threats if they continue to refuse to deny the Lord Jesus Christ.

The Armenian Church, for centuries the largest and most sturdy of the Asiatic Christian churches, has made great progress in moral, intellectual and spiritual life. Its members have been nursed and fed upon the Bible more than those of either of the other branches of the Eastern Church. This ancient Church is now in the throes of annihilation. Unless Christendom acts instantly and overwhelmingly to arrest this infamy, this century of enlightment will be marked in history as the one in which a Christian people was destroyed with the full knowledge and before the eyes of Christendom, no Christian nation being sufficiently moved by the spectacle to lift a hand to prevent it.

Only from a few places comparatively has the cry of the sufferers been heard. From such instances, however, a slight idea of the ferocity of this attack upon Christianity in Turkey can be gained. It will be noticed that wherever a foreign consul is established these things have not been carried to the extent now revealed, for a consul in Turkey is like a single policeman preserving the public order. It must be observed, also, and emphasized that the same hand which beckons to Europe to wait and see if reforms will not be carried out pushes on its work and screens it from the eyes of foreign observers. Hence the facts which have come to light represent only a small part of the horrors which have occurred.

EUROPEAN POWERS ASKED TO ACT.

The Archbishop of Canterbury, head of the Anglican Church, the American Bishops have thus addressed:

To the Most Reverend His Grace the Archbishop of Canterbury:

My Lord Archbishop: We, Bishops of the Protestant Episcopal Church in the United States of America, having learned with deep sorrow the deplorable and continuous persecution of our fellow-Christians in Asiatic Turkey, do hereby appeal to your Grace in their behalf. Is it not possible for us, laying aside at this crisis all questions political, international or commercial, to rise to the higher plane of earnest, sympathetic action, that a stop may be put to the horrible massacre of Armenian Christians? "If one member suffer, all the members suffer with it." It is evident from a careful analysis of the causes and reasons of this determined assault, that the real object of it is the destruction of the Church in Armenia by the slaying of all who refuse to give allegiance to Islam. It is, therefore, a distinctly religious persecution; and the number of martyrs already sacrificed is probably larger than in any of the persecutions of the early Church. It would seem, considering the ferocity of the cruel attack upon our brethren in Armenia, the awful suffering they are enduring, the fact that the offer is made to these Christians that their lives shall be spared if they renounce their faith—that a crusade supported by Christians the world over would be truly warranted.

We therefore respectfully and lovingly plead with your Grace that, for Christ's sake, for the sake of His religion, you interpose the weight of your office and influence to succor and defend this afflicted and persecuted branch of the Christian Church. May we not ask that the great Church of England, through her episcopate, shall take decisive action—that our suffering fellow-Christians may find not only ready sympathy, but speedy deliverance from their foes?

THE ARCHBISHOP OF CANTERBURY URGED TO BRING TO BEAR THE INFLUENCE OF THE CHURCH OF ENGLAND.

In addition to the letter to the Archbishop of Canterbury, petitions have been sent to the President of the French Republic, the Emperors of Germany and Austria and to the Czar of Russia. Following is the letter to the Czar:

To His Imperial Majesty, Nicholas II, Czar of all the Russias:

Sire: We, Bishops of the Protestant Episcopal Church in the United States of America, most respectfully petition your Imperial Majesty, as the head of the Christian Church in Russia, in behalf of your and our fellow-Christians, the Armenians. They have been subjected to the most cruel persecution by the Turks, and, as we are well informed, under the express orders of the Turkish government, because they are Christians. Tens of thousands have been massacred outright, after having refused to renounce Christ and accept Islam, and some hundreds of thousands are at this moment in utter want and destitution, or even fugitives in the mountains, perishing by cold and hunger, for the same cause. We believe the evidence to be conclusive that the purpose of the Turkish government is to exterminate the Armenians as a Christian people, at least in those interior portions of Anatolia and Armenia where there are no foreign consuls. We implore you, in Christ's name, to come to the aid of our persecuted brethren. Even under the most bloody persecutions among the Roman emperors such an atrocious and wholesale massacre was never perpetrated; and no persecution of the early Church reckoned so many martyrs for Christ's sake. And shall the Christian world of the end of the nineteenth century stand carelessly by and see a Christian community utterly exterminated by the infidels? Our differences of doctrine are as nothing in the presence of a crisis like this. All we, who profess and call ourselves Christians, must place the rescue of hundreds of thousands of our fellow-Christians from death, or what is worse than death, above all questions

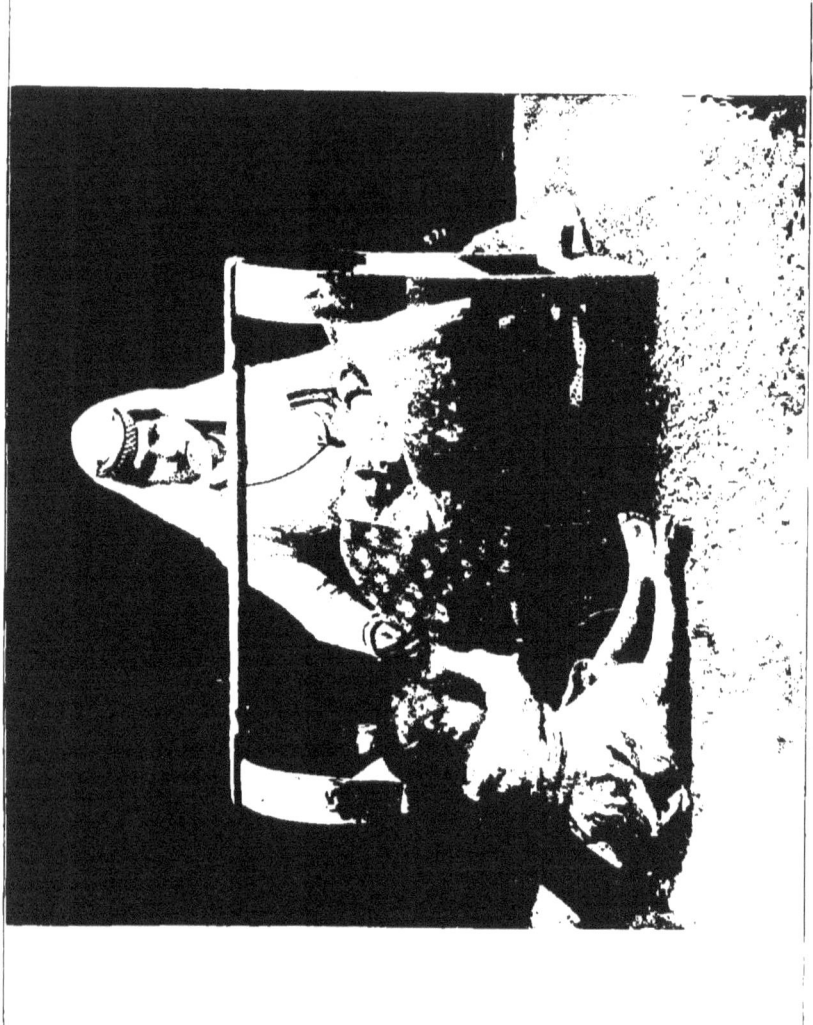

ARMENIAN MOTHER AND CHILDREN

of mere material or national advantage. It is not a question of policy, but of Christianity, and even of common humanity. For Christ's sake save our brothers from death and rescue a Christian community from extinction. In this moment all else should count as nothing in comparison with this. God grant that your Imperial Majesty, whom may God ever guard and guide, may heed our heartfelt cry, for Christ's sake. Amen.

The letters to the Emperor of Germany and the Emperor of Austria and the President of the French Republic are similar to that addressed to the Czar of Russia. The letters have been signed by sixty-two Bishops of the Church in this country.

Authentic reports have been received from the districts of Spargered, Mamardank, Khizan and Gargar, in the Bitlis Vilayet, to the effect that a wholesale conversion of the Armenian population to the ranks of Islam has taken place there. During the recent reign of terror several Sheikhs of Khiza, assisted by their hordes of fanatical followers, among them at least one officer known to the writer, ravaged that whole region, and simply terrorized the helpless people into declaring their faith in Mohammed. First of all, they murdered a certain Sahag Vantabed, as true and brave a man as ever lived, thus cutting off the last hope the people had. They flayed the body, filled the skin with straw and hung it on a tree in front of the beautiful monastery which for twenty-six years he had occupied and defended at the daily risk of his life. Some, at least (the number is not known), followed his noble example and surrendered their lives instead of their Christian faith. The official figures in the possession of an ecclesiastic prelate of these districts gives the number of converts to Islam as 800 families, which would mean at least 4000 individuals.

THE DISGRACE OF EUROPEAN DIPLOMACY.

News of this same grave character comes from Harpoot, whence it was least expected, also from Sert and other places.

For twelve months past those in the interior have been faithfully sending their warnings and urging immediate and effective action, but evidently to no purpose. The representative diplomats of Constantinople no doubt thought they understood their own business, and so they did, if it was their intention to play the leading parts in the most awful tragedy which the nineteenth century has witnessed. If the massacreing of 50,000 people, the forcible conversion of thousands more to Islam, and the reducing of nearly 3,000,000 to the verge of beggary, is the result of diplomacy (and who will deny that it is?), then God spare the world, and especially Turkey, of diplomats. It is the Berlin Treaty and the Anglo-France-Russian farce of 1895 which has ruined the Christians of Turkey. The integrity of the Christian powers stands compromised in the eyes of all Oriental Christendom. It is more than humiliating to watch the mighty nations of Europe bestowing their tenderest solicitude on this most putrid government. The stench which has filled the whole world seems not in the least to offend their political nostrils. How long is the sense of humanity, nay, of decency, to be thus outraged? The tendency now is to think the Turks have done their worst and that anxiety may be suspended;

but let it be known that, as long as Ottoman rule endures, they will not rest content until they have either converted or massacred every Christian in the country. The events of the past three months have given them more encouragement than they have had since the day when the Prophet brandished his sword over the heads of the Jews in Arabia. Is Europe still going to look calmly on while the Turks savagely slaughters or converts the Christians of this land? Is there no conscience, no mercy in the heart of civilized Christendom? If the Christians of this unhappy land are doomed by the decree of Europe, let at least one act of justice be done them by telling them their fate, that they may prepare themselves for the worst.

JAMES BRICE ON ARMENIA.

There is a still more painful subject on which I must speak freely to you. For many years in succession I have described to you the sufferings of the Armenian Christians, have pointed out England's responsibilities, and have repeated to you the predictions of persons who knew the East thoroughly, that before long some massacre would ensue sufficient to endanger the peace of the whole East and to compel the intervention of the Europeans Power. These predictions have been only too completely fulfilled. The massacre of Sassun, an unprovoked massacre, and part of a deliberate scheme for the extermination of the Christian population, was perpetrated on a community of simple mountaineers, the flower of what remained of the Armenian race.

Lord Roseberry's government spoke to the Sultan in the very strongest terms, pressing the need for prompt and sweeping reforms and for the punishment of the guilty, and they endeavored to get Russia and France to join with them. The Turks, of course, resisted, never expressing the slightest regret or remorse for the slaughter, while Russia and France gave a somewhat qualified support, hesitating to adopt what we thought even the irreducible minimum of reforms.

We were still arguing with them and pressing the Sultan when we quitted office last June. The time had not then yet arrived for proceeding to coerce the Turks—though it was plain that it must soon have arrived—because it was deemed proper first to exhaust the resources of remonstance and warning, and if possible to carry Russia and France along with us. When Parliament opened last August, Lord Salisbury addressed to the Turks grave words, which were taken by the country as a pledge that England would do everything she could to secure protection for the Eastern Christians. He repeated this pledge in still stronger and clearer terms in his Guildhall speech. By that time fresh massacres had begun. Massacres have gone on ever since. They have been secretly planned or publicly organized by the Turkish government, and either permitted or actually carried out by Turkish troops; tens of thousands—some accounts seem to put the number above 150,000—of Christians have been slain. Probably as many more have been made homeless, and are dying of famine. Some have sought to escape death by renouncing their religion. Recently we heard of a massacre at Orfah in which 2000 were killed. And now the hardy mountaineers of Zeitun are in danger of a similar fate unless—so the intelligence runs—they surrender their leaders to the mercy of the Turks. With the experience they have of Turkish mercy, and the recollection of the slaughter at Sassun, when the men, women and children who surrendered were massacreed in cold blood, how can they be expected to give up their arms? We may hear any day of a Zeitun massacre surpassing those of the last few months.

And while these things go on, Britain does nothing. Sir M. Hicks-Beach says we have no special responsibility, forgetting the Anglo-Turkish convention, forgetting that it was England that set aside the treaty of San Stefano, by which Russia had undertaken to protect the Armenians, and Britain that substituted for that treaty the Treaty of Berlin, in whose 61st article our obligation stands plainly written, and Mr. Arthur Balfour, while deploring the position, offers no consolation except that "the concert of Europe has been maintained." Six Powers, anyone of which could, by moving a few ironclads, bring the Turk to his knees and stop the massacres, stand helplessly while massacres go on far worse than those which desolated Armenia in the twelfth century, or in those later days when the Turk, now so feeble, except for massacre, was the terror of all Christendom. The concert of Europe is maintained! Six strong men stand by while a ruffian tortures and despatches the victim they have pledged themselves to protect. And it is owing to Britain more than to any other Power that the Turkish government has lived on to do its hideous work, for it was Britain that saved that government in the days of the Crimean war;

Britain that in 1878 deprived the Armenians of the protection which Russia had then promised.

So now Britain is bound, above all the other Powers, to come to the rescue of these victims of ferocity and fanaticism. You may ask whether, for the sake of this rescue, we ought to run the risk of a European war? Certainly no such risk ought to be, or need be, incurred. I speak under the disadvantage of not knowing what communications have passed since June. But everything seems to indicate that Russia and France are reluctant to support so drastic a scheme of reform as our government deem needed, and reluctant also to resort to that coercion by which alone the acceptance and practical application of any reforms can be secured. What, then, ought our course to be? To ask Russia and France whether they will resist the application to the Turks of British coercion, whether in fact they will consider such application to be a casus belli? That they will refuse to allow us to apply coercion can scarcely be expected. If they do refuse, that is to say, if they will neither help us to stop the massacres nor suffer us to stop them alone, they will make themselves responsible for the present horrors, and our hands will henceforth be clean. If they do not refuse, there are several ways and places in which we can soon bring the Turk to reason—Smyrna is one and the Red Sea is another—without danger of further complications. Should the ministry, however, reject this course—and of course there are facts within their knowledge which they have not disclosed to us—then only one other course seems to remain, that of inviting Russia herself to restore peace in the Armenian provinces as the mandatory of Europe.

TURKISH GOVERNMENT METHODS.

The Turkish government is doing its best to make a good appearance to Europe, and one of its latest moves has been to appoint Muavins (assistants) to the governors of the proinces. This office is not a new creation, but had been abolished some ten years ago. Christian Muavins have been appointed to all the six provinces, one to each province in Roumelia except Adrianople, and Moslem Muavins to Aldin, Aleppo and Angora.

Without going into the question whether a Christian assistant ever has influence with a Moslem governor, little real change is expected to be accomplished by them.

It may be remembered that six judicial inspectors were appointed under the reforms, one Moslem and one Christian for each province. None of these has left Constantinople, and now it is announced that Dikran Bey, one of these inspectors for Anatolia, has been appointed Procureur-General for Beirout. One more indication of the seriousness of the reform movement.

Word comes from Erzeroum that the government, under the eye of Shakir Pasha, is distributing flour to the destitute, and this flour is of such a sort that it has brought on an epidemic of sickness.

THE SITUATION AT BITLIS AND ELSEWHERE.

At Bitlis the local authorities are still annoying the missionaries by petty acts. They wish to arrest their servants, and imply rather than say that the missionaries are dangerous characters. Mr. Terrell has denounced the calumnies against Mr. Knapp as lies. At Van everything is quite still, but there is a probability that some effort will be made to bring low the population there. Mr. Terrell has advised the removal of ladies from that place, in which advice he is supported by the missionaries here.

At Erzeroum the exile of the Armenian Bishop has removed one excuse for the Moslems to make trouble. There seems to have been no reason for the exile, save in the fact that the man was an able man. About 1500 persons are being fed. The Porte objects to giving Mr. Barnum a pass to go to Erzeroum, as was desired for the support and comfort of Mr. Chambers.

Harpoot is still in danger of new massacres. The pressure for conversions under threat is still very great. Probably 15,000 persons in the field have accepted the new religion.

Mr. Dewey has returned from Mosul to Mardin in safety, with guards furnished by the government. Mr. Ainslie asks if the government has the right to prevent his touring. The answer is, that the right of travel is not questioned, but only its expediency at this time.

Sivas reports the chapel as packed in the first week of prayer. Mrs. Perry has the cordial support of the Vali in her visit to Guerun. At Marsovan appearances are better. Consul Jewett has been there and is coming to Constantinople this week for consultation. Application has been made for the Red Cross to distribute aid, but the Porte objects. The question is still under discussion. The English embassy has the opinion that the missionaries can do all that is needed in the way of aid without assistance.

The Roman Catholics here and in other places are promising Armenians full protection if they will become Catholic. If France is a party to this, the matter is one for indignation, since it implies an ability to give protection, and a refusal to use the ability for purely selfish reasons.

THE HORRORS OF CAESARIA.

In the district between Guerun and Ghemerig twenty-seven Armenian villages are pillaged and burned. Thirteen villages, five or six hours distant from Ghemezek, such as Dendil, Boorhan, Ilkmen, Karageet, Lisanli, Kyapoonar, etc., are likewise plundered and ruined. Boorhsm was attacked five times and Tekmen seven times. The raiders carried the plunder from Dendil for three days continuously. No clothes, no bedding, no kitchen utensils, and nothing to eat are left to the surviving villagers. They had to live on herbs, which they cooked in the empty tins of the petroleum used by the enemy to burn their houses. In many villages the contents of granaries which the plunderers could not carry away were spoiled with petroleum and filth, so as to make it uneatable. In the district of Tonnooz the Armenian villages, especially Kantavoz, Kazmakara and Patriu, were pillaged and burned, and male inhabitants were butchered and young women were ravished. Some of the villages were entirely ruined. No place inhabited by Armenians in this district has escaped except Talas and Ghemenek. In the latter place the local Turks joined the Armenians to drive back the raiders, who, however, have carried away about 1000 sheep and cattle and about 100 loads of wheat and flour.

A BISHOP'S STATEMENT.

The Bishop of Caesaria gives the following figures as the result of the pillage and massacre of October 30 in that city: Number of killed, 348; wounded, 190; number of young brides and unmarried girls outraged, 50; houses burned, 27; houses plundered, 447; shops pillaged, 250. Many parents, seeing their violated daughters brought back, have exclaimed: "We would that this, our child, also had been among those who fell by the sword, rather than to be brought back to us in this condition." No Christian as yet, Armenian or Greek, dares to open his shop in the city of Caesaria, despite the assurances the authorities are giving to the people that the plundered goods will be found and brought back to their owners. Judging from the wounded, it appears that all kinds of weapons and instruments were used, such as axes, sickles, meat axes, etc.

Mr. Avedis Yeretzian, a medical doctor and pastor, his wife, eldest son and brother-in-law were ruthlessly butchered and thrown into the flames of their burning house because they resisted the raiders.

FEROCITY OF THE TURKS.

In order to give an idea of the ferocity shown by the Turkish mob, the following incidents may serve as examples: The wife of a Turkish military captain happened to be looking from a window when the massacres were going on in the city. She was so much affected by the scenes that she lost her head, and ever since that day her only words have been, "O savage Turks! O beastly Turks!"

In one house there were four young women. The Turks attacked the house and carried away two, leaving the other two to be carried away next time. The two young women, seeing that there was no way of escape, burned the taudir (Oriental oven dug in the floor of the room) very hot and threw themselves into the flames and were burned alive. The raiders, coming back, were very much disappointed to find them dead.

From some places in the interior no letters are sent out unless written in Turkish by the public scribes. This is a censorship not yet ventured in other countries.

TURKEY'S TERROR RECORD.

The work of making out the statistics about the countless smaller villages goes on slowly, but shows that the worst has not been realized. A careful list of those killed at Adaiman, near Aintab, shows the number to have been 1050, but few of whom were women and children. Soldiers were called out after three days' work was done, and are now protecting Christians.

Two strong houses in Adaiman were filled with the prominent and wealthier class of Christians, who, thus inclosed, resisted attacks. The buildings were undermined and fired with kerosene and cotton, and a general holocaust was the result. Over thirty persons were in each dwelling. Both houses contained members of the local governing board. Of the four churches, two were ruined and two burned. It will be noticed in all these accounts that buildings were often spared through fear that the fire might be communicated to Moslem dwellings.

A large number of the villagers had fled for safety into Furnez, near Marash, and finally there was a great slaughter of everybody in Furnez itself, no authentic details of which can be given, but some 300 women and children were brought to Marash, where they were stowed at first in the Third Protestant Church and afterward divided among the committees of the city, seventy-five falling to the Protestants, who received them into their already impoverished homes. At Marash the relief is given at the rate of four cents a head each week.

ENFORCED TELEGRAMS TO SULTAN.

Just before the last massacre at Oorfa, the Christians there paid $20 for the government to send two telegrams to Constantinople, expressing their thanks and love to the Sultan. These telegrams had been wrung out of them by the threat, "If you do not sign you are rebels."

A college graduate, who a few years ago was put into the Marash prison, used often to say that no further experience was needed to set before one a complete idea of hell. There is more comfort in hundreds of the stables in that city than in this overcrowded receptacle of hundreds of men, who are thrown into it with or without reason, and many of whom are kept in there without trial for months.

Preachers, priests, educated men and the lowest criminals are put together almost as closely as cattle in a freight train. No food is ever given to them by the authorities, but the friends of each one must bring it day by day. It first goes into the hands of the Turkish guards, who eat as much of it as they wish, and then give to their friends, whom the government crowds upon the prisoners for support, and the part remaining is handed over to the prisoners.

During the late disturbances and awful massacre of 650 men, not a Moslem was arrested, but Christians were seized without a show of reason, and there they continue in that "Black Hole of Calcutta," month after month, without any prospect of trial, and still less of any show of justice when they are examined. The fact that a man is a human being seems to have no place in the criminal code of the land, and yet an educated Turk can discourse as intelligently upon the humanity that is common to man as an educated European.

DETAILS OF THE HORRORS OF IMPRISONMENT AT MARASH.

The following communication is directly from a man who has been lying in that hell-hole for over a month, and is no more worthy of such treatment than thousands of the readers of this letter. It is given as sent, with the exception of a few words of explanation interspersed to make it fully intelligible to Occidental readers:

Our condition in prison passes description. Only he who

sees can understand it. Most of the occupants of every room are Christians, but many are Moslems. Life would be a shade more tolerable if the subject race were not compelled thus to associate with the dominant race, whose temper, tastes and habits are so different. Into one small room twenty persons are crowded.

Except for a few Moslems, not a single person has room enough on the bare floor to stretch out and lie down. For fully sixteen hours in the night the doors of the rooms are all locked. In one of these small rooms, sometimes twenty cigarettes are smoking at once. Out of the small amount of food which reaches us, the Christians are obliged to feed the Moslems confined there. Instead of eating themselves, the Christians are compelled to supply food to these men. The oppression of the dominant race continues even here. It is a tyranny within a tyranny. In every room there are a few Aghas or principal Moslems, and every Christian must contribute money to their lordships. Those who withhold such contributions are not allowed to sit down.

Among the inmates of the prison are twenty or thirty rowdies and bullies, under whom the Christians must serve as menial slaves. There is no respect, no pity. The horrible blasphemies cannot be described. There is no book, no Bible, no work, no sleep. Every man is covered with the swarming vermin with which the unwashed rooms of the prison teem. To clean ourselves is impossible. Now and then the rumor sweeps through the prison that we are all to be put to death, and all our hearts melt like water.

The terrible darkness of the night, the curses and stripes inflicted from time to time, cause us to live in the valley of the shadow of death. It is a living grave, a visible hell, a world without God. Out of this throng of prisoners more than a hundred are in daily suffering from the gnawings of hunger and from nakedness, but there is no one to pity. Many praying men are tempted to cease praying, many are tempted to change over to the Moslem faith. In truth, all of us are dumb; what we say we know not. We are wearied of the long silence; our eyes are strained with watching, our bones ache, our prayers are despised by the revilers. Night is not night and day is not day. Our grief is our food, our sleep is weeping. For how long a time must we cry? Oh, Lord, wilt Thou hide Thyself forever? How long will Thy anger burn like fire? And yet some of us are saying: "Though He slay me, yet will I trust in Him."

When will the Christian statesmen and philanthropists of the world find a way to cleanse these Augean stables all over Turkey? Long centuries cry out for redress.

CONFESSIONS OF SEDITION EXTORTED BY TORTURE.

Within a month the following incidents have occurred: A Christian confined in this prison was ordered to receive 400 stripes. After 300 had been inflicted he cried out that he could endure no more or he must die. An officer then presented to him a paper with the names of fifty Christians in the city who were accused therein of sedition.

In his great agony he signed it, and this is to be used to incriminate others, wholly regardless of their guilt or innocence. The other victim of unendurable stripes was an old man. When he could endure no more of this inhuman treatment, he also was asked to sign a paper implicating others indiscriminately.

Can anyone living in a free country for a moment understand what it is to live under such a government? There is a great flourish just at present over the reforms that are being instituted in certain parts of this land. No resident of this country can have confidence in the superficial operations. What will you do with a land where lying is the simplest of mental exercises, and where no one was ever known to blush over it if exposed?

TURKS LOST AT ZEITOUN.

In spite of the report spread abroad by the Turkish government regarding the attack on Zeitoun, it has not been a success. The Zeitounlis, fighting against superior numbers, were favored by their impregnable position and by the winter season. The facts that the Turks were able to close in to the Hot Springs, five miles from Zeitoun on the east, and at least to Furnuz, eight miles from Zeitoun on the west, over roads which are supposed to be impassable during the winter, seems to show that the Zeitounlis were not strong enough to defend the approaches.

Zeitoun lies in a deep valley, and there are four roads that lead into it. One is directly over the mountains from Marash to the south. This road is considered impassable in winter, and has to cross the Jihan river by a bridge about six hours from Zeitoun. The second road leads from the direction of Geben on the southwest. This is the usual winter road from Marash, and crosses the Jihan only four hours out of Marash. The third leads from Guksun on the northwest and passes through Furnuz three hours directly west of Zeitoun. The fourth road leads from Albostan and the rugged northeast country and passes through the Hot Springs about two hours east of Zeitoun.

TEN THOUSAND SAID TO HAVE BEEN SLAIN IN THE HOT SPRINGS FIGHT.

It will be remembered that the plan of attack was to approach Zeitoun with the army in three divisions, closing in from Marash, Geben and Guksun. Of these three roads, the mountain road from Marash would be the easiest to defend, because, besides the bridge over the Jihan, there is a high, narrow gorge three hours from Zeitoun at the point where the city is first visible. The road from Guksun is also easily defended, and the 3000 men concentrated at Guksun seem to have taken little part in the attack. The Geben division of 5000 men, weakened by sickness, moved forward slowly, and the main advance was made from Marash over the most difficult road of all. It is possible that, as once reported, the bridge across the Jihan, four hours from Marash, had been destroyed and the main army of about 10,000 men could not take the winter road.

The Zeitounlis, at the very commencement, had succeeded, by cutting off the water supply, and, after an attack of sixty hours, in capturing the barracks of the city, and the Turkish reports say that the Zeitounlis held 593 prisoners. It was in this engagement that the two sons of Babik, once the chief of the Zeitounlis, were killed (Bablik himself died several years ago, confessing on his deathbed that his death was due to a kerosene can of whiskey which he had drunk the night before.

Although the Turks claim to have captured the barracks commanding Zeitoun, the fact that the battle took place at Hot Springs, five miles east of the city, makes it look as though only the heights had been taken, and not the barracks, which are but one-quarter of a mile from Zeitoun. The tributary of the Jihan, which passes through Hot Springs from Zeitoun, is a dry bed in summer, but at this season of the year it is a rushing, unfordable torrent, and is crossed by a stone bridge.

The Zeitounlis made a partial stand at the bridge, and slowly withdrew up the steep road, followed by almost the entire Turkish army. When most of the Turkish army had crossed, the bridge was suddenly blown up, and the Zeitounlis, from the precipitous banks of the stream, rained down bullets and rocks. They had prepared small mines of dynamite down in the valley, and they may have had also dynamite bombs. The Turkish account is "fire burst out from the air or from the ground, and destroyed the army."

The defeat of the army was complete. Since it had not got into Zeitoun, there was no place where it could be sheltered; it was obliged to resign all it had captured and retreat to Marash. The only report from Marash which estimates the killed gives the Turkish losses as 10,000, although this number does not seem possible.

What was left of the army went back into Marash over the direct Zeitoun road the 30th and 31st of December. The wounded were put into some of the Christian churches. The Zeitounlis are said to have enough provisions to last until July. Whatever may be the result of the mediation, no further attack can be made until after March. Whether the detachment of the Turkish army, which had reached Furnuz, on the west, has tried to hold its position has not yet been learned.

Regarding the numerical strength of the Zeitounlis, nothing can be said with certainty. At the start their success in taking four or five hundred prisoners gave an idea of great strength. If, however, they were able to cut off the water supply, this fact would be of less significance, and in the battle of Hot Springs the rebel leaders had every advantage of position and science. There is no doubt that there are wise heads in command at Zeitoun.

That the Turks are waging a war of extermination against Zeitoun is shown by their treatment of the villages around. Furnuz is situated about nine miles east of Zeitoun, and with the approach of the Turkish army, the Christians had fled into Furnuz from the surrounding villages, until finally there were at least 4000 people crowded into the town. They had watchers out on the approaches to give warning of the arrival of the Turkish army, with the intention of fleeing to Zeitoun. In some way the Turkish army eluded those watchers and surrounded the town by night, so that the unfortunate Christians awoke to find a cordon around them.

BRUTAL TREATMENT OF PRISONERS.

Three hundred women and children were brought by the soldiers to Marash. They say that all the rest were killed. This two days' winter journey over the snow was especially hard on the children. Many of them dropped down on the way from exhaustion and were left to die. The soldiers would not permit the mothers to delay the march. On reaching Marash, they were crowded into the Third Protestant Church, and only with the greatest difficulty did a Bible woman push past the guard to get among them.

She found many Catholics, and the Jesuits of Marash

came forward to do their share of the relief work. Many of the orphans were adopted, and the whole 300 were soon distributed among the already impoverished homes of the Christians.

DESTITUTION IN MARASH.

One Christian in Marash took thirteen of these Furnuz refugees into his yard, where he was living with his wife and several children, one three days old, on the ground. Their house and all their clothing, except what they had on, had been lost, and there were no clothes for the newcomers. The father went to the Americans, who made up a little bundle of clothing, and he started home. But, as he returned, even that little bundle was taken from him by the soldiers.

MASSACRE IN ERZEROUM.

The following description of the massacre at Erzeroum, which appeared in the London Times, November 16, 1895, is selected, because it is written by an eye-witness:

On October 30, at noon, I was at lunch, when our Armenian neighbors, with blanched faces, rushed into the hall and breathlessly said, "They've commenced firing in the market." I knew what this meant, for a struggle had been expected every day between the Christians and Mussulmans. We ran to the balcony and heard rifle and revolver shots in every direction, near and far. The neighboring Armenian women with their children came flocking into the American mission building, where I was stopping. This building, being much larger and stronger than the native houses, was looked on as a castle, and then, too, being a residence of foreigners, the people felt safer. But soon the house was simply jammed with two hundred and twenty-five women and children and about seventy-five men. Among these latter were six rifles and about twenty revolvers, with about 1000 rounds of ammunition in all. One of these men, a young fellow named Aram, came running to the mission hotly pursued by Turks with revolvers, which they fired, but fortunately he got off without a scratch.

I went up to the roof of the building and saw the mob and soldiers running pell-mell towards the market, firing right and left into the houses on their route, from a few of which the fire was returned. The whizzing of bullets induced me to go below, for the Turks and Armenians were popping away at any fair mark they could find. Soon Mr. Chambers, the American missionary, returned. We had been anxiously awaiting him. He had been up to the postoffice. On his way back through the long, straggling market he noticed a general uneasiness. Then he passed an Armenian who was running from one shop to the other, telling his brethren to close their shops and run, for the firing would soon commence. He walked on for five minutes from the spot where he had seen Murad, when he heard shots behind him. The people began to run, and he followed suit. Some friends told him afterwards that the Turks had fired at him, but he did not know whether it was the mob or the soldiers. He met one of the patrols of twenty soldiers, under command of an officer, who were supposed to keep the peace. These men had drawn their revolvers and were shooting right and left down the street and into the windows. The bullets whistled unpleasantly near to Mr. Chambers, who walked on until he was with us at his home in the mission building. All this time a perfect fusillade was going on, mostly in the direction of the bazar. In the extreme western part of the city a large fire had broken out, the smoke of which drifted across the large barracks that are situated in that part of the city. There seven Armenians resisted the attack of the soldiers, who fired on them, riddled the house with bullets, and then set fire to it, and it continued to burn for twenty hours.

One of the most curious things was the number of women hanging about the soldiers to carry off the plunder obtained. All the robbing and looting in our section was done entirely by the regular soldiery, commanded by their officers. At the head of the Gumruk street I saw the officers lead a detachment of soldiers to two Armenian houses; the commanding officers themselves knocked open the doors, entered, and looted the whole house, stripping it completely, not leaving even a "haseer" (straw mat). Just before this, an Armenian, with his head bandaged, came to the front door. We took him in. It was an awful sight; the blood was running from the bandage all over his clothes. Mr. Chambers dressed his wound, which was an ugly skull wound. The bullet had entered just above the left eye, and it passed out, apparently, in the left temple; but there was also a hole in the back of the head. The wound continued to bleed for several hours. I was astonished to see a man with such a wound run up to our place from the bazars and never once lose consciousness or faint from loss of blood.

The Demir Sokak (Iron street) suffered fearfully. This street was nearly all Armenian; only a Turkish house here and there. From our windows I saw the soldiers on the roofs robbing every house systematically, making up their bundles, which were carried away by horsemen, whom we saw passing the head of our street towards the Turkish quarter of the city. Next day this street was a woful sight. Every house was wrecked except those of the Protestant minister (Badvilli Krikor), a wealthy Armenian Protestant merchant, Ohanazar Aghajanian, and another, Manovg Agha (also a wealthy merchant), had been wrecked. These, I was told, were protected by a friendly Turkish neighbor, who, however, robbed many of the others. The other houses were stripped bare; every door was either splintered to pieces or broken in, frame and all, by heavy sledge-hammers. This is what the soldiers did in our quarter, and later reports from reliable quarters left no doubt in my mind that they did most of the pillaging and almost all the killing.

The suspense during the afternoon, during all the night, and the next morning, was intense. The house was by this time as foul-smelling as a menagerie. Babies were crying and women were in hysterics. None would sit down, so nervous were they. When night came on there was no room for them to sleep. None of them had anything to eat, but, forfunately, Mr. Chambers was able to give them each a little native bread from a supply that had just been laid in. No one knew where his kinsfolk were. The worst fears haunted them all. Some wept for a brother, for a mother, or sister, or father. Some had left their children at home, too sick to take away, and there was one baby with smallpox in the crowd. It was a beautiful moonlight night, and we could see the Turks carrying away the plunder all night. Occasionally a volley of shots rang out clear on the cold air, or the barking of dogs.

TURKEY FROM THE INSIDE.

By Rev. Edward Riggs, Marsovan.

Yes, we have had our massacre, too, and, although it is seven weeks today since it took place, the impression of it has been so scorched into my consciousness that it seems but yesterday whenever I recall the hideous scenes. For days and weeks it had been prognosticated, but the human mind is slow to take in such strangely improbable things, and no one realized that it was really coming. When, however, the very day and hour were openly talked about, and warnings, friendly and hateful, were greatly multiplied, some of those most likely to be in exposed positions went to the authorities and asked whether they would be safe to open their shops the next day. Let the sheep go and ask the wolf where he had better find shelter! They were assured that nothing should happen to them, and that they should, in any case, be protected, etc. The next day was Friday, and at noon the muezzin called from the minaret the hour of prayer. Hundreds crowded to the mosques, and Moslem fanaticism was at his high-water mark. In the yard of one of these mosques someone fired two shots, and another rolled over and screamed in well-simulated agony. At once the cry arose that the holy assemblage was attacked, and as the crowd surged out of the building, it was only a question where the lightning would strike first. Many were already armed, and others rushed to their houses to seize such arms as they could lay their hands upon. Axes, clubs, knives— anything with which a deadly blow could be struck. At first the mob surged up toward the mission premises. Fugitives, rushing wildly in, brought the dread news, and our gates were at once closed and bolted. But slight defence would they have been against the fanatical mob if they had actually assailed them. The large school buildings were abandoned, and students huddled together in frightened groups in the missionaries' houses. Nearer and yet nearer rolled the volume of mingled sound. Frantic yell, despairing scream, and sickening groan, with rifle and pistol shots, and thundering banging on doomed doors, thud of axe, and crash of useless barriers. Bullets came whistling over toward the school building, rattling on tiles and clapboards. Houses separated from our own premises by but a thin mud wall were gutted, and their occupants butchered, and through cracks in one of our gates a woman was seen lying close by, groaning in the agonies of death. It would seem, however, that these assailants were but skirmishing detachments, and the main body of the mob was met and turned back by influential and humane Turks, as well as by gendarmes and soldiers. Then they headed for the market, with an eye to plunder. In a few minutes 120 Armenians were slain, and their shops looted and left as clean as if they had never contained an article. Indelibly printed on my memory is the scene in our own sitting-room during those awful hours. Pupils and teachers and servants and neighbors crowded together in our small rooms. Tears were few, but pale faces, fixed eyes and rigid features, with suppressed groans, and whispered exclamations, showed the depth of the emotion—the horror and dread that filled all hearts. When the horrid tide was swelling nearest, we expected every moment to see our own gates crashed in. Then we raised our voices to heaven in such a prayer as perhaps no one of us ever poured forth before. Neighbors, unaccustomed to such worship, were hushed in silent awe, and joined in our Amen. When our prayer came to a close, we found that the tide had turned, the din was sounding more distant, and it appeared that our premises were intact. It was the hand of God, working through the friendliness of individual Turks, and through the policy of the government, which desired that so far as convenient no direct harm should come to foreigners. The local governor detailed a detachment of soldiers to surround and protect our premises, and toward night brought us a squad of thirty soldiers, under the command of a lieutenant, who have remained on our grounds ever since.

On the day which followed that terrible 15th of November a ghastly sight was visible from our windows. In the little valley that lies between us and the Armenian cemetery were deposited the corpses of the slain. No tender hand composed the limbs, or washed away the clotted blood. Cartload after cartload, they were brought like so much refuse, and dumped in disordered heaps. Even there they were not let alone, but covetous hands stripped off the few remaining rags, leaving the bodies in every degree of nudity. Then a long trench was dug, and eighty-three corpses were laid in it and covered up to wait till their testimony shall be called for at the last judgment. Among them were five women and several children.

We are conscious that we stand face to face with very threatening possibilities. Present duty seems to be clearly to stand at our post, hoping for the best, and prepared for the worst. If we survive the great changes that are evidently imminent, we shall hope for a broader and more fruitful field of labor than we have ever had before. And if we should be suddenly eliminated from the sphere of this great problem, we know that sooner or later others will take our places, and the work to which our lives are devoted will in due time be accomplished.

TABULAR VIEW OF THE ARMENIAN MASSACRES.

Name of Town.	Date of Massacre.	Number Killed.	By whom done.
Constantinople	Sept. 30	172	Police and Softas
Ak Hissar	Oct. 9	45	Moslem villagers
Trebizond	Oct. 8	800	Soldiers, Lazes, and Turks
Baiburt	Oct. 13	1,000	Lazes and Turks
Gumushane	Oct. 11	No	details
Erzingjan	Oct. 21	1,000	Soldiers and Turks
Bitlis	Oct. 25	900	Soldiers, Kurds, and Turks
Harpoot	Nov. 11	1 000	Soldiers, Kurds, and Turks
Sivas	Nov. 12	1 200	Soldiers and Turks
Palu	Oct. 25	450	Soldiers, Kurds, and Turks
Diarbekr	Oct. 25	2,500	Soldiers, Kurds, and Turks
Albistan	Oct.	300	
Erzeroum	Oct. 30	800	Soldiers and Turks
Ourfa	Nov. 3	300	
Kara Hissar	Oct. 25	500	Circassians and Turks
Ma'atia	Nov. 6	250	
Marash	Nov. 18	1,000	Soldiers and Turks
Aintab	Nov 15	No	details
Gurun	Nov. 10	3.000	Kurds and Turks
Arabkir	Nov. 6	2.000	Kurds and Turks
Argana	No	details	
Severek	No	details	
Mush	Nov. 15	6	Kurds
Tokat	No	details	
Amasia	No	details	
Marsovan	Nov. 15	125	Turks
Cesarea	Nov. 30	1,000	Circassians and Turks
Gemerek	No	details	
Egin	No	details	
Zileh	No	details	
Se'ert	No	details	

TURKISH STATISTICS FOR SEVEN VILAYETS WITH ESTIMATED LOSSES.

Armenian population in larger towns............................. 177,700
Armenian population in villages................................. 588,500
Number killed in towns (estimated).............................. 20,000
Number of Armenian villages (about)............................ 3 300
Number of villages destroyed (estimated)....................... 2,500
Number killed in villages.......................................No data
Number reduced to starvation in towns (estimated)............. 75,000
Number reduced to starvation in villages (estimated).......... 350,000

Note.—All the numbers given above, including the Turkish statistics, are more or less inaccurate, but the estimates are based upon a careful study of all the information which has reached Constantinople from many independent sources.

CHAPTER XVI.

CLARA BARTON AND THE RED CROSS.

By Myrtis Willmot Barton.

The story goes that toward the end of the sixteenth century there lived in Lancashire five brothers, who decided that not only was Lancashire too small, but England not quite large enough, to hold them all; so one went to Ireland, and from him come the Bartons of Grove; another wended his way to the land of the canny Scots, where in time the name became changed to Bartan; a third crossed over to France, where his descendants bear the name of Bartin; a fourth settled in Southern England, under the name of Burton; and, after fifty years, the younger son of that Barton who remained in the old home, one Marmaduke by name, was seized with the wandering spirit of his race, and, coming to America within a dozen years after the landing at Plymouth, founded the family of which Clara Barton is the brightest light. Thus she comes from a race of sturdy pioneers and volunteer soldiers; the very name Barton in the Anglo-Saxon means "defender of the town."

Her father, Captain Stephen (one of the youngest sons of Dr. Stephen Barton and beautiful Dorothy Moore), was a man prominent in the business and political life of his town and State; until incapacitated by age, he was always chosen

"Moderator" to preside at town meetings; he was also a captain of the militia—being a soldier by training and nature, having served for three years in the Indian wars by the time he was of age; and, in short, was a man universally respected and esteemed for his bravery and goodness of heart. The family into which my Aunt Clara was born was already a grown-up one, she being the youngest, by a dozen years, of five children. With her two sisters and eldest brother all teachers themselves, it is not surprising that she began her school-life at the age of three, riding to and from the rude little building on the shoulder of her big brother Stephen, who was a teacher there, and studying quietly in classes by the side of boys and girls many years her senior. She has told me she never remembers possessing a doll, her loving care having been lavished on the pets of the household—a sick cat or dog appealing more strongly to her sympathies than anything else. The only inanimate playthings she had were wooden soldiers fashioned by her brothers, and with these her father would amuse and interest her, as together they fought over the battles of his younger days, until she felt all the fire and enthusiasm of a soldier following the lead of Mad Anthony Wayne, and learned lessons in military tactics and war as though in preparation for the life before her.

Lest I give the idea that her time was devoted entirely to books, I must speak of her outdoor life, for she was one of those fleet-footed, agile girls, strong of limb, clear-headed, and perfectly at home in a saddle. Her younger brother, David, instead of being studiously inclined, as were the others, was passionately fond of horses; so that when she was but a wee child he would put her on the back of a young horse, while he, on another, would hold her hand, and together they would canter around the fields, in and out among the other horses, broken and unbroken. Those who know her now will understand what a sensitive, shrinking girl she must have been, never thrusting herself forward, and avoiding, rather than seeking, strangers; although, in her own home, she was gay and light-hearted, full of fun and jokes, with the keen sense of humor which she has never outgrown, and the power of making the drollest speeches in a quiet, irresistible way; the knack of remembering, and telling well, a good story has always been one of her greatest charms. Remembering her shyness and modesty, one can imagine how soon it must have been tried, when, as a little nine-year-old girl, she went away from home to board in the family of the teacher under whom she was to study. The love and respect she bore this man are things of which she cannot speak now with dry eyes, and his sayings and advice she remembers and often repeats to this day.

Thus the years passed, first in study, then at home caring for a sick brother—nursing him through a dangerous illness though a mere child herself; and, when scarce entering girlhood, away with a school of her own to teach, and later at a college for young women, until she came back to assist her brothers in the counting-rooms of the mills they had built. She was always wise, always helpful—going home when needed, and, when the work in hand was done, going away to earn a little more by her teaching or bookkeeping, and with those earnings to further educate herself—taking a few lessons in one thing here, a few more in another branch there —until she went to Washington as one of the first women in a department of the government.

Her labors in the civil war have been recounted to often and so minutely that I shall not undertake to describe them again in so brief a sketch as this. The story of her courage and self-sacrifice the world can never know in its fullness— except as she consents to give it to us in the autobiography upon which she is now at work.

In Miss Barton's home in Washington is a collection of Andersonville relics—rude cups and plates, and still ruder tools, all made by those poor prisoners, and these, while each speaking of heartache and misery, bear also, to those who know how to read between the lines, a story of that melancholy comfort that makes a woman rejoice, even though her loved ones be dead, in knowing that they were given Christian burial, and that a woman's hand, with pity and tenderness, marked their last resting-place. To see Miss Barton before a group of Grand Army men shows how she must have worked and ministered through those long, hard years of war to have so won the esteem and admiration of these strong men.

Clara Barton's connection with the Red Cross began when, at the end of the sixties, worn out and broken down in health, she went to Switzerland to rest and grow strong again, only to find there more work to do, and, finding it, to so enter into it, heart and soul, as never to lay it down. At the breaking out of the Franco-Prussian war there came to her, in her Swiss cottage, several members of the International Committee of the Red Cross, en route for the scene of action. They explained their errand, begged her to join them, and finally so filled her with enthusiasm that, ill as she was, she promised to follow them within a fortnight.

She was at once presented to the sweet, unassuming daughter of Kaiser William I, the Grand Duchess of Baden, who, with her ladies of the court around her, was working as hard and unceasingly as any simple woman of our own land worked during our great conflict; and, as they worked together, these two women found themselves mutually helpful —my aunt bringing forward her practical experience, and the Grand Duchess being able to teach her the methods and objects of the Red Cross, its workings and its ways; so that, all through her months there, in the field, at court, or in the hospitals, while she was doing good in her own way, she was acquiring the knowledge necessary for the fulfillment of her ultimate promise—to work unceasingly until she should have brought her own country into the treaty; for the international character of the Red Cross is a feature of the greatest importance, though often forgotten.

It would be impossible to enter here into a detailed account of her life during the Franco-Prussian strife; it would be too long a story, however interesting, to follow her about from hospital to battle-field, and from Strassburg to Paris, which latter place she entered the day after the siege was raised; but, as an illustration of her work there, and as showing the sorrows of the weaker sex during war, there stands out in my mind one picture. Among the recollections of a dozen years ago I remember seeing in a little Frenchwoman's studio a large, unfinished painting of a scene in a Strassburg hospital. It was a picture to appeal to my childish eyes, for there stood my aunt with her head turned away toward a baby in a woman's arms, while women leaned toward her to catch a word, and children clung to her skirts, and one little boy, half afraid, had lifted a corner of her gown to his lips. I hope that picture may be finished some day. The gown in this picture, by the way, is green, my aunt's favorite color. The story is told that one of her sisters once said: "When Clara goes to town to buy a brown dress, a brown dress I know she will get, for Clara always does as she says. But, one way or another, that dress always manages to turn green before she can get home."

I have said that as regards the international character of the Red Cross so little seems to be known; the name, as a general rule, brings to people's minds a hazy idea of "trained nurses," and "something to do with hospitals," when in reality it stands for a great treaty entered into by the nations of the earth for the purpose of alleviating the sufferings of war. It shows that, although that glorious day when war shall be over and all difficulties settled by arbitration has not yet come, still the time has arrived when a wounded man is no longer left to die on the field, nor shut up in a prison to expire little by little—that the time has even now come when the sick and wounded of the enemy are cared for with the same tenderness shown one's own.

Under the flag of the Red Cross all ground is neutral; all persons lawfully wearing its brassard can go unmolested; in its hospitals are found friend and foe, side by side, with every thought of personal strife left outside its walls, and only the motto of humanity and neutrality in mind. One by one, nearly every civilized nation of the world has accepted the invitation to enter, becoming a party to the great treaty; and the reasons that the United States did not join sooner are, first, that the idea was never presented to the people themselves, the knowledge of the treaty never having gone beyond the State Department; and, second, that the possibility of war for us was so remote that our Government seemed to think it a useless step until the new feature known as the American Amendment was suggested, whereby relief was to be given to the victims of the terrible national calamities so frequent here; this additional to the original scope of the treaty, in its purely war character, made it appeal more fully to our people and our officials. Since the adhesion of the United States, in 1882, several succeeding nations, in joining, have added the American Amendment to the provisions of the treaty.

It is a long story, that of those ten years between the close of the Continental war and the final accession of the United States—a long story, full of discouragements, false hopes and disappointments, full of weary months, I may say years, of nervous prostration, when my aunt was so ill that it seemed as if she were a weak little child, and had to grow up again. But, as soon as she was able, she was up from her sick-bed and in Washington, ready to begin the work to which she had pledged herself; and, at last, through the interest and co-operation of those great statesmen, Garfield, Windom and Blaine, steps were taken necessary for making the United

States one of the Red Cross nations—the untimely death of the martyred President leaving the honor of signing the treaty to his successor, President Arthur, who affixed his signature and made proclamation of the fact in 1882.

We have had no wars in the past fifteen years to call the Red Cross into its original field of action, but in the time of suffering from the elements it has come nobly to the front, doing the work of humanity in the quiet, unostentatious way characteristic of its American president; asking nothing, distributing what was given with a wise and generous, though frugal, hand, bringing order out of chaos, feeding the hungry and clothing the destitute, at first; teaching the people to help themselves rather than making them objects of charity; so that, in every case where the Red Cross has quitted a field, it has left the mass of the people better off than before the disaster—better off because of the practical lessons inculcated as well as from the gifts distributed.

It has worked at such times as those of the forest fires of Michigan, the Texas drought, the Mount Vernon cyclone, the Johnstown flood, twice on the Ohio at the time of the floods, for ten months at the Sea Islands after the cyclone and floods there; and, after being at home but one year, preparations are even now being made whereby, if so decided, Miss Barton will start with a few of her staff for the East, to carry food, money and clothes to the suffering Armenians. This, if undertaken, will be a new and terrible kind of work—an undertaking full of peril and danger, and one requiring the head of a diplomat and a heart of courage, as well as the hand and soul of a philanthropist.

Altogether, the work of the Red Cross here has been of a different nature from that in other countries; that it is not conducted on quite the same plans and principles as in Germany of Italy, for instance, is due to the difference between the governments of those countries and ours, the difference in the character of the people, and to the entirely different kind of work needed. That there are so few authorized sub-societies is owing mainly to lack of knowledge and even to indifference on the part of many. In New York city there is, however, an association under its direct patronage, which, since its founding, has done good and faithful work in its nursing among the poor, as well as in its hospital and training school, which is to supply all the nurses used by the National Red Cross.

The New York branch, of which Mrs. Charles H. Raymond is president, is at present located on One Hundredth street, between the Boulevard and West End avenue, and is under the supervision of Miss Bettina Hofker, who, although but a young girl, has won laurels for her self-sacrifice and devotion while working in the slums of this city, before she undertook the larger and more responsible position of training "Sisters" for true Red Cross work. It will be a gratification to the people of New York to know that their institution is the especial pride of Miss Barton, it being begun and carried out on the genuine Red Cross ideas, brought straight from Germany.

The American National Red Cross has its headquarters at Miss Barton's home in Washington—in a house well fitted, because of its location and history, to be the centre of such a work as that of the Red Cross. On the corner of Seventeenth and F streets, across the street from the War, State and Navy Departments, and on the opposite corner from the famous old Winder Building, stands a large, old-fashioned house, a place of great, high-studded rooms—plain, comfortable, staid and substantial, but with a total absence of any suggestion of luxury. Here live Clara Barton and the Red Cross. The house was built in Jefferson's time, and for many years was the private residence of General Jessup, of the old army; then, during the civil war, it was the headquarters of the army of Generals Halleck and Grant; and my aunt has pointed out to me the room in which, for months, lived the famous Indian, General Eli Parker, and has told me a story of his singular life and ways. In another room General Horace Porter had his office, and out of General Grant's great room was that of Colonel Dent, while many other well-known names are associated with the various rooms.

It is a house in which to remember half-forgotten stories and bits of history, each and all suggested by the rooms themselves or their contents. Thus, in a vase in the reception-room one sees a large bunch of wild rice, gathered and dried by my aunt at the siege of Fort Wagner—gathered from a spot over which had rained shot and shell for a whole long day; close beside it stands a modern photograph of her Highness the Grand Duchess of Baden; while upstairs, in my aunt's own room, there hangs, in its quaint frame of twenty-five years ago, a larger portrait of her, showing the sweet, womanly face as my aunt first knew it in its youthful beauty. Again, one finds some curious and beautiful pillows of Russia leather in all colors, sent home at the time of the relief work of our Red Cross during the Russian famine; and in an out-of-the-way corner, as far from being on exhibition as possible, lies a bit of wood from the fence of the dead-line within Andersonville prison.

The walls of the corridors are hung with banners and immense flags of all nations. Norway and Sweden greet one upon opening the door; on either side hang the crown of Italy and the cross of St. George and St. Andrew; in the drawing-room are two beautiful flags of silk—the dainty blue and white of Greece, surmounted by the silver ball and crescent; and the flag of brave little Switzerland, of which our Red Cross is the reverse. The most magnificent of these is the enormous black eagle of Prussia; in the upper corridor hangs the flag of United Germany, the large eagle, with its circle of smaller ones; then come the tri-color of France, the Russian ensign, and many others, all sent as personal gifts in appreciation and acknowledgment of her service under the one little flag to which they all bow.

As is the case with all the rest of the house, Miss Barton's office is devoid of useless luxuries; it is plain, simple and devoted entirely to business. Here she works from early in the morning until late at night, answering personally and by dictation the enormous daily correspondence from all parts of the world, transacting business of all kinds, working quietly and steadily for hours, forgetting to eat, and, one is tempted to say, to sleep as well, for she is always the first one up in the morning, and frequently works until away into the small hours of the night.

The question naturally arises, How has she preserved her strength and youth so marvelously? The only answer to my mind seems to lie in the fact that she is so quiet and calm that she never wastes her strength, coupled with a thoroughly acquired knowledge of how to live and keep well; and as for sleep, she has the happy faculty of being able, at any time and in any place, to curl up, sometimes in the most cramped positions, and sleep for fifteen minutes, then, waking, to take up the conversation or work just where it was dropped and go on.

The letters she receives are most curious, interesting and touching; all of them showing love—and all receive the same kind attention. Indeed, I have seen her, on several occasions, toss aside, until she had more time, some delicate letter in the unintelligible fashionable hand of the day—from some stranger who thinks she has more time to study over the writer's words than the latter has to write them distinctly in the first place—only to take up reverently and lovingly a poor, misspelled, badly written, much-blotted letter of love and thanks written by a Southern negro whom the Red Cross had helped at some time.

Questions are frequently asked concerning Miss Barton's religious belief; on that score I can say that she comes of a family of most liberal-minded people, and this, combined with her life, has led her to adopt the true Red Cross spirit, making no distinction in the race, nationality, nor creed—the word "humanity" embracing everything—so that it may well be said of her, as Thomas Paine said of himself: "The world is my country; to do good is my religion."

That she is a fluent writer, everyone knows; but not everyone knows of the dainty bits of verse she has been in the habit of writing since her girlhood. She also adds to her other accomplishments that of reading aloud most charmingly, and sometimes gives her family and a few friends delightful treats in that way.

At home, as in the field, she is never idle; and when traveling is never distressed by inconveniences by the way. I have journeyed with her throughout the Western country, in parts unsettled and wild; I have ridden miles with her over rough Western trails while she told of roads during wartimes—roads rough and unbroken, with mud to the hubs of the wheels, over which she rode on a springless wagon, the only woman, with a band of mutinous men, when, to show one sign of fear or fatigue, would have meant failure to her; and when the wagon stuck and the men refused to help, delicate little woman that she was, she was out in the mud with her own shoulder to the wheel, until, for very shame, the men fell to work with a will.

I have seen her in camp, where she has taught us how really comfortable and delightful an out-of-door life can be made without any of the conveniences of modern appliances.

Again, on the Atlantic coast, in her native State, I have seen her in a State's prison, in a group of the most hardened, obstreperous of women offenders, still quiet and gentle, but controlling them so that not one would disobey her, and even the most ugly had a word of praise. This was at Sherborn, Mass., to which place General Butler asked her to come as superintendent of the Woman's Reformatory Prison for the year 1883. She, remembering his kindness and goodness to her and her family in the years gone by, gladly went to help straighten out one of the tangles of his governorship. Her home in Dansville was another place where for a few years she was able to live in quiet, peace and retirement among the trees and vines of that beautiful spot on the hillside, resting in preparation for the greater work of after years.

In conclusion, I can say that if Clara Barton ever had a motto or watchword, she has kept it so modestly in the background that even I never heard of it; but her idea of life, I often think, lies in what she once said to me when, with the feverish haste and impatience of youth, I was longing for great things to do. "Be always calm, my child," she said; "keep yourself quiet and in restraint, reserve your energies, doing those little things that lie in your way, each one as well as you can, saving your strength, so that when God does call you to do something good and great you will not have wasted your force and strength with useless strivings, but will be ready to do the work quickly and well. Go slowly, my child—and keep ready."

www.ingramcontent.com/pod-product-compliance
Lightning Source LLC
Chambersburg PA
CBHW051159300426
44116CB00006B/370